*Domestic Crimes, Family Violence
and Child Abuse*

ALSO BY R. BARRI FLOWERS

Drugs, Alcohol and Criminality in American Society
(McFarland, 1999)

The Prostitution of Women and Girls
(McFarland, 1998)

Female Crime, Criminals and Cellmates:
An Exploration of Female Criminality and Delinquency
(McFarland, 1995)

The Victimization and Exploitation of Women and Children:
A Study of Physical, Mental and Sexual
Maltreatment in the United States
(McFarland, 1994)

The Adolescent Criminal:
An Examination of Today's Juvenile Offender
(McFarland, 1990)

DOMESTIC CRIMES, FAMILY VIOLENCE AND CHILD ABUSE

A Study of Contemporary American Society

by
R. BARRI FLOWERS

McFarland & Company, Inc., Publishers
Jefferson, North Carolina, and London

Library of Congress Cataloguing-in-Publication Data

Flowers, Ronald B.
    Domestic crimes, family violence and child abuse : a study of
contemporary American society / by R. Barri Flowers
        p.   cm.
    Includes bibliographical references and index.
    ISBN 0-7864-0823-5 (softcover : 50# alkaline paper) ∞
    1. Family violence — United States.   I. Title.
HV6626.2.F56   2000
362.82'92'0973 — dc21   00-30483

British Library cataloguing data are available

Cover image © Art Today

Manufactured in the United States of America

*McFarland & Company, Inc., Publishers
    Box 611, Jefferson, North Carolina 28640
        www.mcfarlandpub.com*

For Loraine, Marjah, Jacquelyn, and Julie

And to the many victims and survivors of domestic violence, elderly abuse, and child abuse and the prevention of such in future years

Contents

Tables and Figures

Tables

Figures

Preface

At the dawn of the twenty-first century, American society is beset by an epidemic of violence and abuse within the home and between intimates. Millions of women, men, children, and elderly persons in the United States are being victimized every year by those closest to them. Wife battering, marital rape, domestic violence, child abuse and neglect, child sexual abuse, elderly abuse, parent abuse, and sibling violence show little sign of abating.

Indeed the evidence suggests that most, if not all, forms of domestic crimes are growing at an alarming rate. The vast majority of such offenses involving family or intimates remain hidden from view and can only be estimated by professional and law enforcement authorities. This secretive nature of family and intimate violence makes it all the more frightening — and all the more necessary that we uncover, understand, and prevent it.

Much of what we do know about crimes between members of the same family or intimate partners tells us that they are often interrelated to one another in a cycle of abuse and violence. Abused children typically become child abusers or spouse abusers. Batterers were once beaten themselves. Psychological abuse is often passed from generation to generation. Child sexual abuse can lead to victims sexually abusing their own children or others, as well as marital rape or other sexual assaults.

Familial violence is also related to violent criminality outside the family such as homicide, aggravated assault, school violence, and delinquency. Other offenses such as running away, prostitution, and illicit drug use have been shown to correlate with child abuse, domestic violence, sibling violence, and other types of abuse and violence at home.

A common thread among offenders and victims of family and intimate

1

criminality is substance abuse. Studies show that alcohol and drugs are factors in a high percentage of conflicts and crises between family members, or those romantically involved, or former lovers. Other important factors appear to be stress, depression, pressure in life, insecurity, jealousy, children-related problems, and financial troubles.

Although men are largely responsible for violence against wives, girlfriends, ex-partners, parents, or children, perpetrators of familial violence are also wives, mothers, girlfriends, children, and even grandparents. This reflects the diversity of violent activity in the home setting as well as the complexities in addressing it.

The costs of treating domestic violence and child abuse victims in hospital emergency departments and physicians' offices, as well as incarcerating perpetrators of such victimization, are enormous. The same can be said of educating the public about family violence and formulating public policies in dealing with the issues. These costs will likely rise as more victims are identified and treated and perpetrators are arrested, convicted, and confined.

In light of the enormity of the problem, *Domestic Crimes, Family Violence and Child Abuse* seeks to add a new and compelling chapter to the body of literature in assessing the incidence, nature, and dimensions of domestic criminality. The aim is to bridge the gap between existing studies and to influence efforts in devising strategies to decrease the level of assaultive behavior tearing families and intimates apart in our society.

This book should be a useful resource for years to come for educators, students, and professionals in the disciplines of domestic violence, wife abuse, conjugal rape, child abuse and neglect, child sexual abuse, violent crimes, delinquency, and related areas. As a textbook, it should be appropriate reading material for undergraduate and graduate level study in the fields of child health and welfare, criminal justice, psychology, psychiatry, medicine, sociology, social science, women's studies, and elderly studies. Laypersons with an interest in violence in the home and between intimate partners should also find the book educational and easy to read.

I offer my undying gratitude and appreciation to the woman who has been the glue to hold this writer together from the very beginning, and never stopped believing that dreams really can come true: H. Loraine (BJ).

Introduction

Most experts agree that the risk of being the victim of a violent offense may be greater at home than away from home, with the offender more likely to be a member of one's own family, an intimate, or an acquaintance than a total stranger. This goes against the grain of family values and unity, often promoted in society as a means of stability and reducing crime and violence. The reality is that in spite of laws that exist in every state making acts such as spouse battering, child abuse, child sexual abuse and elderly abuse a crime, family and domestic violence is a fact of life in the United States and elsewhere.

The majority of victims and offenders never come into contact with the criminal justice system. Those who do may be inadequately assisted or unfairly penalized, such as battered women sentenced to prison for defending themselves against abusive men, or children held in custody as abuse or neglect victims. Others simply fall through the cracks as far as official intervention, proper diagnostic treatment, or assistance by social service agencies is concerned.

The problems related to violence in the family (or involving spouses, girlfriends, boyfriends, or ex-mates) are many. Identifying and directing attention to these problems is important in coming to terms with such violence as well as working towards preventative mechanisms, legal remedies, and treatment of victims and offenders.

This study will examine the types of intrafamilial and intimate violence that fall under the broad umbrella of family or domestic violence. The intent is to create a greater understanding and recognition of the prevalence, dynamics, and severity of domestic violence as well as to assess related aspects of abuse within the home.

Domestic Crimes, Family Violence and Child Abuse is divided into seven parts. Tables and figures are used where appropriate to illustrate relevant data.

Part I focuses on the general dynamics of domestic criminality including a historical review of woman abuse and child maltreatment, the magnitude of family and intimate offenses, demographic characteristics of family violence, and medical treatment for victims of violence in the home.

Part II explores issues in family and intimate violence including domestic fatalities, battered women, conjugal rape, and sexual factors in battering; battered men; and elderly abuse.

Part III examines child maltreatment including child abuse and neglect, child sexual abuse, incest, other child sexual abuses, sibling abuse, and parent abuse.

Part IV studies symptoms of domestic criminality such as the relationship between substance abuse and intimate violence as well as family abuses. Also examined is the cycle of child abuse, family violence, and other crimes.

Part V looks at theories about the causes of domestic violence and child abuse and neglect.

Part VI explores the characteristics of jail and prison inmates incarcerated for intimate violence and violence against children.

Part VII focuses on strategies in responding to domestic crimes.

Notes and a bibliography can be found at the end of the text, along with suggested additional readings in the study of domestic and family violence, child maltreatment, child sexual abuse, and elderly victimization.

As life begins in a new century, it is more important than ever that we address the conditions that create violence among family members and between intimate partners. We must seek constructive ways to reduce the incidence of such violence and its consequences in the family and society.

PART I

Dynamics of Domestic Criminality

1. The Abuse of Women and Children: Historical Precedents

Family violence and abuse today takes on many forms, commonly referred to in terms such as domestic violence, spouse abuse, child abuse and neglect, child sexual abuse, elderly abuse, and sibling violence. Most of these family offenses tend to be interrelated, coexisting, intergenerational, and underestimated and underreported. They also tend to be spoken of as relatively recent phenomenons. In fact, much of the family violence and child abuses we know of have deep roots in history, often dating back to the beginning of recorded history.

In many respects, here lies the difficulty in recognizing, reporting, controlling, and preventing familial crimes. Before examining domestic violence, child abuse, and victimization in present times, it might be a good idea to take a look historically at the mistreatment of women, children, and family.

Family Violence

Long before family violence became a household term, history tells us that it was already firmly established. Adam and Eve's progeny, Cain, murdered his brother, Abel, because of sibling rivalry and jealousy.[1] The Greek myth of Oedipus describes episodes of fratricide, parricide, filicide, and multiple suicides over several generations in one family.[2] The *Report of the Commissioners* in 1833 on the employment of children in factories noted "acts of severity and cruelty towards children [by] parents."[3] Novelists such as Charles Dickens offer numerous "examples of violence perpetrated on wives, their husbands, as well as other forms of working-class domestic brutality."[4] Many studies found that homicide "as a paradigm of violence" has been largely family related.[5]

In a sad commentary on family violence, M. Freeman observed: "The home is a very dangerous place and we have more to fear from close members of our family than from total strangers."[6] Richard Gelles and Murray Straus echoed these sentiments in an article on violence in the American family:

> With the exception of the police and the military, the family is perhaps the most violent social group, and the home the most violent social setting in our society. A person is more likely to be hit or killed in his or her home by another family member than anywhere else or by anyone else.[7]

Unfortunately, far too often the statistics tend to bear this out.

Wife Abuse

The battering of wives and other women has existed since ancient times, often encouraged or accepted in the societies in which it occurred. Historical literature is filled with examples of the cruel mistreatment of women by their mates, including references in the Bible.[8] For instance, one book tells of the "scalding death of Fausta ordered by her husband, the Emperor Constantine, which was to serve as a precedent for the next fourteen centuries."[9] Around AD 1140, Gratian systematized church law in his work, *The Decretum*, which held that

> Women should be subject to their men.... The image of God is in man and it is one. Women were drawn from man, who has God's jurisdiction as if he were God's vicar.... Therefore, woman is not made in God's image.... Adam was beguiled by Eve, not she by him. It is right that he whom woman led into wrongdoing should have her under his direction, so that he may not fail a second time through female levity.[10]

Frederick Engels contended that wife abuse began with "the emergence of the first monogamous pairing relationships, which replaced group marriage and the extended family of early promiscuous society."[11] Another hypothesis on battered women is that the condoning of wife abuse, historically, is a reflection of the

> subjugation and oppression of women through the male partner exercising his authority as head of the family. The notion of the nearly limitless

right of the husband and father as undisputed leader of the family, and father-family relationships defined as a proprietary interest, can be traced to the doctrines of such ancient civilizations as Babylonia, Greece, and Rome.[12]

Such doctrines had a significant effect on the early English Common Law and the American statutory system.[13]

In western societies, abuse of women has been supported since the Middle Ages. European male violence against their wives made its way into American society with the colonists and legal precedents.[14] At one point, a husband "was permitted by law to beat his wife so long as his weaponry was not bigger than his thumb."[15] Such laws remained in existence until the end of the nineteenth century.

Conjugal Rape

Conjugal or marital rape is another branch of wife abuse rooted in history and tradition. Forcible rape was once the means by which a man could "seize or steal" a woman to be his wife. "She represented little more than a trophy — with no legal, social or human rights."[16]

Over time, the tolerance of rape declined in society while, in many instances, culpability was placed on the victim rather than offender. This view was expressed by Herodotus, often referred to as "the father of history," when he advanced:

> Abducting young women is not, indeed, a lawful act, but it is stupid after the event to make a fuss about it. The only sensible thing is to take no notice; for it is obvious that no young woman allows herself to be abducted if she does not want to be.[17]

Sadly, many conjugal and stranger rapists and even victims of rape continue to take this view of forcible rape and other sexual assaults.

In a historical review of rape, Susan Brownmiller described rapists as "shock troops" whose sexual violence against females essentially forced women into marriage as a means of protecting themselves from sexual predators.[18] Brownmiller further postulated that the predatory nature of men and their desire to acquire property are the fundamental causes of rape and sexual inequality (see Chapter 7).

Child Abuse and Neglect

Perhaps no form of family violence and mistreatment has been as pervasive historically as child abuse and neglect. Children have long been viewed as unequal to adults in society and therefore subject to various acts of cruelty and exploitation, often at the whim of parents or others. Physical abuse was particularly used as a means of discipline and punishment in early societies. Expressed in 1633 in the *Bibliotheca Scholastica* was the dictum: "Spare the rod, spoil the child."[19] The Bible itself has a number of passages encouraging child physical abuse. Examples can be found in Proverbs, such as "A youngster's heart is filled with rebellion, but punishment will drive it out of him" (22:15) and "Discipline your son in his early years while there is hope" (19:18).

Whippings, floggings and other forms of violence against children have not only been the prerogative of parents but of schoolmates as well. In the schools of Sumer some 5,000 years ago, boys were punished "upon the slightest pretext by a 'man in charge of the whip.'"[20] At one point in most Christian countries, children were whipped on Innocents Day to force them to remember the massacre of the innocents by Herod.[21]

The history of parental violence towards children is reflected in two important rights: (1) the right to property and (2) the right to *own* children. Aristotle asserted: "The justice of a master or a father is a different thing from that of a citizen, for a son or slave is property and there can be no injustice to one's own property."[22] In ancient Rome, the *patria potestas* gave a father the absolute right to sell, abandon, sacrifice, or even murder his own child.[23]

Although this right to own children "was proclaimed most often in antiquity, the concept of children as property was a tradition that the English colonists brought with them" to America.[24] It was not until 1967 that children in the United States were assigned rights through the juvenile justice system.[25]

INFANTICIDE

The killing of infants by their parents, known as infanticide, is believed to be responsible for more child deaths than any single cause in history, with the possible exception of the bubonic plague.[26] The literature on infanticide is extensive. In the Bible, the New Testament refers to the "slaughter of the innocents,"[27] while in the Old Testament, the killing of countless children in Jericho by Joshua and his nomadic warriors is described.[28] King Nimrod "slew every first-born in his kingdom after being told by his astrologer that a boy would be born in Mesopotamia who would declare war upon the king."[29] An estimated 70,000 children were killed.[30]

Many children were burned at the stake during Queen Mary's reign.[31] "In rural areas of Ireland 'changeling babies' (usually babies with congenital

defects — but sometimes ugly, screaming or hungry babies) were sometimes roasted alive over fires, even in the twentieth century."[32] Killing
female infants was once so common that in many societies the male population was 4 or 5 times that of the female population.[33]

Up until the nineteenth century, dead or abandoned infants were
almost commonplace in the United States. In 1892, "100 dead infants and
200 foundlings were found on the streets of New York City alone."[34]

Historically, infanticide has often been a reflection of "religious
appeasement, collective acts of faith, Darwinian survival, and Malthusian
population control."[35] Modern day infanticide is often attributed to mental illness on the part of the mother killer, illegitimate births, the young
age of the mother, fear, and ignorance (see also Chapter 5).

CHILD ABANDONMENT

In historical times, many parents also rid themselves of unwanted
children through abandonment. Inadequate birth control, ignorance,
poverty, and societal norms often left parents with a surplus of children
they could not afford to care for or did not desire to. During times of social
upheaval or war, foundlings were particularly numerous. Since the beginning of Christianity, the church founded institutions for such unwanted
or unclaimed infants.[36] The first modern institution was established in
AD 787 by Datheus, the archpriest of Milan.[37]

As recently as the early nineteenth century there were no foundling
homes in the United States. Abandoned infants instead were often taken
to almshouses.[38] Lacking the knowledge of artificial feeding, the need for
wet nurses in these hospitals reached critical proportions. As a result, some
almshouses were forced to place such infants in foster homes; however, the
abuse and neglect they endured there was so great that there was a public
outcry and demands for reform. Things began to improve gradually with
the establishment of the Nursery and Children's Hospital of New York in
1854 and the New York Foundling Asylum of Randall's Island in 1869.[39]

CHILD SEXUAL MISUSE AND EXPLOITATION

Sexual maltreatment of children by parents and relatives has existed
throughout history in one form or another. Incest is one such example.
Traditionally defined as sexual relations between blood relatives, incest
has long been taboo in most societies. Prohibitions against incestuous relations have been severe and precise, as indicated in Leviticus, the Book of
Laws (18:6–18; 20:11–21).

In spite of this, particularly in western societies, incest has flourished. Moses was the offspring of an aunt and nephew marriage (Numbers 26:59; Exodus 6:20); while Abraham married his paternal sister, Sarah (Genesis 20:12).

In some nonliterate and folk groups, incest existed among the privileged classes only. In ancient Ireland, the prince married the princess, and sometimes the king married his daughter.[40] In ancient Peru, the Incas wed their sisters; while in ancient Egypt, during the 10 generations of the Ptolemaic dynasty, virtually every kind of incestuous marriage was practiced.[41] Among sectarian groups, the Mormons sanctioned every type of incest.[42] (See also Chapter 12.)

Children have also been sexually exploited in other ways historically. Many children have been forced into prostitution by parents through the centuries. For instance, in ancient Egypt, the most "beautiful and highest born Egyptian maidens were forced into prostitution as a religious practice, and they continued as prostitutes until their first menstruation."[43] In China and India children were often sold by their parents into prostitution, and for centuries Persia was renowned for its child brothels.[44]

In some countries it was once considered hospitable to "loan" one's daughter or wife to guests for sexual purposes.[45] Defloration rites at puberty or in preparing for marriage is another practice once common. "Enthusiasts [have] always claimed that there is a special pleasure in deflowering a virgin, because of the emotional thrill, a blend of aggression, possessiveness, and mild sadism."[46]

CHILD LABOR AND MALTREATMENT

The mistreatment and exploitation of children through child labor has existed for centuries but became particularly prevalent as urbanization and industrialization altered the value of children to parents. In the 1600s, child labor was encouraged by England and the American colonies. Children were regularly placed in apprenticeships, work houses, orphanage placement mills, mines, factories, and other industries.[47] In England it was not uncommon to find young children "shackled in chains, working sixteen hours in factories."[48] Brutal overseers often "goaded laggards with whips and prods."[49]

Transportation was a means used in many European countries to reduce overcrowding. England transported thousands of children to the American colonies to work in the New World. It was considered punishment for children who had committed crimes. Transcripts from seventeenth century court record that two 9-year-old boys who stole "a till containing upwards of £1 [one pound]" were sentenced to 7 years transportation for their offenses.[50]

Though child labor laws began to bring about reform in the nineteenth century, as recently as 1866 a Massachusetts legislative report saw child labor as "a boon to society."[51] At the turn of the century, Louise Bowen noted that many children were working in 40 nut factories in Chicago, "cracking nuts with hammers from 4:00 p.m. until midnight."[52]

Identifying Physical Abuse of Children

Up until the end of the eighteenth century, very little was known or acknowledged about infantile pathology or other forms of child abuse. Hippocrates discussed childhood mistreatment as did Galen.[53] In the tenth century, Rhazes became the first to gather medical information concerning young children in a single monograph.[54]

The first major step towards recognizing child abuse and neglect in the United States came in 1874. The case of Mary Ellen, an 8-year-old girl who was severely abused and malnourished by her mother, was brought before the Supreme Court of New York. This led to the establishment of the Society for the Prevention of Cruelty to Children in New York and a number of similar organizations across the country.[55] Such efforts helped set a precedence for protecting children from abusive parents and having the right not to be severely abused or inhumanely treated.

With a new discipline of pediatric radiology at the turn of the century, advances in diagnosing child abuse began to take place. As early as 1906, Thomas Rotch presented studies in infant x-rays.[56] Twenty years later, Ralph Bromer became the head of the country's first x-ray department in a children's hospital. It was not until 1946 that J. Caffey presented his original findings on the "relation of subdural hematoma and abnormal x-ray changes in the long bones."[57]

In the early '60s, C. Henry Kempe's "battered child syndrome" drew attention to the problem of child abuse.[58] Alarmed by the high number of children admitted to his pediatric service suffering from nonaccidental injuries, Kempe contacted 8 district attorneys to investigate the problem. In 1961, he directed a symposium on child abuse sponsored by the American Academy of Pediatrics. The following year, Kempe and his associates published "The Battered Child Syndrome" in the *Journal of the American Medical Association*.[59] This helped lead the way to greater recognition and understanding of child abuse and its implications.

2. The Magnitude of Domestic Crimes

Domestic crimes, abuses, and violence have taken on all forms over the years and continue to be of great concern to medical workers, criminal justice personnel, researchers, and others. In the process of identifying and labeling criminality involving family members, many terms have been used, including *domestic violence, family violence, conjugal violence, child abuse, child sexual abuse, child neglect, sibling violence,* and *elderly abuse.* Sometimes these are used interchangeably, other times in distinguishing specific types of abuse. For the purposes of this book, in general, and this chapter in specific, the terms *domestic crimes* and *domestic criminality* will be used to refer to any and all crimes, abuses, acts of violence, and victimization that involves members of the same family, ex-spouses, intimates, ex-intimates, or others related to victims in a romantic or familial way.

The Nature of Domestic Crimes

Domestic criminality spans the range of violent and abusive offenses and includes physical assaults, sexual assaults, verbal assaults, threats, intimidation, emotional abuse, neglect, and death. The perpetrator-to-victim relationship varies, depending on the nature of the offense. Most commonly recognized are intimate violence (domestic violence), parent-to-child violence (child abuse), parent-to-child neglect (child neglect), child-to-parent violence (parent abuse or elderly abuse), and child-to-child violence (sibling abuse). When there are multiple offenders and victims in the domestic arena, it is often referred to as family violence.

Regardless of what type of domestic crime, what is clear is that the numbers of victims and offenders in the United States are staggering. The following statistics illustrate the severity of the problem:

• Every 9 seconds a woman is battered by her spouse.
• Four million spouses are battered each year.
• Two million women are victims of severe intimate abuse annually.
• One-third of female homicide victims are killed by an intimate.
• Ninety-five percent of assaults on spouses or ex-spouses are perpetrated by men against women.
• One in 5 battered women were victims of at least 3 assaults in the last 6 months.
• The rate of abuse among college students by intimates on some campuses is similar to that in marriages.
• More than 1 million children are abused or neglected annually.
• The rate of child abuse is 15 victims per 1,000 children.
• More than half of child abuse victims were neglected.
• More than 1 in 10 children are sexually abused each year.
• Every day 3 children die from abuse.
• Eight in 10 child abusers are parents.
• One in 25 elderly persons are abused; one-third of the perpetrators are adult children.[1]

A recent 9-year study on family violence yielded the following results on its nature:

• Spouse-to-spouse violence occurred most frequently.
• Nine in 10 cases of domestic violence involved assaults.
• One-third of the assaults involved the use of a weapon or resulted in serious injury.
• Two percent of the abuses included rape.
• Fifteen percent of the parent-to-child violent incidents occurred at least 3 times over 6 months.[2]

Domestic crimes occur among all socioeconomic classes, racial and ethnic groups, and educational levels. Like a cancer, its hideous nature has affected all of us in some manner.

The Extent of Domestic Violence

Domestic violence, or violence between people presently or previously involved romantically, has been defined in various ways with the intent of being all inclusive and/or legally functional in its criteria. For instance, the Family Violence Prevention Fund defines domestic violence as "the actual or threatened physical, sexual, psychological or economic abuse of an individual by someone with whom they have or had an intimate relationship."[3] While a researcher and expert on domestic violence defines it as "a pattern of assaultive and coercive behaviors, including physical, sexual, and psychological attacks, as well as economic coercion, that adults or adolescents use against their intimate partners."[4]

What is clear is that the problem is widespread and epidemic in nature. So how extensive is domestic violence? According to the American Medical Association, 4 million spouses are beaten each year in the United States.[5] Murray Straus estimated that 65 percent of all married couples were involved in spousal abuse, with 25 percent of a serious nature.[6]

The Family Violence Prevention Fund reported that 7 percent of American women or 3.9 million, married or living with someone, were physically beaten in the last year.[7] A 1996 survey found that the rate of domestic violence was 9.3 cases per 1,000 adults, including physical and psychological abuse.[8]

Gallup Polls reflect the high incidence of battered women in this country. A 1997 poll found that 22 percent of the women in the United States have been the victims of abuse by their spouse or boyfriend.[9] This is more than 3 times the percentage of women in Canada and more than twice that of women in Mexico.[10] Another poll revealed that 53 percent of the respondents knew of women who had been physically abused by an intimate.[11] Six in 10 of the female respondents reported personally knowing other females who were victims of domestic violence.[12]

Men are also battered by their partners. Robert Langley and Richard Levy estimated that 12 million men have been victims of spouse abuse in the United States at some point during their marriage.[13] Suzanne Steinmetz reported that approximately 280,000 men are beaten by their partners each year in this country.[14] Another study estimated that 2 million husbands have been the victims of severe marital violence, compared to 1.8 million wives.[15]

Domestic violence is also experienced among non-married couples and adolescents who are dating. Surveys reveal a high rate of abusive treatment in dating relationships. Around 1 in 3 females will be the victims of violence perpetrated by boyfriends prior to reaching adulthood.[16] One study found that dating violence is "remarkably similar to marital violence."[17] Some jurisdictions have revised definitions of domestic violence to reflect dating. For example, the California Code's definition of domestic abuse now includes people involved in a "dating, courtship, or engagement relationship."[18]

Significant findings on the dimensions of domestic violence can be seen below:

- One-third of men and women have witnessed an act of domestic violence.[19]
- Fourteen percent of women have been the victims of severe domestic violence.[20]
- Divorced or separated women are 14 times more likely to have reported being a victim of domestic violence by a spouse or ex-spouse than married women.[21]
- Thirty percent of women admitted to an emergency department had injuries identified as due to battering.[22]
- Anywhere from 8 percent to 26 percent of pregnant women in public and private clinics have been abused by partners.[23]
- Forty-two percent of murdered women are killed by male intimates.[24]
- More than 9 in 10 battered women did not report it to their doctors; over half the victims told no one of the abuse.[25]

VICTIMIZATION SURVEYS AND DOMESTIC VIOLENCE

Much of what we know about domestic violence comes from victimization data obtained from victims themselves. The most comprehensive victimization survey is conducted by the U.S. Department of Justice's Bureau of Justice Statistics (BJS). Its National Crime Victimization Survey (NCVS) gathers information on crime and its nature from a national representative sample of persons age 12 or older regarding criminality in which they may have been victims. In the BJS Factbook, *Violence by Intimates*, information was compiled from the NCVS on domestic violence, defined as "violence between people who have had an intimate relationship — spouses, ex-spouses, boyfriends, girlfriends, and former boyfriends and girlfriends."[26]

According to the NCVS, women were victims of an estimated 840,000 nonlethal crimes of violence involving an intimate in 1996.[27] These included rape, sexual assault, robbery, aggravated assault, and simple assaults. Men were victims of approximately 150,000 nonlethal violent crimes perpetrated by an intimate in 1996.[28]

Between 1992 and 1996, there were, on average, more than 960,000 violent victimizations against intimates.[29] Approximately 85 percent of the victims were women. The number of female victims of intimate violence declined from 1993 to 1996, with 1.1 million violent victimizations in 1993.[30]

From 1992 to 1996, "series victimizations" or intimate violence involving 6 or more incidents represented 11.5 percent of all domestic violence against female victims, compared to 9.8 percent of intimate violence against males.[31] More than 88 percent of the female victims and over 90 percent of the male victims of intimate violence between 1992 and 1996 experienced non-series victimizations.[32]

Data on domestic violence are also collected by the Federal Bureau of Investigation (FBI). Through its National Incident-Based Reporting System (NIBRS), detailed information on victims and offenders is gathered, based on individual crime reports recorded by law enforcement at the time the incident occurred. In Table 2-1, various characteristics of the incidents of intimate violence in 1995 are shown. According to the NIBRS, in more than 53 percent of the victimizations, the offender was a spouse. Forty-two percent of the perpetrators were other intimates. Aggravated assault was the offense most often committed by spouses and other intimates. More than 4 times as many intimidations were committed by ex-spouses as other incidents of intimate violence.

Over 40 percent of the victims of domestic violence were between 20 and 29, with over 35 percent between ages 30 and 39. In 81 percent of the incidents, an argument led to the violence. Eight in 10 incidents of intimate violence occurred in the home, while nearly 38 percent of the offenses took place on the weekends. Nearly 25 percent of the offenders had been drinking at the time of the violence.

Other trends in nonlethal violence against intimates include:

- Females are 5 to 8 times as likely as males to experience violence by an intimate.
- Intimate violence accounts for about one-fifth of all crimes of violence against females.
- Violence by relatives aside from intimates comprises less than 10 percent of all violent crimes against women.
- Women age 16 to 24 have the highest rate of nonlethal intimate violence.
- Black women have a higher rate of intimate violence than white women.
- White and black males have the same rate of violence by intimates.
- The rate of male intimate victimization is around one-fifth of the rate for females.
- Women in low income households have a higher rate of nonlethal intimate violence than women in high income households.
- Seven in 10 female victims of violence by intimates were physically assaulted.
- Three in 10 women victims of intimate violence were threatened or an attack attempted.
- Three-quarters of nonlethal intimate violence occurs at or close to the victim's home.

Table 2-1
Characteristics of Violence
Between Intimates[a]

	Percent of incidents of intimate violence			
	All intimate assaults[b]	Aggravated assault	Simple assault	Intimi- dation
Victim/offender relationship				
Spouse	53.1	52.5	54.8	41.0
Ex-spouse	4.9	3.3	3.8	16.4
Other intimate	42.0	44.2	41.4	42.6
Age of victim				
Under 20	8.8	7.1	9.1	9.1
20-29	40.2	37.0	41.3	38.2
30-39	35.7	37.0	35.5	35.5
40 or older	15.2	18.9	14.2	17.2
Circumstances				
Argument	81.0	81.2	84.7	76.4
Lovers' quarrel	14.4	14.3	11.0	13.9
Other	4.6	4.5	4.3	9.7
Location				
Home	80.0	78.2	81.0	75.6
Bar/club	1.2	1.1	1.3	0.7
Hotel	1.2	1.2	1.2	0.7
Road/garage	8.1	10.6	7.5	7.5
Other	9.5	8.9	9.0	15.3
Day of the week				
Sunday	18.6	18.9	19.0	14.8
Monday	12.1	11.8	12.0	13.4
Tuesday	12.4	12.1	12.2	15.0
Wednesday	12.0	11.7	11.9	14.0
Thursday	12.2	12.0	12.0	13.6
Friday	13.9	14.0	13.7	14.9
Saturday	18.8	19.4	19.2	14.3
Alcohol use				
Evidence of offender drinking	24.9	28.0	25.8	12.7

[a] These data were obtained from law enforcement agencies in 9 states. Coverage for these data is estimated to be about 2% of murders, 4% of reported aggravated assaults, and an unknown percentage of simple assaults and intimidation offenses.
[b] *All intimate assaults* includes murder but excludes violent sex crimes.

Source: U.S. Department of Justice, Bureau of Justice Statistics Factbook, *Violence by Intimates* (Washington, D.C.: Government Printing Office, 1998), p. 16.

Table 2-2
Trends in Reporting of Intimate
Violence to Police, 1992–1996

Female victims of intimate violence	
Violent crime against an intimate reported to the police	52.1%
Violent crime against an intimate not reported to the police	47.8%
Most important reasons given for not reporting	
Private or personal matter	15.4%
Afraid of offender retaliation	7.3%
Police would do nothing	4.4%
Incident was not important enough	3.5%
No one reason most important	1.7%
Reported to another official	1.1%
Don't know	0.7%[a]
Other	13.6%
Percent of female victims of intimate violence	
White	49.0%
Black	68.0%
Other	44.0%

[a] Fewer than 10 cases.

Source: Constructed from U.S. Department of Justice, Bureau of Justice Statistics Factbook, *Violence by Intimates* (Washington, D.C.: Government Printing Office, 1998), p. 19.

- A higher percentage of female than male victims of nonlethal violence by intimates live in households with children under the age of 12.
- Urban women have a higher rate of nonlethal violent victimization than women in the suburbs or rural areas.
- Almost one-third of females victimized by nonlethal intimate violence experienced at least 2 incidents of violence during the past 6 months.[33]

REPORTING INTIMATE VIOLENCE TO LAW ENFORCEMENT

Just over half the incidents of intimate violence are reported to law enforcement agencies, according to the NCVS. As shown in Table 2-2, between 1992 and 1996, just over 52 percent of the female victims of intimate violence reported the crime to police, while just under 48 percent did not. The most important reason given for not reporting domestic violence was that it was considered a private or personal matter. One in 3 female victims of violence by an intimate and 1 in 6 of all female victims of domestic violence gave this reason for not reporting.

Table 2-3
Number of Victimizations, by Type of Crime and Relationship to Offender, 1994

Type of crime	Total number of victimizations[a]	Number of victimizations					
		Related					
		Total[a]	Spouse	Ex-spouse	Parent	Own child	Other relatives
Crimes of violence	**10,860,630**	**924,760**	**328,820**	**111,250**	**80,340**	**84,620**	**319,730**
Completed violence	3,205,410	392,940	192,250	38,550	33,620	35,250	93,280
Attempted/threatened violence	7,655,220	531,820	136,580	72,700	46,720	49,370	226,450
Rape/Sexual assault[b]	432,750	45,890	23,610	12,200[c]	2,630[c]	0[c]	7,450[c]
Robbery	1,298,750	76,580	19,350[c]	9,590[c]	10,110[c]	12,170[c]	25,360
Completed/property taken	795,130	41,970	6,860[c]	4,930[c]	7,490[c]	10,140[c]	12,550[c]
Attempted to take property	503,620	34,610	12,490[c]	4,660[c]	2,620[c]	2,030[c]	12,810[c]
Assault	9,129,120	802,290	285,860	89,470	67,600	72,450	286,920
Aggravated	2,478,150	169,090	61,400	16,600[c]	17,840[c]	20,640[c]	52,610
Simple	6,650,970	633,200	224,450	72,870	49,760	51,810	234,300

[a] Detail may not add to total shown because of rounding.

[b] Includes verbal threats of rape and threats of sexual assault.

[c] Estimate is based on about 10 or fewer sample cases.

Source: Adapted from U.S. Department of Justice, Bureau of Justice Statistics, *Criminal Victimization in the United States, 1994: A National Criminal Victimization Survey Report* (Washington, D.C.: Government Printing Office, 1997), p. 33.

Black women were most likely to report intimate violence. Nearly 70 percent reported the crime to the police from 1993 to 1996, compared to 49 percent of white women and 44 percent of women of other races.

For women who did report the intimate violence, the police responded or the victim went to the police in nearly 9 out of 10 cases.[34] Almost 6 in 10 female victims of intimate violence reported that police response time to a call for assistance was within 10 minutes. In 7 in 10 of the cases of reported domestic violence, police took an official report.[35]

Family Violence

Family violence involving spouses, children, and other relatives affects many families across the country and represents a much broader problem than violence between intimates. Victimization surveys indicate that hundreds of thousands of people are victimized by some form of family violence each year. A recent survey found that over an 8-year period almost 6 million violent victimizations occurred in which the victim and offender were related.[36] Nearly 21,000 females were estimated to be the victims of violence by parents annually.[37] Another study found that parents' violence against children averaged 29,000 cases per year.[38]

The most comprehensive victimization survey is the BJS's annual report, *Criminal Victimization in the United States: A National Crime Victimization Survey Report* (NCVS). In the most recently published report, the NCVS indicated that there were 924,760 violent crime victimizations involving relatives as offenders in 1994.[39] The type of victim-offender relationship can be seen in Table 2-3. More than 484,000 victimizations were perpetrated by parents, children, and other relatives. Comparatively, just over 440,000 victimizations were committed by spouses and ex-spouses. Most of the crimes were assaults and attempted or threatened violence.

Among the single-offender victimizations for crimes of violence in 1994, more than 11 percent were perpetrated by family members.[40] Nearly 6 percent of these victimizations were committed by family members other than spouses or ex-spouses. Multiple-offender victimization data indicate that in familial crimes of violence, the victim's children, siblings, or other relatives were more likely to be the perpetrator of violence than spouses or ex-spouses.[41]

Child Abuse

Few would argue that child abuse and neglect represent our most critical problem with respect to domestic crimes. A fairly encompassing definition of child abuse and neglect is included in the Child Abuse Prevention and Treatment Act which defines it as "the physical or mental injury, sexual abuse or exploitation, negligent treatment, or maltreatment of a child by a person who is responsible for the child's welfare, under circumstances which indicate that the child's health or welfare is harmed or threatened thereby."[42]

Most estimates of child abuse in the United States are alarming and give rise to the severity of the problem. The National Incidence Study of Child Abuse and Neglect (NIS) estimated that there were 2.8 million reported cases of child abuse and neglect in 1996, for a rate of 41.9 per 1,000 children.[43] The National Child Abuse and Neglect Data System (NCANDS), whose information is derived from state child protective service agencies' data on abused and neglected children, estimated that there were over 2 million reports of child abuse and neglect involving more than 3 million children in 1996.[44] The rate of reports was 44 per 1,000 children, an increase from 41 per 1,000 children in 1990. The figures are rising even higher, according to the American Medical Association, which reported that 3.2 million cases of child maltreatment were reported to child protective service agencies in 1997.[45]

Table 2-4 compares national estimates of reported child abuse and neglect between 1986 and 1997. The figures indicate that more than twice as many cases of alleged child maltreatment were reported in 1997 compared to 1986. Indeed, since 1990 nearly 700,000 more reports of child abuse and neglect were estimated to have been made to child protection agencies.

Though not all such allegations proved to be founded, it is estimated that upwards of 1.5 million children are victims of moderate to severe abuse or neglect each year.[46] Child protective services found that nearly 1 million child abuse or neglect cases were substantiated in 1996.[47] This represented an increase of approximately 18 percent since 1990.[48]

Nearly 80 percent of perpetrators of child maltreatment were parents, while another 11 percent were other family members or relatives of the victim.

Children of all ages are victims of all forms of child abuse. The NCANDS data indicated that while the percent of neglect and medical neglect victims tended to decrease with age, the child victims of physical, sexual, and emotional maltreatment increased with age.[49]

Figure 2-1 breaks down types of maltreatment experienced by children in 1990 and 1996. In both years, more than half the maltreatment was for neglect and medical neglect, with physical abuse accounting for more than 2 in 10 cases of child abuse. This was followed by sexual abuse, which accounted for over 12 percent of the maltreatment cases in 1996, and

Table 2-4
Comparison of National Estimates of
Reported Child Abuse and Neglect

Year	Source	Estimates of children reported abused or neglected
1986	National Incidence Study (NIS-2)	1,424,400
1987	American Humane Association	2,178,000
1988	National Committee for Prevention of Child Abuse (NCPCA)	2,265,000
1989	NCPCA	2,435,000
1990	NCPCA	2,557,000
1990	National Child Abuse and Neglect Data System (NCANDS)	2,600,000
1991	NCANDS	2,700,000
1991	NCPCA	2,723,000
1992	NCPCA	2,936,000
1996	NCANDS	3,000,000
1997	American Medical Association	3,200,000

Source: R. Barri Flowers, *The Victimization and Exploitation of Women and Children: A Study of Physical, Mental and Sexual Maltreatment in the United States* (Jefferson, N.C.: McFarland, 1994), p. 9; John M. Leventhal, "The Challenges of Recognizing Child Abuse: Seeing Is Believing," *Journal of the American Medical Association* 281 (February 17, 1999): 657.

Figure 2-1
Types of Maltreatment, 1990 and 1996

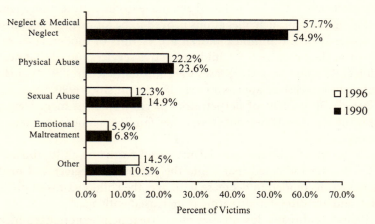

1990: 558,234 victims in 31 states.
1996: 572,943 victims in 31 states.

Source: U.S. Department of Health and Human Services, Children's Bureau, *Child Maltreatment 1996: Reports From the States to the National Child Abuse and Neglect Data System* (Washington, D.C.: Government Printing Office, 1998), p. 2-8.

emotional maltreatment, representing under 7 percent of the child abuse both years. Other types of maltreatment increased by 4 points in 1996 over 1990. Every other type of child abuse decreased slightly between the years, except neglect and medical neglect.

Deaths and Family Violence

The most extreme instance of family violence is when death occurs. Though official statistics show a decline in deaths attributable to domestic crimes in recent years, the sad fact remains that too many women and children are being murdered in this country by intimates, parents, and children. In 1996, there were more than 1,800 murders involving intimates in the United States.[50] There were nearly 1,100 child fatalities resulting from child maltreatment.[51] The U.S. Justice Department estimates that there are 600 cases a year of filicide, or mothers killing their children.[52]

According to FBI figures, there were 15,289 murders in the U.S. in 1997 (see Table 2-5). Of these, 2,514 were committed by family members, boyfriends, or girlfriends. Thirteen percent of all murder victims were related to their killers, while 35 percent were acquaintances. Twenty-nine percent of female murder victims were killed by husbands or boyfriends; whereas only 3 percent of male victims were slain by wives or girlfriends. Most domestic murders involved other arguments as the circumstance.

Murder trends involving intimates indicate declining numbers of people killed by a current or former romantic partner. From 1976 to 1996, the number of intimate murders dropped from nearly 3,000 — representing 13.6 percent of all murders — to less than 2,000 or 8.8 percent of total homicides.[53] During this period, nearly 1 in 5 women murder victims were killed by husbands, with nearly 11 percent murdered by ex-spouses and other intimates. Comparatively, less than 6 percent of the male murder victims were killed by an intimate over the same span.[54]

Studies on intimate murder further reveal:

- More than twice as many women are murdered by intimates as by strangers.[55]
- Seven in 10 women are killed by an intimate or ex-intimate.[56]
- Female murder followed by suicide of the male intimate is often preceded by spouse or intimate abuse.[57]
- Intimate murder among blacks is 4 times the rate of that among whites.
- The black male rate of intimate murder is 8 times greater than the white male rate.

Table 2-5
Murder Circumstances, by Relationship,[a] 1997

Circumstances	Total[b]	Husband	Wife	Mother	Father	Son	Daughter	Brother	Sister	Other Family	Acquaint-ance	Friend	Boy-friend	Girl-friend
Total[c]	15,289	183	583	83	147	274	211	120	20	311	4,237	432	156	426
Felony type total	2,908	4	17	10	7	25	23	3	1	38	837	54	3	12
Rape	66	-	-	-	-	-	1	-	-	-	21	1	-	-
Robbery	1,458	1	-	5	4	1	-	1	-	11	315	21	-	-
Burglary	100	-	-	-	-	-	-	-	-	3	23	1	-	-
Larceny-theft	18	-	-	-	-	-	-	-	-	-	7	-	-	-
Motor vehicle theft	18	-	1	-	-	-	-	-	-	-	3	1	-	-
Arson	88	1	2	-	-	-	1	-	-	10	15	2	-	3
Prostitution and commercialized vice	6	-	-	-	-	-	-	-	-	-	4	-	-	-
Other sex offenses	24	-	-	-	-	-	1	1	-	2	8	-	1	-
Narcotic drug laws	786	-	1	1	2	1	1	1	1	2	348	23	1	5
Gambling	19	-	-	-	-	-	-	-	-	1	10	1	-	-
Other - not specified	325	2	16	1	1	23	19	-	-	9	83	4	1	4
Suspected felony type	153	-	-	-	-	-	3	1	-	2	11	-	-	-
Other than felony type total	7,438	167	499	61	118	231	165	107	12	223	2,841	324	139	369
Romantic triangle	171	3	10	-	-	2	1	-	-	1	101	8	9	10
Child killed by babysitter	24	-	-	-	-	-	-	-	-	2	21	1	-	-
Brawl due to influence of alcohol	240	2	6	-	4	2	-	6	-	6	122	27	1	2
Brawl due to influence of narcotics	105	-	-	1	1	2	-	-	-	2	57	4	-	2
Argument over money or property	286	1	1	2	5	3	-	3	-	7	183	18	4	4
Other arguments	4,297	144	357	41	88	54	30	82	10	161	1,598	235	118	308
Gangland killings	84	-	-	-	1	-	-	-	-	-	33	-	-	-
Juvenile gang killings	780	-	-	-	-	-	-	-	-	-	297	3	-	-
Institutional killings	19	-	-	-	-	-	-	-	-	-	15	-	-	-
Sniper attack	8	-	-	-	-	1	2	-	-	-	-	-	-	-
Other - not specified	1,424	17	125	17	19	169	132	16	2	44	414	28	7	43
Unknown	4,790	12	67	12	22	18	20	9	7	48	548	24	14	45

[a] Relationship is that of victim to offender. [b] Includes other categories not shown. [c] Total murder victims for whom supplemental homicide data were received.

Source: Derived from U.S. Department of Justice, FBI. Crime in the United States: Uniform Crime Reports 1997 (Washington, D.C.: GPO, 1998), p. 21.

Figure 2-2
Arrest Trends for Offenses Against
Family and Children, by Sex, 1988–1997

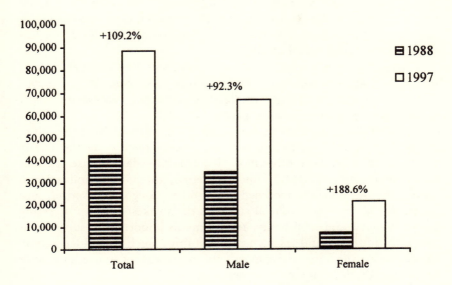

Source: U.S. Department of Justice, Federal Bureau of Investigation, *Crime in the United States: Uniform Crime Reports 1997* (Washington, D.C.: Government Printing Office, 1998), p. 226–27.

• The black female rate of murder by an intimate is 3 times higher than the rate of white females.[58]

Arrest Statistics and Family Offenses

Another measurement of tracking family violence, although somewhat limited in its effectiveness, is through the FBI's criminal report on crime statistics, *Crime in the United States: Uniform Crime Reports* (UCR). It contains a number of crime categories that may include family violence and abuse, including murder and nonnegligent manslaughter, aggravated assault, forcible rape, and other assaults. However, the one offense category specifically geared towards family-related crimes is "offenses against family and children." The UCR defines this as "nonsupport, neglect, desertion, or abuse of family and children."[59] For domestic violence incidents in which the police are called for assistance, approximately 20 percent of calls result in arrest of the offender.[60]

In 1997, there were 104,997 arrests for offenses against family and children.[61] More than 3 out of 4 of those arrested were male, while over 93 percent of the arrestees were age 18 or over.[62] Whites were arrested in more than 65 percent of the offenses against family and children, and blacks in nearly 32 percent of the arrests.[63] Other racial groups accounted for less than 3 percent of the total arrests.[64]

Arrest trends in Figure 2-2 show that between 1988 and 1997 arrests for offenses against family and children rose 109.2 percent. For males, arrests increased 92.3 percent. Female arrests grew even more dramatically at 188.6 percent over the 10-year period.

Notwithstanding these figures, most experts agree that arrest statistics reflect only a fraction of the true incidence of offenses against family and children, even when other more detailed crime data are used such as the earlier mentioned NIBRS. Police discretion, unreported family crimes, family offenses officially recorded under other categories of crime, and additional factors make official statistics the weakest area for assessing family violence and criminality. Yet it remains important to supplement victimization data and its own shortcomings, such as hidden family offenses and truthfulness of respondents, in presenting an overall picture of the magnitude of domestic crimes.

3. Demographic Features of Family Violence

Violence within the family has proven to be one of our toughest challenges in society. It comes at us in many forms including intimate violence, child abuse, sexual abuse, elderly victimization, and sibling violence. But the core of family violence continues to be spousal or domestic violence and child abuses. As we move into the twenty-first century, much of the familial violence involves guns and other killing weapons. The proliferation of firearms in America, both legal and illegal, has only increased the incidence of violence between relatives or the threat thereof. This suggests that more effective strategies are necessary to deal with the growing problem of family violence and weapons, along with insufficient laws and social controls on both fronts.

What are the demographic characteristics of those caught in the middle of family violence and their social and economic circumstances? This chapter will examine these important aspects of family violence.

Spouse Abuse

INCIDENCE

No one knows for certain how many women and men spouses are being battered and beaten, but every indicator is that the numbers are staggering (see Chapter 2). One study estimated that 3.9 million women were physically abused by a husband or live-in intimate in the United States in a given year.[1] Nearly 21 million were verbally or emotionally battered by an intimate. Another study estimated that 12 million men were victims of spouse abuse by their wives over the course of their marriage.[2] Richard Gelles found that 55 percent of married couples had experienced at least one episode of marital violence[3]; while Murray Straus approximated that 65 percent of all married couples engaged in one form or another of domestic violence during their marriage, with 25 percent of a serious nature.[4] An extrapolation of spouse abuse findings revealed that an estimated 1.8 million wives and 2 million husbands nationwide had experienced one or more incidents of severe spousal violence.[5]

GENDER

The typical perpetrator-victim pattern of spouse abuse is the male aggressor and female victim. This is largely supported in the literature. The National Crime Victimization Survey (NCVS) found that the rate of female victimization by an intimate was 5 times greater than the male rate of victimization.[6] Gelles found that 47 percent of the husbands sampled had ever been violent towards their spouse, compared to 32 percent of the wives.[7] A study of college students revealed that 16.7 percent of their fathers and 10 percent of their mothers had perpetrated physical abuse upon the other parent during the students' senior year in high school.[8]

Official data further support the contention that there are considerably more abusive men than women in domestic violence. Police reports estimate that complaints of spousal abuse perpetrated by males outnumber complaints of spousal abuse perpetrated by females by a ratio of 12 to 1.[9] Similarly, victimization surveys have found the ratio to be 13 abused wives for every abused husband.[10] Research by Rebecca Dobash and Russell Dobash yielded a ratio of male to female domestic violence of 66 to 1.[11]

Some studies have cast doubt on the disparity between male and female marital violence as indicated by the majority of findings. Straus and associates found roughly equal aggregate rates of spousal abuse among men and women, with women inflicting more severe abuse than men.[12] Another study reported that women and men committed approximately the same number of incidents of domestic violence, with men committing the more serious acts.[13] Suzanne Steinmetz advanced that husband abuse may be the most underreported type of domestic violence.[14]

Overall, most evidence supports the view that women are more likely to be the victims of spouse abuse, particularly involving serious injuries, than men.[15]

AGE

According to the FBI's National Incident-Based Reporting System (NIBRS), 3 out of every 4 victims of intimate violence are between the ages of 20 and 39.[16] Four in 10 are between 20 and 29, while more than 1 in 3 women victims of intimate violence are between ages 30 and 39. More than 15 percent of the victims are age 40 and over; just under 9 percent are under the age of 20. These patterns tend to be consistent whether the type of assault is aggravated, simple, or intimidation. Around 4 in 10 victims of aggravated assault are between the ages of 20 and 39.

The NCVS found that the actual rates of intimate violence are highest among women ages 16 to 24, followed by ages 25 to 34.[17] Women age 65 and over have the lowest rate of intimate violence.

Batterers of women tend to be of every age, though typically they appear to be in the greatest numbers under the age of 40.

MARITAL STATUS

Though much of the research on domestic violence focuses on married couples living together, many studies show that the incidence of violence among non-married intimates or estranged couples may be even higher than legally married intimates. Kersti Yllo and Straus found that cohabiting couples reported more incidents of domestic violence than did married couples.[18] A disproportionate number of cohabiting couples have been shown to be participants of intimate violence.[19] Separated or divorced women are 14 times as likely as married women to report having been the victim of abuse by a spouse or ex-spouse, according to the Bureau of Justice Statistics.[20] While separated or divorced women represent 10 percent of all women, they reported 75 percent of the violence between intimates.[21] Studies further show that women who leave their abusive spouse or threaten to do so are at higher risk to be killed by their partner than women who remain in the marriage.[22]

RACE/ETHNICITY

The race or ethnicity of the victim or offender does appear to be a factor in domestic violence, even though it occurs across racial and ethnic lines. Straus and associates' research indicated that the rate of spouse abuse among black couples was double that of white couples.[23] The rate of wife abuse was 3 times greater for blacks than whites, and husband abuse was twice as high among blacks.[24] Between 1992 and 1996, the NCVS reported

Table 3-1
Intimate Violence Rates,
by Race, Ethnicity, and Sex,
1994–1996

Victim characteristic	Average annual rate of nonlethal violent victimization by an intimate per 1,000[a]	
	Male	Female
White	1.4	8.2
Black	2.1	11.7
Other[b]	0.5	5.6
Hispanic[c]	1.3	7.2
Non-Hispanic	1.4	8.7

[a] Nonlethal intimate violence includes rape, sexual assault, robbery, and aggravated and simple assault. Because it is based on interviews with victims, the NCVS does not include murder. Intimates include current and former spouses, boyfriends, and girlfriends.

[b] Denotes Asians, Native Hawaiians or other Pacific Islanders, Alaska Natives, and American Indians.

[c] Hispanic or Latino persons could be of any race.

Source: Adapted from U.S. Department of Justice, Bureau of Justice Statistics Factbook, *Violence by Intimates* (Washington, D.C.: Government Printing Office, 1998), p. 43.

that about 12 per 1,000 black women were battered by an intimate, compared to 8 per 1,000 white women.[25]

Rates of domestic violence victimization by race, ethnicity, and sex for 1994 to 1996 can be seen in Table 3-1. Black females had the highest rate of intimate violence among all females and males of each racial and ethnic category. The black female rate of intimate violence was more than 22 times greater than the rate for men of races other than black or white. The rate of intimate violence for females of all races was considerably higher than that of males of all races. White females were more likely to be victims of intimate violence than females of other races, excluding black.

With respect to Hispanics, the rate for female victims of intimate violence was better than 5 times the rate of males. Non-Hispanic women were more likely than Hispanic women to be beaten by an intimate.

CLASS AND COMMUNITY SIZE

Research on the relationship between class and spouse abuse has shown mixed results, while reflecting the prevalence of domestic violence across class lines. G. Levinger found in a study of couples seeking divorce that intimate violence was reported most often among lower class women.[26] M. Bulcroft and Straus found spouse abuse for females and males to be higher in the working class than in the middle class.[27] Other research has suggested that spousal violence may be as prevalent, if not higher, in the middle and upper classes as in the lower classes.[28]

The type of community has been shown to be related to the prevalence of domestic violence. The NCVS found that urban women have a higher rate of nonlethal intimate violence than suburban and rural women, with the rates of violence among suburban and rural women roughly equal.[29] Male rates of intimate violence relative to community size are much lower than the rates of female intimate violence, with little variation between urban, suburban, and rural males.

INCOME

The evidence supports the theory that the rate of spousal violence decreases as income levels rise, or increases as income levels lower. A national survey of family violence revealed that 11 percent of the families with an annual income under $6,000 reported spouse abuse, compared to only 2 percent of the families with incomes of $20,000 or more.[30] Gelles's study found the rate of violence to be similar with respect to declining levels of income.[31]

Table 3-2 illustrates household income and rates of nonlethal intimate violence, by sex, nationally between 1992 and 1996. Women living in low income households experienced a higher rate of nonlethal violence from an intimate than women in households with higher incomes. Those females who lived in households with an income less than $7,500 had a rate of intimate violence more than 7 times that of females living in households with an income of $75,000 or more.

Male rates of nonlethal intimate violence were highest at the lowest household income level and lowest at the highest household income level. However, the rates did not decrease relative to an increase in household income. For instance, the male rate of intimate violence was lower for the

Table 3-2
Intimate Violence Rates,
by Household Income and Sex,
1992–1996

Household income	Average annual rate of nonlethal intimate violence per 1,000 persons[a]	
	Male	Female
Less than $7,500	2.7	21.3
$7,500 - $14,999	1.4	12.3
$15,000 - $24,999	1.8	10.4
$25,000 - $34,999	1.8	7.2
$35,000 - $49,999	1.1	5.8
$50,000 - $74,999	1.5	4.4
$75,000 or more	0.5	2.7

[a] Nonlethal intimate violence includes rape, sexual assault, robbery, and aggravated and simple assault. Because it is based on interviews with victims, the NCVS does not include murder. Intimates include current and former spouses, boyfriends, and girlfriends.

Source: Derived from U.S. Department of Justice, Bureau of Justice Statistics Factbook, *Violence by Intimates* (Washington, D.C.: Government Printing Office, 1998), p. 43.

household income level of $7,500–$14,999 than for several higher income levels. Women tended to have much higher rates of nonlethal intimate violence at all household income levels than men.

Some studies have shown a correlation between satisfaction with a level of income and domestic violence. For instance, in J. E. O'Brien's sample, the wife displayed serious dissatisfaction with her husband's income in 84 percent of the violent marriages and in only 24 percent of the nonviolent marriages.[32]

OCCUPATIONAL STATUS

Domestic violence has been shown to be more prevalent among blue-collar than white-collar workers. Straus and colleagues found the rate of severe spousal violence among blue-collar workers to be twice that of white-collar workers.[33] Gelles found that 82 percent of the violent husbands in his sample were of a lower occupational status than their nonviolent neighboring male spouses.[34] The highest rates of total and frequent violence occurred in married couples where the male spouse's occupational status was lower than that of the female spouse.

EMPLOYMENT

Employment status appears to be a significant indicator of domestic violence. A number of studies have shown a higher rate of spouse abuse among the unemployed than employed. Straus and colleagues found the rate of severe spousal violence to be 2 or 3 times greater in families where the male spouse was unemployed or employed only part-time than among families where the male spouse had a full-time job.[35] They also found severe domestic violence to be most common when the male spouse was disabled, as opposed to employed full-time, and least common among married couples when the male partner was retired. One study found that part-time employment was more closely related to violence in the family than unemployment.[36]

EDUCATIONAL LEVELS

An association between educational level and intimate violence has been documented through a number of studies, though with inconsistent findings. Gelles found rates of wife abuse to be highest among male spouses without a high school diploma, with rates steadily decreasing as the level of education increased.[37] However, the most violent wives in Gelles's sample were those with college degrees. Straus and associates' study also produced conflicting results, with male spouses who graduated from high school being the most abusive and men with less than 8 years of schooling or with some college but without a degree being the least abusive spouses.[38] With respect to gender differences, education, and intimate violence, studies tend to show that the rate of violence is greater for both spouses when the husband is less educated than the wife.[39]

WHERE AND WHEN INTIMATE VIOLENCE OCCURS

Eighty percent of all intimate violence takes place in the home, as reported by the NIBRS.[40] As seen in Table 3-3, which breaks down the percent of nonlethal intimate violence by sex, more than 7 in 10 female victims of intimate violence are victimized at or near their own home. Comparatively,

Table 3-3
Places Where Intimate
Violence Occurs

	Percent of nonlethal violence by intimates[a]	
	Male	Female
At or near own home	63.0	72.2
At or near other's home	18.3	12.2
Commercial place	3.4	2.8
At school	1.1	1.2
Open area of parking lot	12.2	9.1
Other	2.0	2.5

[a] Nonlethal intimate violence includes rape, sexual assault, robbery, and aggravated and simple assault. Because it is based on interviews with victims, the NCVS does not include murder. Intimates include current and former spouses, boyfriends, and girlfriends.

Source: Derived from U.S. Department of Justice, Bureau of Justice Statistics Factbook, *Violence by Intimates* (Washington, D.C.: Government Printing Office, 1998), p. 44.

just over 6 in 10 nonlethal intimate victimizations of males occur at or near their own home. Over 12 percent of females experience nonlethal violence at or near other's home, while more than 18 percent of the male victim's intimate violence occurs at or near other's home. Intimate violence is least likely to occur at school, in a commercial place, or other location.

Forty percent of intimate violence takes place on the weekend, with Friday the next most likely day of occurrence.[41] Three in 10 violent incidents between intimates occur between 9 p.m. and midnight.[42]

Child Abuse

INCIDENCE

Child abuse is arguably the most frequent form of family violence, and certainly the most devastating. Estimates of child abuse and neglect range from the National Center on Child Abuse and Neglect's estimate that 1 million children are maltreated by parents each year in the United States,[43] to David Gil's approximation of anywhere from 2.5 million to 4 million children are abused or neglected annually.[44] One study estimated that 1.5 million children are moderately or seriously abused each year in this country.[45]

According to the National Child Abuse and Neglect Data System (NCANDS), there were nearly 1 million substantiated cases of child abuse or neglect in 1996.[46] This number increased to approximately 1 million cases of confirmed child maltreatment in 1997.[47] Of these, 54 percent involved neglect, 22 percent physical abuse, 8 percent sexual abuse, 4 percent emotional abuse, and 12 percent other types of child mistreatment.

Studies have shown that between 84 and 97 percent of all families engage in spanking.[48] A national study of family violence by Straus and colleagues of 2,143 American families with children ages 3 to 17 living at home during the year of the survey found that among the families in which abuse had "ever happened," 8 percent of the children "were kicked, punched, or bitten approximately 9 times per year; 4 percent were beaten about 6 times yearly; and 3 percent were victimized by a knife or gun."[49] One expert estimated that 3.3 million children between the ages of 3 and 17 were at risk for violence committed by parents.[50]

ABUSIVE PARENTS

Gender

Parents account for more than 3 out of every 4 cases of child maltreatment.[51] Research indicates that mothers are more likely to abuse or neglect their children than fathers. Findings from the NCANDS Detailed Case Data Component (DCDC) revealed that 61 percent of the perpetrators of child maltreatment in 1996 were female.[52] Gelles's study found that 94 percent of the mothers, compared to 65 percent of the fathers, sampled physically mistreated their children at least once.[53] Brandt Steele and C. B. Pollock found that the mother was the abusing parent in 50 of the 57 cases studied.[54]

Age

The majority of child abusers fall between the ages of 20 and 40, the typical child-bearing, child-rearing years. Gil's sample indicated that 71 percent of the mothers or mother substitutes and 66 percent of the fathers or father substitutes were within this age range.[55] Blair and Rita Justice found that 3 in 4 of their sample group of parents were between 20 and 40 years of age.[56]

As shown in Table 3-4, the DCDC found that nearly 81 percent of the perpetrators of child abuse and neglect in 1996 were under the age of 40. The majority (39 percent) were between the ages of 30 and 39. Less than 6 percent were over the age of 50. More than 85 percent of the female abusers were under age 40, compared to 73.5 percent of the male abusers.

Race and Ethnicity

Much of the child abuse research indicates that there is little relationship between child maltreatment and the abuser's race or ethnicity. Some studies have found the rate of child abuse in black and white families to be similar.[57] Official data have shown child abuse to be more prevalent among blacks than whites.[58] However, other research such as the National Study of the Incidence and Severity of Child Abuse and Neglect suggests that child abuse may actually be lower in black families than white families.[59] More study is needed on race and ethnicity in relation to child maltreatment, particularly within racial or ethnic groups other than white or black.

Socioeconomics

Child maltreatment occurs at all socioeconomic levels in society. However, there is evidence that a higher incidence of child abuse exists among families of lower incomes. One study found that parents were 22 times more likely to abuse their children if their income level was under $15,000 a year compared to those with incomes of more than $30,000 a year.[60] A study by E. Bennie and A. Sclare found that 8 out of every 10 child abuse cases involved low income families.[61] Gil found that most of the abusive parents in his study did not graduate from high school and that nearly half the abusers were unemployed during some point in the year preceding the child maltreatment.[62]

ABUSED CHILDREN

Age

Studies reveal that there is some correlation between age and child maltreatment. However, this relationship tends to vary depending on both age and the types of maltreatment. In Table 3-5, types of child maltreatment by age are broken down for 1996 from DCDC data. The percent of physical, sexual, and emotional maltreatment generally increased with age; whereas neglect and medical neglect decreased with the age group of the child. More than 3 in 10 victims of physical abuse were age 12 and over, while nearly 36 percent of those sexually abused fell into this age category.

Table 3-4
Perpetrators of Child Maltreatment,
by Sex and Age, 1996

Age Group	Sex		Totals
	Male	Female	
19 and younger	5,727 (10.4%)	6,205 (7.2%)	11,932 (8.5%)
20-29	13,468 (24.5%)	33,464 (39.0%)	46,932 (33.3%)
30-39	21,241 (38.6%)	33,516 (39.1%)	54,757 (38.9%)
40-49	9,984 (18.2%)	8,885 (10.4%)	18,869 (13.4%)
50 and older	4,586 (8.3%)	3,681 (4.3%)	8,267 (5.9%)
Totals	55,006 (100.0%)	85,751 (100.0%)	140,757 (100.0%)

Source: U.S. Department of Health and Human Services, Children's Bureau, *Child Maltreatment 1996: Reports From the States to the National Child Abuse and Neglect Data System* (Washington, D.C.: Government Printing Office, 1998), p. 2-14.

Nearly half of all physical abuse victims were between the ages of 4 and 11, with 1 in every 5 victims under the age of 4. Almost 54 percent of the victims of sexual abuse were ages 4 to 11.

Over 30 percent of the victims of emotional maltreatment were age 12 and over, with nearly 54 percent between the ages of 4 and 11. More than half the medical neglect victims and over one-third of the victims of neglect were under the age of 4. Nearly 50 percent of the neglect victims fell between the ages of 4 and 11.

In all, 28 percent of the victims of maltreatment were under the age of 4, 27.8 percent ages 4 to 7, 21.5 percent between 8 and 11, and 22.7 percent age 12 and over.

Other research has yielded similar findings. C. Henry Kempe found abuse to be most common among children under the age of 3.[63] R. Galdston found the highest incidence of abuse to be among children 3 months to 3½ years old.[64] P. Resnick's study of child fatalities committed by parents

Table 3-5
Type of Child Maltreatment,
by Age of Victim, 1996

Age Group	Type of Maltreatment					Totals
	Physical Abuse	Neglect	Medical Neglect	Sexual Abuse	Emotional Maltreatment	
0-3	12,010	50,400	5,339	2,873	1,644	72,266
	(20.0%)	(33.7%)	(51.7%)	(10.3%)	(15.7%)	(28.0%)
4-7	15,454	43,559	2,169	7,932	2,710	71,824
	(25.7%)	(29.2%)	(21.0%)	(28.4%)	(26.0%)	(27.8%)
8-11	13,681	30,370	1,501	7,123	2,905	55,580
	(22.8%)	(20.3%)	(14.5%)	(25.5%)	(27.8%)	(21.5%)
12 and over	18,960	25,096	1,313	10,037	3,182	58,588
	(31.5%)	(16.8%)	(12.7%)	(35.9%)	(30.5%)	(22.7%)
Totals	60,285	149,425	10,322	27,965	10,441	258,438
	(100.0%)	(100.0%)	(100.0%)	(100.0%)	(100.0%)	(100.0%)

Source: U.S. Department of Health and Human Services, Children's Bureau, *Child Maltreatment 1996: Reports From the States to the National Child Abuse and Neglect Data System* (Washington, D.C.: Government Printing Office, 1998), p. 2-9.

indicated that most deaths occurred during the first year of life.[65] Gelles's study of physical violence against children 3 years of age and older found the percentage of abuse to be greater the younger the age group.[66]

GENDER

In general, the rate of child abuse and neglect appears to be similar between girls and boys though the rates tend to vary when speaking of specific types of maltreatment. Justice and Justice found that over half the abused children in their sample were female[67]; whereas Gil reported that more than half his sample of abused children were male.[68] The National Incidence Study (NIS) found neglect of girls and boys to be relatively equal.[69]

Data from the DCDC on types of child maltreatment by sex of victim in 1996 can be seen in Table 3-6. Fifty-two percent of the maltreatment victims were female, compared to 48 percent male. Sexual abuse showed the greatest disparity between girls and boys. More than 77 percent of the sexual maltreatment was perpetrated against females. Males were more likely than females to be victims of physical abuse, neglect, and medical neglect, with over half the totals in these types of maltreatment. Victims of emotional maltreatment were more likely to be female than male. Girls constituted 53 percent of the victims of emotional abuse.

Table 3-6
Type of Child Maltreatment,
by Sex of Victim, 1996

| Sex | Type of Maltreatment | | | | | Totals |
	Physical Abuse	Neglect	Medical Neglect	Sexual Abuse	Emotional Maltreatment	
Male	31,316	76,955	5,386	6,454	4,989	125,100
	(51.6%)	(51.2%)	(52.0%)	(22.8%)	(47.0%)	(48.0%)
Female	29,367	73,426	4,975	21,867	5,622	135,257
	(48.4%)	(48.8%)	(48.0%)	(77.2%)	(53.0%)	(52.0%)
Totals	60,683	150,381	10,361	28,321	10,611	260,357
	(100.0%)	(100.0%)	(100.0%)	(100.0%)	(100.0%)	(100.0%)

Source: U.S. Department of Health and Human Services, Children's Bureau, *Child Maltreatment 1996: Reports From the States to the National Child Abuse and Neglect Data System* (Washington, D.C.: Government Printing Office, 1998), p. 2-10.

Straus, Gelles, and Steinmetz found that child abuse rates peaked at ages 3 to 4 and 15 to 17, with boys experiencing abuse slightly more than girls.[70] American Humane Association (AHA) data found girls to be at a greater risk for physical and sexual abuse than boys.[71] The rate of child sexual abuse for females was more than 3 times the rate for males.

RACE AND ETHNICITY

Child abuse is not significantly related to race and/or ethnicity. However, certain groups such as African Americans and Native Americans have been shown to be disproportionately maltreated relative to their population figures in the United States. The types of child maltreatment by race or ethnicity of the victim in 1996 is shown in Table 3-7. Nearly 55 percent of the victims for all types of maltreatment were white, while almost 31 percent were African American, 12.2 percent Hispanic, 1.3 percent American Indian or Alaskan Native, and 1 percent Asian or Pacific Islander.

For African Americans, the percentage of total maltreatment is more than twice their proportion of the national child population; and the 44 percent of all victims of medical neglect over 3 times their population figures.[72] However, African American children had a disproportionately low percentage of sexual abuse and emotional maltreatment, each under 20 percent.

While white victims were underrepresented in overall maltreatment figures, they were disproportionately represented as victims of sexual abuse and emotional maltreatment, accounting for more than 6 in every 10 victims.

Table 3-7
Type of Child Maltreatment,
by Race/Ethnicity of Victim, 1996

Race/Ethnicity	Type of Maltreatment					Totals
	Physical Abuse	Neglect	Medical Neglect	Sexual Abuse	Emotional Maltreatment	
White	33,181 (56.1%)	76,967 (52.3%)	4,224 (41.3%)	17,978 (64.8%)	7,130 (68.9%)	139,480 (54.8%)
African American	16,406 (27.7%)	50,401 (34.3%)	4,509 (44.0%)	5,339 (19.2%)	1,684 (16.3%)	78,339 (30.8%)
Hispanic	8,053 (13.6%)	16,447 (11.2%)	1,299 (12.7%)	3,901 (14.1%)	1,265 (12.2%)	30,965 (12.2%)
American Indian/Alaska Native	670 (1.1%)	2,018 (1.4%)	145 (1.4%)	349 (1.3%)	167 (1.6%)	3,349 (1.3%)
Asian/Pacific Islander	842 (1.4%)	1,275 (0.9%)	61 (0.6%)	198 (0.7%)	104 (1.0%)	2,480 (1.0%)
Totals	59,152 (100.0%)	147,108 (100.0%)	10,238 (100.0%)	27,765 (100.0%)	10,350 (100.0%)	254,613 (100.0%)

Source: U.S. Department of Health and Human Services, Children's Bureau, *Child Maltreatment 1996: Reports from the States to the National Child Abuse and Neglect Data System* (Washington, D.C.: Government Printing Office, 1998), p. 2-12.)

Hispanics' percentage of sexual abuse was greater than their numbers in the population; while American Indian and Alaskan Native children had disproportionately high numbers for every type of maltreatment.

In spite of being underrepresented in national child maltreatment figures, Asians may be suffering from more child abuse than previously recognized. A recent study of abuse of high school boys revealed that 1 in 8 had been physically or sexually abused. Asian Americans and Hispanics had the highest rates of abuse.[73] Seventeen percent of the Asian boys said they were physically abused and 9 percent reported being sexually abused. Thirteen percent of the Hispanic boys had been physically abused and 7 percent sexually abused. Two-thirds of the reported physical abuse was perpetrated by a member of the family. One in 5 of the boys in the study reported being victims of medical neglect.

SOCIOECONOMICS

Child abuse and neglect crosses the social and economic strata. Some studies have found children at greater risk for maltreatment in lower income families. The NIS reported that children from families with an annual income below $15,000 had a victimization rate almost 7 times that of children from higher income families.[74] In Gil's study, 77 percent of the abusive fathers and 68 percent of the abusive mothers were in skilled or semiskilled jobs.[75] The majority of the abusive parents did not graduate from high school, with nearly one-fourth failing to complete the 8th grade.

4. Medical Treatment for Victims of Family Violence

Familial crimes such as domestic violence and child abuse and neglect can often require medical treatment of one sort or another for the victim. A high percentage of hospital emergency rooms around the country treat abuse victims every day, many of whom suffer from severe injuries as a direct result of spousal battering, child maltreatment, elderly abuse, or other types of family violence.[1] Many victims of battering and abuse receive treatment through primary care providers or family clinics. Some victims' injuries are serious enough to require hospitalization, or even result in death. In all, hundreds of thousands of women, children, elderly, and men are injured through mistreatment and violence within the family each year, necessitating medical attention.[2]

The cost of providing medical services to domestic crimes victims can be staggering. According to a study conducted at the Rush Medical Center in Chicago, the average charge for medical treatment given to abused women, children, and elderly victims was $1,633 per person each year. Nationally, this adds up to an annual total cost of more than $857 million.[3]

In spite of such figures, many believe the totals would be much higher were more victims of family violence and child abuse identified, recognized, reported, treated, and properly diagnosed.[4] A national health promotion objective for the year 2000 was for no less than 90 percent of the hospital emergency departments to have plans in place for routinely identifying, treating, and referring victims of family violence and sexual assault.[5]

What follows are some findings with respect to injuries and medical treatment related to domestic violence and child maltreatment:

- Around half the victims of domestic violence report an injury of a physical nature.[6]
- One in 10 women beaten by an intimate seeks medical attention.
- One in 5 *injured* female victims of violence committed by an intimate seeks medical treatment.
- Three in 10 injured women in emergency departments were identified as having injuries sustained from domestic violence.[7]
- More than 8 in 10 of those seeking medical treatment from an intentional injury perpetrated by an intimate are women.[8]
- About half of such injured victims of intimate violence are treated for bruises or similar type trauma.
- Nearly 3 in 10 injured women in an emergency department as a result of domestic violence required hospital admission; 13 percent needed major medical treatment.[9]
- Four in 10 severely injured battered women in emergency departments required previous medical treatment due to intimate violence.[10]
- One in 4 injured patients in emergency departments as a result of violence were victimized by a family member or intimate.
- Nearly 4 in 10 female victims of violence in emergency departments were injured by a spouse, ex-spouse, or boyfriend.[11]
- More than half the child emergency department patients under age 12 were injured by a family member.[12]
- Nearly 4 in 10 emergency department sexual abuse cases involving children younger than 12 are family child sexual abuse cases.[13]

Intimate Violence Injuries and Treatment in Hospital Emergency Departments

Violence by intimates resulting in hospital emergency department (ED) treatment for injuries sustained by the victim has reached epidemic proportions. In 1994, the most recent year in which comprehensive data are available, an estimated 1.4 million people were treated in EDs for non-fatal injuries related to interpersonal violence (see Table 4-1). Three-fifths of the injured were males and around half were under the age of 25. Just over half of all persons injured by violence in the ED were white. Black ED patients treated for injuries caused by violent acts were overrepresented relative to their population figures.

Table 4-1
Characteristics of Persons Treated in
Hospital Emergency Departments for
Violence-Related Injuries

Characteristic of emergency department patients injured by violence	Number treated	Percent	Rate per 1,000 U.S. residents
Total[a]	**1,417,500**	**100.0%**	**5.5**
Sex			
Male	862,000	60.8%	6.8
Female	554,700	39.1%	4.2
Not specified	900	0.1%	N/A
Race			
White	744,400	52.5%	3.4
Black	344,300	24.3%	10.5
Other	161,600	11.4%	14.4
Not recorded	167,200	11.8%	N/A
Age			
Under 12	75,600	5.3%	1.6
12-14	87,100	6.1%	7.8
15-18	199,600	14.1%	14.2
19-24	325,800	23.0%	14.9
25-34	389,600	27.5%	9.4
35-64	318,700	22.5%	3.5
65+	20,300	1.4%	0.6
Not recorded	900	0.1%	N/A

[a] Detail may not add to total shown because of rounding.

Source: U.S. Department of Justice, Bureau of Justice Statistics Special Report, *Violence-Related Injuries Treated in Hospital Emergency Departments* (Washington, D.C.: Government Printing Office, 1997), p. 2.

Among the injured patients, 17 percent were victims of violence perpetrated by intimates, such as spouses, ex-spouses, boyfriends, girlfriends, or ex-partners.[14] Women were significantly more likely than men to be treated for injuries caused by an intimate. The number of persons treated in EDs for injuries perpetrated by intimates was estimated at 4 times greater than estimates from the National Crime Victimization Survey.[15]

Table 4-2 reflects the number of injury cases treated in hospital EDs by type of violence and sex of victim in 1994. Women injured by intimates comprised around 1 in 5 visits to EDs as a result of intentional violence. Females were more than 5 times as likely as males to be treated for intimate violence-related injuries. Although females represented 39 percent of all hospital ED visits as a result of injuries arising from violence, they accounted for 84 percent of the persons being treated for injuries brought on by intimates in 1994.[16]

The patient-offender relationship in injuries sustained through violence, by the sex of the ED patient in 1994, can be seen in Table 4-3. Nearly 37 percent of female ED patients' violence-related injuries were inflicted by a spouse, ex-spouse, boyfriend, or ex-boyfriend. Comparatively, less than 5 percent of the male ED patients injured by violence were victims of someone they were intimately involved with. Women patients were nearly 6 times as likely as men patients to have been injured by a spouse or ex-spouse, and almost 5 times more likely to have injuries committed by a significant other, such as a boyfriend or ex-boyfriend.

Table 4-4 shows the general characteristics of injuries through violence treated at hospital EDs in 1994. Approximately one-third of injuries received by patients were bruises or similar type injuries. Nearly another one-third of patients were victims of cuts, stab wounds, or internal injuries. Around one-sixth of the injured were treated for muscular or skeletal injuries such as sprains, fractures, dislocations, or dental injuries. About one-tenth of the ED injuries were for gunshot wounds or sexual assaults.

In nearly 60 percent of injuries, there was no weapon used. Most patients were injured by being punched or kicked; others suffered falls during attacks or by being thrown into a wall, an object, or to the ground. etc. When a weapon was used, it was most likely something other than a firearm. In nearly 19 percent of the injuries, another object was used by the offender. Just over 4 percent of the injuries came as a result of a firearm.

A comparison of data on ED victims of intimate violence and violence by nonintimates, by the victim's age, weapon used to inflict violence, and type of injury in 1994, can be found in Table 4-5. According to the data from the National Electronic Injury Surveillance System, based on a national sample of hospital EDs, around 1 in 4 of the injuries caused by intentional violence was committed by an intimate. Most victims of intimate violence fell between the ages of 20 and 45, while nonintimate victims were more evenly spread between the ages of 13 to 45.

Table 4-2
Persons Treated in Hospital Emergency
Departments for Violence-Related Injuries,
by Type of Violence and Sex, 1994

	Number of injury cases treated in hospital emergency departments		
	Intimate violence[a]	Other types of violence	Unrecorded relationship
Total	243,316	700,777	383,633
Males	38,958	487,814	287,233
Females	204,358	212,963	96,400

[a] Intimates include current and former spouses and current boyfriends and girlfriends.

Source: U.S. Department of Justice, Bureau of Justice Statistics Factbook, *Violence by Intimates* (Washington, D.C.: Government Printing Office, 1998), p. 45; BJS, *Study of Injured Victims of Violence, 1994.*

Table 4-3
Patient/Offender Relationship
in Violence-Related Injuries, by the Sex
of Emergency Department Patient, 1994

	Hospital ED patients injured by violence			
	Male		Female	
	Number	Percent	Number	Percent
Total[a]	862,000	100.0%	554,700	100.0%
Spouse/ex-spouse	15,400	1.8%	88,400	15.9%
Other relative	56,900	6.6%	52,600	9.5%
Boy/girlfriend	23,600	2.7%	116,000	20.9%
Other friend	142,100	16.5%	86,100	15.5%
Other acquaintance	75,200	8.7%	27,200	4.9%
Stranger	248,800	28.9%	77,500	14.0%
Not reported	300,100	34.8%	106,900	19.3%

[a] Detail may not add to total shown because of rounding.

Source: U.S. Department of Justice, Bureau of Justice Statistics Special Report, *Violence-Related Injuries Treated in Hospital Emergency Departments* (Washington, D.C.: Government Printing Office, 1997), p. 5.

In nearly 3 in 4 cases of ED patients injured from intimate violence, there was no weapon used, compared to around 6 in 10 violent incidents involving nonintimates. Knives, sharp objects, bats, and other objects were used most often as weapons for both intimates and nonintimates who were injured; however, the proportion was lower for intimates. Nonintimates were more than 3 times as likely to be victims of a firearm than intimate victims of violence.

Almost half the persons treated for intimate violence suffered from bruises, with around one-fourth of the injuries cuts, stab wounds, or internal injuries. Approximately one-third of injuries sustained by nonintimates were bruises, and another one-third cuts, stab wounds, and internal injuries.

Slightly more than half the victims of intimate and nonintimate violence were treated for head or facial injuries. Nearly 1 in 5 intimate ED victims were treated for hand or arm injuries, and around 1 in 10 were injured in the upper trunk area. A similar pattern existed for victims of nonintimate violence.

Nearly 3 in 10 violence-related injuries of ED patients occurred at home. Less than 1 in 5 took place in stores, offices, or factories; while just under 1 in 10 took place in the street. The month in which violence resulting in injuries occurred was fairly evenly distributed across the 12 months, with the peak months being June through September — each accounting for more than 9 percent of the violence-related injuries experienced by ED patients.

More than 14 percent of injuries sustained by ED patients involved illegal drugs or alcohol. This was true for nearly 17 percent of the male patients and over 10 percent of the female patients.[17] Studies show that there is a high incidence of substance abuse in domestic violence situations (see Chapter 14).

Family Violence Injuries Treated in Hospital Emergency Departments

Family violence and child abuses are responsible for thousands of injuries being treated annually at hospital emergency departments nationwide. The relationship between ED patients injured through violence and the perpetrator of such violence in 1994 is shown in Table 4-6. A family member such as spouse, parent, child, sibling, or other relative were responsible for an estimated 15 percent of all intentional or possibly intentionally perpetrated injuries. A parent was more than 3 times as likely to

Table 4-4
Characteristics of Violence-Related Injuries
Treated at Hospital Emergency Departments, 1994

Characteristic of injury and violent event	Number	Percent	Characteristic of injury and violent event	Number	Percent
Injury diagnosis			**Place of occurrence**		
Total[a]	1,417,500	100.0%	Total[a]	1,417,500	100.0%
Shot	70,300	5.0%	Home	410,300	28.9%
Concussion/head injury	50,900	3.6%	Street	128,300	9.0%
Muscular/skeletal injury	234,800	16.6%	Store, office, factory	246,400	17.3%
Cut/stab wound/internal injury	433,500	30.6%	School	54,800	3.9%
Bruise	477,600	33.7%	Recreational area	20,300	1.4%
Burns/chemical injury	13,300	0.9%	Not recorded	557,300	39.4%
Poisoned	1,400	0.1%			
Rape/sexual assault	63,800	4.5%	**Month of occurrence**		
Other	72,000	5.1%	Total[a]	1,417,500	100.0%
			January	101,300	7.1%
			February	90,700	6.4%
Weapon used			March	102,400	7.2%
Total[a]	1,417,500	100.0%	April	115,600	8.2%
No weapon	827,700	58.4%	May	114,300	8.1%
Firearm	60,900	4.3%	June	135,200	9.5%
Hit with gun	15,300	1.1%	July	136,100	9.6%
Knife/sharp object	100,100	7.0%	August	139,800	9.9%
Other object	264,900	18.7%	September	129,600	9.1%
BB/pellet gun	9,400	0.7%	October	124,100	8.8%
Not recorded	139,200	9.8%	November	115,700	8.2%
			December	112,700	8.0%

[a] Detail may not add to total shown because of rounding.

Source: U.S. Department of Justice, Bureau of Justice Statistics Special Report, *Violence-Related Injuries Treated in Hospital Emergency Departments* (Washington, D.C.: Government Printing Office, 1997), p. 3.

Table 4-5
Emergency Department Victims of Violence, by Type of Violence, Weapon Used, and Injuries, 1994

	Patients treated in hospital emergency departments[a]	
	Victims of intimate violence	Victims of violence by nonintimate
Victim's age		
13-19	9.7%	29.7%
20-29	42.2%	32.4%
30-45	41.6%	29.2%
46 or older	6.5%	8.7%
Weapons used to injure victim		
No weapon used	73.5%	61.9%
Weapon used	21.0%	32.0%
Firearm	1.1%	3.5%
Knife/sharp object	7.4%	6.6%
Bat, or object used to hit	9.6%	15.9%
Other	2.9%	6.0%
Not recorded	5.6%	6.1%
Diagnosis of injury		
Bruise	48.6%	32.7%
Cut/stab wound/internal injury	24.1%	31.3%
Muscular/skeletal injury	16.9%	20.6%
Concussion/head injury	0.9%	1.4%
Rape/sexual assault	2.2%	4.1%
Gunshot wound	1.0%	3.4%
All other	6.4%	6.3%
Part of body injured		
Head/face	51.1%	57.4%
Upper trunk	9.6%	9.9%
Lower trunk	4.8%	3.5%
Hands/arms	18.1%	14.5%
Feet/legs	4.5%	5.1%
Other	2.1%	3.5%
25%-50% of body	6.4%	3.6%
All parts of the body	2.5%	2.2%
Not recorded	0.9%	0.3%
Number	243,000	701,000

[a] The table excludes 384,000 patients who either could not or did not report the victim-offender relationship. Intimates include spouses, ex-spouses, boyfriends, and girlfriends.

Source: Adapted from U.S. Department of Justice, Bureau of Justice Statistics Factbook, *Violence by Intimates* (Washington, D.C.: Government Printing Office, 1998), p. 22.

Table 4-6
Relationship Between the Emergency Department Patient Injured by Violence and the Person Committing That Violence, 1994

Relationship to patient	Number	Percent
Total[a]	1,417,500	100.0%
Spouse/ex-spouse	103,800	7.3%
Parent	40,400	2.8%
Child	11,500	0.8%
Other relative	57,700	4.1%
Boy/girlfriend	139,600	9.8%
Other friend	228,200	16.1%
Other acquaintance	102,400	7.2%
Stranger	326,400	23.0%
Not reported	407,600	28.8%

[a]Detail may not add to total shown because of rounding.

Source: U.S. Department of Justice, Bureau of Justice Statistics Special Report, *Violence-Related Injuries Treated in Hospital Emergency Departments* (Washington, D.C.: Government Printing Office, 1997), p. 5.

have injured a child ED patient than the other way around. Boyfriends, girlfriends, or former intimates were the offenders in almost 10 percent of the violence-related injuries sustained by ED patients.

Children under the age of 12 treated in emergency departments for injuries caused by violence were far more likely to have been injured by a relative than a stranger, as seen in Table 4-7. More than 56 percent of the child patients younger than 12 received injuries from a relative, illustrating the significant relationship between child abuse and injuries to the victim requiring ED treatment.[18] Just over 34 percent of the perpetrators of violence-related child injuries were acquaintances, while less than 10 percent of the injuries were caused by a stranger.

ED teenage patients were injured by relatives in less than 12 percent of the cases, while more than 58 percent were victims of violence by acquaintances. More than 20 percent of adult patients age 20 and over received violence-related injuries from a relative, while nearly 44 percent were victimized by acquaintances.

Table 4-8 indicates the type of offense in violence-related injuries

Table 4-7
Emergency Department
Patient-Offender Relationship,
by Type and Age of Patient, 1994

Age of ED Patient	Total	Relationship to the patient of the person who inflicted the injury		
		Relative	Acquaintance	Stranger
Child (younger than 12)	100%	56.3%	34.1%	9.7%
Teenager (age 12-19)	100%	11.9%	58.2%	29.9%
Adult (age 20 or older)	100%	20.9%	43.9%	35.2%

Source: Derived from U.S. Department of Justice, Bureau of Justice Statistics Special Report, *Violence-Related Injuries Treated in Hospital Emergency Departments* (Washington, D.C.: Government Printing Office, 1997), p. 6.

treated in hospital EDs, by age of patient, in 1994. Most patients among all age groups were most likely to be treated for injuries arising from assaults. Around 30 percent of the teenage and adult patient assault victimizations involved fights or altercations, compared to under 10 percent of the child patients under age 12.

Young children were far more likely than teenagers or adults to be treated for suspected or confirmed rape or sexual assault. More than 29 percent of the injuries suffered by ED child patients under 12 were for rape or sexual assault, while less than 5 percent of the teen injuries and under 3 percent of the adult injuries were a reflection of sexual assaults of any kind.

Of the children younger than 12 receiving ED treatment in 1994, half of those being treated for sexual abuse were age 4 and under, while half the child patients receiving treatment for other types of violence-related injuries were age 5 or under.[19] In 39 percent of the rape and sexual abuse cases involving children under the age of 12, the patients were brought to the ED by parents or guardians who suspected the child may have been sexually abused or assaulted.[20]

Identifying Family Violence Victims

The evidence suggests that many victims of domestic violence and child abuse are not being identified by physicians and other medical staff during examination or treatment. Consider the following findings:

Table 4-8
Offense Type in Violence-Related Injuries
Treated in Hospital Emergency Departments,
by Age of Patient, 1994[a]

	Total	Child (under age 12)	Teen (age 12-19)	Adult (age 20 or older)
Number				
Total[b]	1,416,700	75,600	341,000	1,000,000
Rape/sexual assault	65,100	22,100	15,500	27,500
Robbery	22,000	100	2,300	19,600
Assault	1,329,600	53,500	323,200	952,900
Fight/altercation	416,500	7,100	113,200	296,200
Assault	913,100	46,400	210,000	656,700
Percent				
Total[b]	100.0%	100.0%	100.0%	100.0%
Rape/sexual assault	4.6%	29.2%	4.5%	2.8%
Robbery	1.6%	0.1%	0.7%	2.0%
Assault	93.9%	70.7%	94.8%	95.3%
Fight/altercation	29.4%	9.4%	33.2%	29.6%
Assault	64.5%	61.3%	61.6%	65.7%

[a] Table excludes cases for which age of patient was not ascertained.

[b] Detail may not add to totals shown because of rounding.

Source: U.S. Department of Justice, Bureau of Justice Statistics Special Report, *Violence-Related Injuries Treated in Hospital Emergency Departments* (Washington, D.C.: Government Printing Office, 1997), p. 7.

- Ninety-two percent of battered women do not discuss the domestic violence with their physicians.[21]
- In 40 percent of cases in a study of battered women being treated in a hospital emergency department, physicians failed to discuss the battering with the patients.[22]
- In a study of women at a family clinic, nearly 23 percent reported being physically abused by an intimate within the past year, with a lifetime rate of battering at around 39 percent. Only 6 of the 394 women surveyed had ever been questioned by their physician about domestic violence.[23]
- In one study of a metropolitan emergency department with a protocol for domestic violence, the ED physician did not get a psychosocial history from the battered woman, ask about abuse, or inquire concerning the victim's safety in 92 percent of the cases of domestic violence.[24]

- A high percentage of abused elderly victims' clinical symptoms are mis-diagnosed as due to aging.[25]
- Most battered parents do not admit being abused by their progeny to physicians or others.[26]
- A national study of 143 accredited medical schools in the United States and Canada found that 53 percent of the schools did not require medical students to be educated about domestic violence.[27]

Other studies have supported the lack of preparedness, education, ability to recognize, and indifference of many physicians, other hospital staff, and medical schools with respect to domestic crimes and family violence. In a recent survey of hospital personnel, it was found that less than 5 percent of the evidence of domestic violence was recognized in women patients.[28] In another study of the prevalence of domestic violence among an inpatient female population at a nontrauma urban teaching hospital, 26 percent of the respondents reported ever being in a violent relationship. Not one of the 181 patients, ages 18 to 60, were asked by hospital staff about domestic violence or victimization by an intimate.[29]

Of great concern is the inadequate training of medical students on domestic violence and its dynamics. In a survey of medical school education regarding domestic violence sent to member schools of the Association of American Medical Colleges, 53 percent of the schools that responded gave no instruction to students concerning domestic violence.[30] Forty-two percent had at least one required course on the subject, while 5 percent of the colleges reported that there were elective courses available containing information on domestic violence.

CHILD ABUSE–RELATED INJURIES

Child abuse victims are also at risk for nondetection or misdiagnosis of injuries as a result of child abuse or neglect. Many children being treated in hospitals and clinics across the country have abuse-related injuries that are being misidentified or unrecognized as to their cause. Young children are especially susceptible to sustaining injuries due to child abuse that may be overlooked or given the wrong diagnosis by medical workers. "Because diagnostic reasoning is often shaped by the history provided" of an abused child patient, usually by the parent or guardian, "a misleading history can misdirect the diagnostic process and result in an incorrect diagnosis."[31] In a study of fractures in 52 abused children under 3 years of age, in only 1 instance did a parent initially report a case of child abuse.[32] In nearly 9 out of 10 cases the most common victims' history as reported by the parent or caretaker was a fall or abnormality, such as a seizure, in explaining the fracture; or sibling abuse. Another study of undetected maltreatment found that in nearly one-third of the cases of head injuries in toddlers and babies caused by child abuse, doctors failed to notice the injuries.[33] This was particularly true when such injuries occurred in white children from two-parent households. The study found that doctors even failed to detect life threatening problems such as brain hemorrhaging and skull fractures. The researchers contended that 80 percent of the child fatality victims of injuries due to child maltreatment might have lived had the abuse been recognized sooner.

Supporting these findings of misidentification of child abuse are two other studies. In C. Jenny and colleagues' analysis of a study on doctors' failure to recognize head injuries caused by child abuse, it was found that nearly 1 in 3 children under the age of 3 with a final diagnosis of child abuse–related head injury had visited a physician at least once previously and there had been a misdiagnosis of the injuries.[34] Twenty-eight of the victims were reinjured as a result and 4 child deaths may have been averted with an earlier correct diagnosis.

The National Committee to Prevent Child Abuse found that 41 percent of abused children who died between 1995 and 1997 had been seen by staff from child protective services agencies.[35] Reflecting misconceptions about child abuse with respect to socioeconomics and race factors, the study reported that physicians misdiagnosed abuse in nearly 40 percent of head injury cases due to child maltreatment in white children or children from two-parent families, while not identifying the abuse in around 20 percent of cases involving minority children or children living in single parent homes.

ELDERLY ABUSE–RELATED INJURIES

Similar to child victims of abuse, elderly abuse victims are vulnerable to an incorrect diagnosis by physicians of injuries due to familial or custodial abuse or neglect. Clinicians for elderly patients frequently ignore signs of maltreatment often "attributable to the normal process of aging. Recurrent fractures, for instance, may be automatically ascribed to the brittle bones of osteoporosis. Malnourishment may be attributed to the nutritional problems and poor appetite that often accompany old age."[36] This unfortunate misinterpretation of elderly victimization, along with the difficulty in getting victims to report abuse, makes it all the more critical for medical personnel to be able to recognize and treat such maltreatment for what it is.

The same sense of urgency holds true for properly diagnosing all forms of family violence. More education and training is needed across the board in the medical community in understanding and identifying familial and intimate-related battering and sexual abuse, asking the right questions of victims, reporting suspected cases of violence in the home to authorities, and properly diagnosing and treating domestic violence, child abuse, and elderly abuse victims.

PART II

Family and Intimate Violence

5. Domestic Fatalities

Undeniably the worst possible consequence of family violence is a fatality. Each year in the United States thousands are homicide victims of family members. These include wives, husbands, children, parents, siblings, and grandparents. Most of the victims have been abused, beaten, or neglected by the perpetrator, sometimes for years. In many instances, the circumstances and warning signs leading up to domestic fatalities have been either minimized or ignored altogether. In other cases, intervention by family members, law enforcement, or other agencies was inadequate, or came too late to prevent the tragedy.

Fueling domestic homicides is the increasing availability of handguns, often bought legally and kept inside the home. According to a study on domestic fatalities and gun ownership, the risk of homicide committed by a family member of the victim is higher when firearms are kept in the household.[1] The risks of homicidal violence are even greater when there is a history of domestic violence, child abuse, or substance abuse. Illustrating the relationship between guns and familial deaths, 6 in 10 intimate murders in 1996 involved the use of a firearm.[2]

This chapter will examine the specter of familial and intimate homicides in this country.

Homicide in the Family

The murder of a family member may be the most tragic type of homicide. Unfortunately, it is becoming all too common in a society where aggression, family violence, drugs or alcohol, and handguns can merge into deadly domestic confrontations. According to FBI statistics, in 1997 there were more than 2,500 murders or nonnegligent manslaughters committed by relatives or intimates in the United States.[3] Nearly half of all murder victims knew their killers. Thirteen percent were related to the perpetrator, and 35 percent of the victims were acquainted with their assailants.[4]

Several studies have found a "special interpersonal relationship" between murder victims and their perpetrators, in which violence comes as a result of built-up hostilities that have reached a boiling point after years of the murderer being taunted, teased, or suppressed.[5] Perpetrators of domestic murders have been described as "passive and submissive, preferring to avoid open conflict when possible, especially if playing a masochistic role leads to gaining their affection."[6] Marvin Wolfgang cited the suicidal nature of some victims of familial homicide who so aggressively provoke violence towards themselves by a family member that they can be viewed as suicides.[7]

Intimate Murders

Murder by an intimate accounts for the majority of domestic homicides. Women are most likely to be the victims of intimate murders. Of total female murder victims in the United States in 1997, 29 percent were slain by husbands or boyfriends.[8] This compares to just 3 percent of male victims being killed by wives or girlfriends. More than twice the number of women are murdered by intimates as by strangers.[9] Studies have found that 7 in 10 murdered women are killed by a husband, boyfriend, or ex-intimate partner.[10] Around two-thirds of the victims were battered women.[11]

Separated or divorced women appear at particular high risk to be murdered by an ex-intimate. One study approximated that half the female homicides by intimates were perpetrated after the victim separated from the abusive male.[12] Another study found that 1 in 4 women killed by intimate partners were murdered while seeking to separate.[13]

TRENDS IN INTIMATE MURDERS

According to the Bureau of Justice Statistics Factbook, *Violence by Intimates*, between 1976 and 1996, nearly 52,000 men and women were murdered in the United States by someone with whom they had an intimate relationship.[14] Intimate murders constituted 30 percent of all female murders over the period and 6 percent of total male murders. A percentage breakdown of murder victims killed by an intimate, by age of victim and sex, from 1976 to 1996 is shown in Table 5-1. Females of every age

Table 5-1
Intimate Murder Victims, by Age and Sex,
1976–1996

Age of victim	Percent of murder victim killed by intimates	
	Male	Female
17 or younger	0.8	5.8
18-24	2.5	28.5
25-29	5.5	36.3
30-34	7.6	41.3
35-39	9.3	44.3
40-44	10.6	41.4
45-49	11.7	40.2
50-59	10.8	31.8
60 or older	6.9	19.3

[a] Intimates include spouses, ex-spouses, common-law spouses, same sex partners, boyfriends, and girlfriends. Murder includes nonnegligent manslaughter.

Source: Derived from U.S. Department of Justice, Bureau of Justice Statistics Factbook, *Violence by Intimates* (Washington, D.C.: Government Printing Office, 19⋅ Federal Bureau of Investigation, Supplementary Hoi Reports, 1976-1996.

bracket were far more likely to be murdered by an intimate than males. More than 4 in 10 female murder victims between the ages of 30 and 49 were murdered by someone they had been intimately involved with. Over one-third of the murdered women age 25 to 29 were killed by intimates. Male murder victims aged 40 to 59 were most likely to have been killed by an intimate partner, but only represented just over 1 in every 10 murdered men.

Figures 5-1 and 5-2 reflect the breakdown by percent of victim-offender relationship in intimate murders between 1976 and 1996. Over the two decades, 31,260 women were slain by intimates. Sixty-four percent were killed by husbands, 32 percent by nonmarital partners, and 5 percent by ex-husbands. Of the 20,311 male intimate murder victims, 62 percent were murdered by wives, 34 percent by nonmarital partners, and 4 percent by ex-wives.

Figure 5-1
Female Intimate Murder Victims,
by Type of Relationship to Intimate, 1976–1996

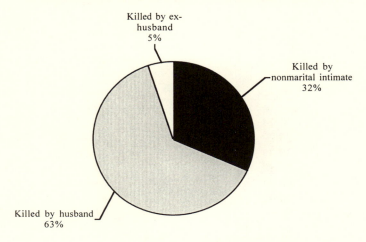

Based on 31,260 total female victims

Source: Constructed from U.S. Department of Justice, Bureau of Justice Statistics Factbook, *Violence by Intimates* (Washington, D.C.: Government Printing Office, 1998), p. 6; Federal Bureau of Investigation, Supplementary Homicide Reports, 1976-1996.

In spite of these disturbing figures of domestic homicides, between 1976 and 1996 the number of intimate murders dropped sharply (see Table 5-2). Overall, intimate murders declined 36 percent during the two decades, while spouse murders decreased by 52 percent.

With respect to race, the number of intimate murders involving blacks declined at a greater rate than those involving whites between 1976 and 1996. As seen in Table 5-3, the rate of intimate murders among blacks dropped from 11 times that of whites to just over 4 times higher than the intimate murder rate among whites. Over the two decades, the number of murders of black intimates fell from 14 per 100,000 blacks age 20 to 44, to just below 4 per 100,000, decreasing an average of 6 percent every year. Comparatively, the number of murders of white intimates dropped from around 1.3 per 100,000 age 20 to 44, to 0.85 intimate murders per 100,000, declining by an average of 2 percent each year.

Annually, between 1976 and 1996, the per capita rates of intimate homicides decreased an average of 8 percent for black males, 5 percent for black females, 4 percent for white males, and 1 percent for white females.[15]

Figure 5-2
Male Intimate Murder Victims,
by Type of Relationship to Intimate, 1976–1996

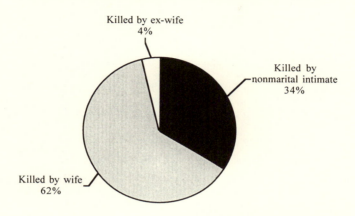

Killed by ex-wife
4%

Killed by
nonmarital intimate
34%

Killed by wife
62%

Based on 20,311 total male victims

Source: Constructed from U.S. Department of Justice, Bureau of Justice Statistics Factbook, *Violence by Intimates* (Washington, D.C.: Government Printing Office, 1998), p. 6; Federal Bureau of Investigation, Supplementary Homicide Reports, 1976-1996.

Child Abuse Fatalities

Child deaths due to child abuse and neglect are occurring across this country with alarming regularity. Estimates of the number of children dying by their parents' hands vary, but illustrate the epidemic nature of this branch of domestic criminality. Vincent Fontana conservatively estimated that 700 children are killed by parents or guardians in the United States every year.[16] *Pediatric News* reported that a child dies from abuse each day of the year.[17] The National Incidence Study estimated that 1,000 children die each year due to child abuse or neglect.[18] Sandra Arbetter estimated there are 600 cases of women alone killing their children each year.[19]

Alex Morales contends that 3,000 children will die from abuse each year in this country, with half the victims younger than age 1 and 90 percent under 4 years of age.[20] Ray Helfer warned that unless steps were taken to stop child abuse, there could be over 5,000 child deaths a year.[21]

According to the National Child Abuse and Neglect Data System, nearly 1,100 child maltreatment fatalities occurred in the 50 states and the District of Columbia in 1996.[22] More than 3 out of every 4 children killed were under the age of 4.

Table 5-2
Intimate Murders,[a] by Type,
1976–1996

	Number of intimate murder victims		
Year	Spouse	Ex-spouse	Boy/ girlfriend
1976	2,174	123	662
1977	2,017	110	603
1978	1,940	116	629
1979	1,940	146	683
1980	1,911	115	744
1981	1,946	136	768
1982	1,722	136	763
1983	1,676	128	770
1984	1,501	97	833
1985	1,581	111	811
1986	1,542	127	901
1987	1,489	96	841
1988	1,467	100	869
1989	1,326	78	913
1990	1,371	110	879
1991	1,297	82	918
1992	1,262	81	834
1993	1,232	94	964
1994	1,145	91	861
1995	1,030	60	776
1996	987	73	749

[a] Murder includes nonnegligent manslaughter.
Data are for all ages of victims.

Source: Derived from U.S. Department of Justice,
Bureau of Justice Statistics Factbook, *Violence
by Intimates* (Washington, D.C.: Government
Printing Office, 1998), p. 39; Federal Bureau of
Investigation, Supplementary Homicide Reports,
1976-1996.

Table 5-4 provides a breakdown of child fatalities, by age and sex in 11 states, in 1996, representing approximately one-third of the child fatalities by maltreatment in the United States. Seventy-six percent of the victims were younger than 4 years of age, with an additional 14.3 percent

Table 5-3
Intimate Murder Rates, by Race and Sex,
1976–1996

| | Rate of murder by an intimate per 100,000 persons age 20-44 | | | | | |
| | White | | | Black | | |
Year	Total	Male	Female	Total	Male	Female
1976	1.31	0.89	1.72	14.01	16.51	12.01
1977	1.27	0.93	1.61	11.94	14.97	9.49
1978	1.30	0.88	1.72	11.38	13.32	9.83
1979	1.35	0.97	1.73	11.10	13.34	9.33
1980	1.37	0.91	1.81	10.66	12.36	9.30
1981	1.33	0.92	1.73	9.64	11.14	8.40
1982	1.30	0.82	1.77	8.33	9.72	7.17
1983	1.22	0.82	1.61	8.35	9.20	7.65
1984	1.17	0.69	1.65	7.06	7.75	6.47
1985	1.20	0.70	1.70	6.95	7.46	6.53
1986	1.21	0.70	1.73	7.36	7.55	7.19
1987	1.14	0.65	1.63	6.46	6.90	6.10
1988	1.13	0.59	1.68	6.60	6.62	6.58
1989	1.01	0.56	1.45	6.36	6.70	6.07
1990	1.06	0.58	1.54	6.24	6.08	6.39
1991	1.02	0.53	1.51	6.02	5.36	6.58
1992	0.98	0.54	1.42	5.35	4.59	6.00
1993	1.03	0.49	1.57	5.62	4.75	6.36
1994	0.99	0.47	1.51	4.84	4.55	5.09
1995	0.89	0.38	1.40	3.87	3.33	4.32
1996	0.85	0.36	1.34	3.74	2.83	4.51

Source: Derived from U.S. Department of Justice, Bureau of Justice
Statistics Factbook, *Violence by Intimates* (Washington, D.C.: Government
Printing Office, 1998), p. 40; Federal Bureau of Investigation, Supplementary
Homicide Reports, 1976-1996.

between ages 4 and 7. Nearly 1 in 5 children killed due to child abuse or
neglect were between the ages of 8 and 11, while just over 3 percent were
12 and over.

Male child fatality victims outnumbered female child victims overall. However, percentage-wise, females were more likely than males to be
victims of fatalities when considering children age 7 and under.

The typical mother and father who kill their children are characterized as follows:

Table 5-4
Child Fatality Victims by Sex and Age,
1996

Age Group	Child Sex		Totals[a]
	Male	Female	
0-3	128	106	234
	(74.4%)	(78.5%)	(76.2%)
4-7	23	21	44
	(13.4%)	(15.6%)	(14.3%)
8-11	15	4	19
	(8.7%)	(3.0%)	(6.2%)
12 and over	6	4	10
	(3.5%)	(3.0%)	(3.3%)
Totals	172	135	307
	(100.0%)	(100.0%)	(100.0%)

[a]Totals are for 11 states using the Detailed Case Data Component (DCDC) of the National Child Abuse and Neglect Data System.

Source: U.S. Department of Health and Human Services, Children's Bureau, *Child Maltreatment 1996: Reports from the States to the National Child Abuse and Neglect Data System* (Washington, D.C.: Government Printing Office, 1998), p. 2-13.

Women who kill their infants or young children usually are severely disturbed, suffer from extreme bouts of depression and may experience delusions. Before a woman kills her offspring, she is likely to go through a preliminary period when she thinks about how to commit the crime, visualizes the dead child and considers suicide. Fathers rarely kill their young children, but when they do, they also build up to the crime and often have a history of child abuse.

Fathers who murder are more likely to kill their teenage sons. These men are marginally adequate husbands and fathers who feel inferior and frustrated by life. Guns and alcohol play significant roles in their lives. Their criminal records, if any, usually involve drinking, drunk driving, and disorderly conduct. They rarely have a history of psychiatric illness. They simply are explosive individuals who kill impulsively.[23]

INFANTICIDE

Infanticide is defined as the killing of an infant, usually soon after birth. Mothers are primarily the perpetrators of this form of familial homicide.

Infanticide has traditionally been regarded as a sex-specific offense, or one that "actually excludes the members of one sex by legal definition."[24] In describing the English legal system, it has been noted that "infanticide does not apply to the British principle of equal applicability because it is an offense in which only women are considered the perpetrators."[25]

No one knows for sure how many infants are killed by mothers in the United States each year, but it is believed that the numbers may be higher than official statistics may indicate. In 1991, around 9 newborn infants per 100,000 were killed by parents.[26] Most such deaths occur from unintentional fatal injuries, abuse, or neglect. A recent study found that young, unmarried, undereducated mothers were more likely to kill their infants than other mothers.[27] Poverty is also believed to be a factor in infanticide, as well as depression. As many as 40 percent of all new mothers suffer from depression after childbirth.[28]

Maria Piers described the horrors of infanticide in modern society:

> A doctoral candidate in the social sciences at one of the large midwestern universities, who was teaching courses in the social sciences to employees of a large city sewer system, learned from these employees that during the previous year, four corpses of newborns had been found on the sewer screen. The newborns had been thrown directly after birth into the sewers, a preferred place for children's corpses for millennia. No identification or investigation was attempted in these cases of infant death.[29]

Familial Homicide by Children

Although relatively rare, familial fatalities and homicides perpetrated by children do occur. Recent years have seen some high profile cases of children murdering family members. Typically abuse is involved, along with firearms. In 1997, there were nearly 400 murders committed against fathers, mothers, sisters, and brothers in the United States.[30] Many others are seriously injured or physically threatened by persons under the age of 18.

D. Sargeant hypothesized that in some instances child killers are the unwitting "lethal agent" of an adult, usually a parent, who "unconsciously incites them to kill in order that the adult can vicariously enjoy the benefits of the act."[31] L. Bender and F. J. Curran advanced that the most common factor in child homicides or attempted murder is the "child's tendency to identify himself with aggressive parents, and pattern after their behavior."[32] The *American Journal of Psychiatry* found that homicidal behavior among children is often associated with very violent parents (particularly the father), a history of psychomotor seizures and suicidal behavior, and/or previous psychiatric treatment by the mother.[33] According to B. M. Cormier and colleagues: "Amongst those adolescents who kill within the nuclear group, there is an inability to displace the problems encountered with the parents on to a broader group, such as their peers, where the problem can be defused and new gratifications experienced."[34]

Some evidence suggests that parents may actually encourage homicidal aggression on the part of their children. C. H. King cited the case of 9 adolescents who had committed homicide at about the age of 14.[35] Each had been subjected to extreme child abuse. In another study of adolescent murder and assaults, W. M. Easson and R. M. Steinhilber found that all the adolescents came "from socially acceptable normal family homes.... All cases demonstrate that one or both parents had fostered and had condoned murderous assault."[36]

6. Battered Women

The battering of women by their husbands, boyfriends, and others with whom they are or were intimately involved continues to occur in this country with alarming regularity. In spite of the considerable efforts to attract attention to domestic violence, society has fallen short in significantly reducing the problem, much less eliminating the violence. As a result, battered wives, ex-wives, girlfriends, and ex-girlfriends are still living in fear of male batterers (and sometimes female batterers) and, in some instances, paying the ultimate price in battering by being murdered by their significant others.

This chapter will examine the issue of women battered by men as well as subgroups of abused women.

Defining the Battered Woman

The battering of women has been identified through a number of terms, including wife beating, wife abuse, domestic violence, spouse abuse, conjugal violence, and the "battered woman's syndrome." Though the terms may be interchangeable, the basic definition of the battered woman is fairly clear and explicit. In its broadest sense, woman battering is defined as "physical beatings with fists or other objects, choking, stabbing, burning, whipping — any form of [intimate] — inflicted physical violence — as well as psychological mistreatment in the form of threats, intimidation, isolation, degradation [and] mind games."[1] Also within the definition of battering is sexual abuse or violation of the woman including rape or other assaults, and economic abuse perpetrated by an intimate.

Some professionals have chosen to narrowly define battering in terms

71

of physical abuse. One study defined battered women as "adult women who were intentionally physically abused in ways that caused pain or injury, or who were forced into involuntary action or restrained by force from voluntary action by adult men with whom they have or had established relationships, usually involving sexual intimacy."[2] Murray Straus supported such a physical definition of woman battering because of its "easier method of documentation."[3] In his study of domestic violence, Richard Gelles added police contact to his definition of battered women.[4]

Many experts believe that psychological battering of women may be even more devastating and extensive than physical battering. Patricia Hoffman, who conducted the first research program on psychological abuse in marriage in the United States, defined this type of woman abuse as "behavior sufficiently threatening to a woman that she believes her capacity to work, to interact in the family or society, or to enjoy good physical or mental health, has been or might be endangered."[5]

Psychological woman battering became more recognized in the 1970s when the number of refugees from abusive men increased and "it became obvious that large numbers of women were seeking safety from psychological abuse."[6] In a study of physical and psychological coercion, Lenore Walker found that both types of domestic violence were present in abusive couples and "cannot be separated, despite the difficulty in documentation."[7] Hoffman estimated that as many as 1 in 3 women may be in a psychologically abusive relationship.[8]

Economic abuse of women by their male partners is defined as various means of controlling the economic resources in the family, including preventing the woman from working or keeping a job, taking any money she does earn, giving her an insufficient allowance to meet family needs, forcing her to beg for money for basic items such as food and children's clothing, and not telling her about or allowing access to family income or financial resources.[9]

The Prevalence of Battered Women

Most experts agree that domestic violence is a serious problem in this country. Women are much more likely to be victims of severe spousal violence, injury, and death than men.[10] A woman is physically abused by her husband every 9 seconds in the United States.[11] Some estimates of battered women have gone as high as 1 victim out of every 2 women in the U.S.[12] An estimated 95 percent of all assaults on spouses or ex-spouses are perpetrated by men against women.[13] Around 20 percent of women battered by a husband or ex-husband have reported being victimized by a series of at least 3 assaults within the previous 6 months.[14]

Nearly 1 in 3 women admitted to a hospital emergency department are identified as having injuries due to domestic violence.[15] In a 1997 Gallup Poll, 22 percent of the female respondents reported having ever been physically abused by a spouse or companion.[16]

The risk of death from battering is high for abused women. More than 4 out of every 10 murdered women in the United States are killed by a male intimate.[17]

In spite of these staggering figures, much of the domestic violence against women goes unreported. According to the National Crime Victimization Survey, around half the female victims of intimate violence report the abuse to law enforcement.[18] However, some experts believe the actual number who report spouse abuse may be considerably lower. One researcher recently estimated that only 1 in every 270 incidents of wife beating is ever reported to the police.[19] Walker found in her study of battered women that fewer than 10 percent ever reported serious violence to law enforcement authorities.[20] The most common reasons attributed to abused women not reporting domestic violence include:

- Victim denial of the abuse.
- The incident was considered a private or personal matter.
- Fear of retaliation.
- Protection of the abusive partner.
- Shame.
- Fear of loss of financial support.
- Lack of confidence that police intervention would make a difference.

Despite this "cloak of silence," researchers in domestic violence have used a "wide variety of techniques to obtain data including intensive studies of small samples of marital dyads, the examination of police incident reports, analyzing groups of cases from agency treatment files, and gathering data on families that are in the process of divorcing."[21] In virtually every instance, studies have supported a high incidence of the battering of women. P. D. Scott reported that 25 percent of the child abusing fathers studied also abused their wives.[22] In an analysis of reported cases of violence, Rebecca Dobash and Russell Dobash found that wife assaults represented the second largest offense category that police recorded.[23] In a study of sexual assaults in marriage, Diana Russell found that more than 2 in 10 women who had ever been married reported being physically abused by a spouse at some point in their lives.[24]

According to victimization data, there were an average of 960,000 female victims of intimate violence between 1992 and 1996 (see Figure 6-1). The rate of victimization was approximately 8 in 1,000 women during the period or around 8 times the rate for male violence victimization by an intimate.[25] Figure 6-2 illustrates murder trends of female victims of intimate violence from 1976 to 1997. Though the number of overall female murder victims decreased over the period, there were still on average 1,467 women murdered by a husband, ex-husband, boyfriend, or former boyfriend each year during the period (see also Chapter 5).

Characteristics of Battered Women

In spite of some data that suggest a greater rate of battering amongst minorities, lower income, or undereducated women, the reality is that women and girls are being battered and beaten by intimates across the socioeconomic spectrum. Recent studies have indicated that as many as 80 percent of battered women cases have gone unrecognized and undiagnosed because "of the more privileged environment in which they occur. Age, income, education, ethnicity, race, class, and occupation offer no protection from this domestic affliction."[26]

What abused women have in common is a "characteristically low self-esteem, generally the result of repeated victimization. Some victims' feeling of powerlessness is limited only to their relationship with men; others find that this trait applies to all areas of their lives."[27] Battered women typically see themselves as inferior to men, tend to cope with anger through denial or turning it inward, and suffer from guilt, depression, and psychosomatic illnesses.[28]

In a study of conjugal violence, Terry Davidson contended that battered wives were characterized by outdated images of ideal womanhood such as being submissive, religious, and nonassertive. She posited that such women tended to put the husband above all else and saw themselves as having little to no control over many aspects of their own lives.[29]

Characteristics of Abusive Men

Like abused women, abusive men exist across the social and economic strata as many female victims will attest to. Researchers have been able to identify some characteristics of male batterers, as noted in the book *Women and Criminality*:

Figure 6-1
Female Violent Intimate Victimization Trends, 1992–1996

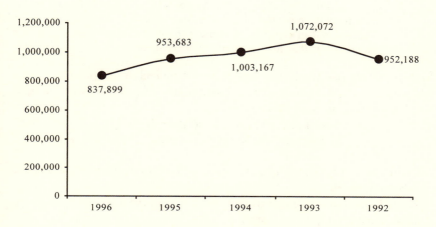

Source: Constructed from U.S. Department of Justice, Bureau of Justice Statistics Factbook, *Violence by Intimates* (Washington, D.C.: Government Printing Office, 1998), p. 37.

Figure 6-2
Female Homicide Victims of Male Intimates, 1976–1997[a]

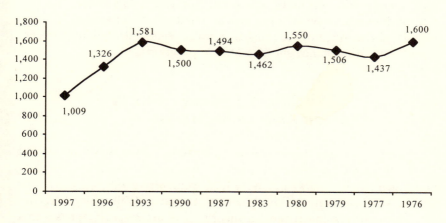

[a] Figures for 1997 include only wives and girlfriends as murder victims.

Source: Derived from U.S. Department of Justice, Federal Bureau of Investigation, *Crime in the United States: Uniform Crime Reports 1997* (Washington, D.C.: Government Printing Office, 1998), p. 21; FBI Supplementary Homicide Reports, 1976–1996.

The battering man is typically seen as possessing a dual personality. He is regarded as either extremely charming or especially cruel. Selfishness and generosity are parts of his personality and depend upon his mood. Substance abuse, while sometimes present, is not a central feature in the battering pattern itself. On the other hand, jealousy and possessiveness are considered an integral part of mate-inflicted violence. Most batterer's greatest fear is that their woman will leave them.[30]

Male batterers also tend to be characterized by feelings of powerlessness, low self-esteem, dependency, and loneliness — and they expect the battered woman to meet all their needs.

Based on a 4-year study of abusive relationships, Maria Roy profiled abusive men and intimate violence as follows:

- The majority of abusive men are between the ages of 26 and 35, followed by ages 36 to 50.
- Most children of violent intimates are between the ages of 1 and 13.
- Most abusive couples have joint incomes.
- Most spouse abuse occurs during the first 15 years of the relationship.
- In 70 percent of the cases, woman battering took place almost immediately after the relationship started.
- Ninety percent of abusive men do not have a criminal record.
- More than 80 percent of abusive men were victims of child abuse, or came from abusive families.
- Major changes in life (such as loss of income or death) increases the likelihood or level of intimate violence in long-term relationships.
- Most domestic violence is physical and without use of weapons.
- Thirty-five percent of the abusive men also abused alcohol; only 10 percent were in substance abuse treatment programs.[31]

Why Battered Women Stay in an Abusive Relationship

On the surface, it seems hard to imagine why any woman would remain in an abusive relationship beyond the first time being hit by a partner, much less for years of abuse. Many women stay with the abuser for various and common reasons. According to Lenore Walker's cycle theory of violence or tension reduction theory, there are 3 specific phases that exist in a recurring cycle of abuse: (1) tension building, (2) the acute battering incident, and (3) loving contrition.[32]

The *tension building* stage usually consists of a series of minor or verbal attacks. The woman victim is able to cope with these episodes by "minimizing their significance and/or severity and using anger reduction techniques."[33] She tries to appease her abuser by doing whatever she deems necessary to calm him down. In the process, the victim becomes even more submissive.

The second phase, *the acute battering incident,* is characterized by the "uncontrollable discharge of the tensions that have been built up during phase one."[34] The abusive mate typically unleashes a combination of physical and verbal abuse upon the wife, which she is not able to prevent. It is during this phase that most injuries, sometimes severe, occur.

The final phase is that of *loving contrition* or the "honeymoon period." The batterer often becomes charming, apologetic, loving, remorseful—a complete turnaround from his violent side. He is willing to do almost anything to be forgiven by his intimate victim. Laura Schlessinger describes the effectiveness of this loving contrition: "Suddenly he's giving her gifts, good sex, pampering. She wants to believe he's really sorry and that he will change this time. In the glow of all this attention, she does believe it."[35] Unfortunately, for most abuse victims caught in this pattern, stage one tension begins again and a new cycle is started.

Walker's cycle theory has been supported by other professionals studying domestic violence, such as P. M. Lewinsohn[36] and E. M. Lewis.[37] However, critics have pointed out that the theory falls short in accounting for the many women who do leave abusive spouses, some of whom do so "without ever having a chance to 'practice' necessary behaviors such as initiating legal proceedings, organizing finances, and finding a safe place to stay."[38]

Experts have found that women typically choose to stay in abusive relationships based on a number of serious factors and reasons, such as:

- *Fear*—of the abusive mate, being humiliated, exposed, left alone.
- *Finances*—loss of income, the house, standard of living.
- *Children*—losing financial support, children, safety threatened.
- *Social stigma*—shame, embarrassment, being labeled.
- *Self-blame*—for causing the abuse to occur.
- *Role expectations*—accepting abuse as normal in a relationship.
- *History of abuse*—victims of child abuse or in a previous abusive relationship.
- *Belief that batterer will change*—accepts his sorrow for abuse and promises it will not happen again and to get counseling.
- *Isolation*—abusive mate has isolated victim, leaving her without support system.

- *Rejection by society* — fear that no one will believe the abuse occurred, often because of the abuser's charms, denials, and stature in society.
- *Dangerous consequences* — legitimate fear of being severely injured or killed by batterer.[39]

Subgroups of Battered Women

Violence in Dating Relationships

Though much of the research on intimate violence focuses on married or previously married intimates, studies also show a high incidence of abuse exists as well in dating relationships, including teenage dating. In a recent study at the Young Women's Resource Center in Des Moines, Iowa, it was found that over a 6-month period, 60 percent of the women were in a current abusive relationship.[40] Almost all the participants of the study reported having been abused in a dating relationship. According to the National Crime Victimization Survey, there were nearly 838,000 violent victimizations of women by an intimate in the United States in 1996, including boyfriends and ex-boyfriends.[41] One in 3 dating females will be battered by a boyfriend before reaching adult age.[42] Many believe that the number of females abused by the men they date may be just as high as women battered by husbands or ex-spouses.

Dating violence has been shown to be similar to marital violence in many respects.[43] "Victims dating their batterers experience the same patterns of power and control as their counterparts in abusive marriages or cohabitations, and clearly dating violence can be just as lethal."[44]

There are also differences between dating violence and domestic violence involving married or divorced intimates. Dating partners typically have no legal standing with respect to financial, property, and custody issues existing in a marital arrangement. This could have an impact on the reporting of dating violence as well as legal intervention. A second difference in dating abuse is the indifference many people have with it compared to traditional domestic violence. Some studies have noted "an apparent lack of social stigma attached to the behavior by participants."[45]

Reasons why dating males abuse appear to differ from those given by abusive husbands. "Young men admit to abusing their young partners in order to intimidate them into giving into their demands, while violent husbands more commonly blame their aggression on reasons out of their control, such as drinking, drugs, anger, and stress."[46]

ELDERLY WOMEN ABUSE

Abuse of elderly women by their partners has not received the same attention as domestic violence involving younger women. According to one writer: "Battered older women have been virtually invisible in the battered women's movement."[47] Studies show that elderly spousal abuse may be much more common than realized. It is estimated that 1 million people age 60 or over are victims of family violence in the United States each year.[48] A sample survey on elderly victimization by intimates suggested that most of the estimated 701,000 to 1,093,560 abused elderly people in this country were victims of spousal abuse.[49] Some authorities estimate that only 1 in 14 cases of elderly abuse is ever reported.[50]

Despite the common ground shared by younger and older female victims of domestic violence, elderly abuse has been "much more frequently compared to child abuse than spouse abuse. These trends have led to making abused older women invisible victims and to viewing them as child-like victims of family violence."[51] (See also Chapter 9.)

ABUSED WOMEN IN RURAL COMMUNITIES

Rural women in the United States face even greater risks for intimate violence than their urban or suburban counterparts.[52] Most abusers typically isolate their victims to prevent discovery or escape. Living in rural communities where there is often great distance between farms, towns, and from more populated areas, battered women are often at the mercy of their batterers. This is compounded by such common rural circumstances as poor roads, limited phone service, and inaccessible transportation (some abused rural women are not even allowed to have a driver's license). Seasonal work on farms can further contribute to abuse in the relationship, as rural males are often left with "months of unemployment; resulting in women being trapped in a house with an abusive partner for long stretches of time."[53]

Hunting weapons and tools commonly kept in rural homes add to the sometimes deadly risks abused rural women face.[54] Injuries sustained by battered women may never be detected because of limited contact with neighbors, giving bruises time to heal and fade. Even injuries that are noticed can easily be attributed to farm work, and thus, misdiagnosed and unreported as wife battering.

LESBIAN BATTERING

There are few studies on intimate battering by same sex partners. This is particularly true of lesbian women. Because of homophobia and

denial, battered lesbians are considered the most "under-served population of battered women in the nation."[55] Dispelling the myths that lesbian
abuse is usually consensual and never as violent as heterosexual domestic
violence, researchers have found that lesbian violence "is almost never
mutual and can be every bit as lethal as when men batter women."[56] It is
estimated that intimate violence in homosexual relationships is as prevalent as in heterosexual relationships.[57] One recent article cited the "high
rates of violence in lesbian homes."[58] Clearly more study is needed on this
segment of violence between intimates.

BATTERED IMMIGRANT WOMEN

Immigrant women, particularly those from Third World countries in
Asia, Latin America and Africa, or the former Soviet bloc may face additional risk of being battered by intimates than nonimmigrant women; along
with higher rates of unreported abuse and nonintervention by law enforcement personnel. This is due in part to different cultures, customs, lan-
guages, and backgrounds; as well as racism and poverty.[59] "The rigors of
immigrant life put battered women from many of these communities in a
particularly vulnerable position."[60] Language barriers can sometimes make
it difficult, if not impossible, for battered immigrant women to communicate with social service agencies such as police, hospitals, and courts. These
institutions "are not structured to accommodate language and cultural differences, a reality which alienates and isolates many immigrant women."[61]

The isolation of undocumented abused women puts them in an even
more perilous position to be victimized by intimates.[62] Many such women
are totally dependent on their husbands who are typically their sponsors
in the United States. Batterers may use the threat of deportation as a form
of spousal abuse. Victims, often speaking little or no English and without
money or other resources, are unlikely to press charges against their abuser
for fear of deportation and/or loss of children or future citizenship.

PROSTITUTES AND BATTERING

Women in prostitution face a number of hazards, including battering and rape by their pimps, whom many prostitutes also consider their
lover or intimate partner. Studies have found that prostitutes are routinely
subjected to "extreme sexual, physical, and psychological abuse" by
pimps.[63] More than two-thirds of streetwalkers report being regularly battered by pimps.[64] The physical abuse can range from "being hit with fists,
slapped, whipped, burned, or even killed."[65]

Most female prostitutes seeking to escape abusive pimp-lovers share the same obstacles and needs as women battered in traditional domestic abuse situations. This can often include needing shelter for children and fear for their lives. The majority of these women have few occupational skills, little education, and a history of physical and sexual abuse.[66] (See also Chapter 15.)

WIFE ABUSE IN THE MILITARY

Wife abuse in the armed forces appears to be an even more serious problem than in the general population, according to studies. The rate of domestic violence in the military has been estimated at 5 times that of civilian domestic violence.[67] Further, research has suggested that the military "routinely fails" to adequately punish servicemen convicted of spouse abuse. According to New York Representative Carolyn Maloney: "There are indications that the military is not taking this issue seriously. It is undisputed that there are more cases of domestic violence in the military than in civilian life, and that they go unpunished or with just a slap on the wrist."[68] This was supported by a finding at Kentucky's Fort Campbell that the Army typically ignores court orders aimed at protecting battered women.[69]

The Department of Defense's (DoD) Family Advocacy Program is in charge of identifying armed forces' domestic violence and intervention through military law enforcement authorities, counseling, and treatment of spouse abuse victims. The DoD has defended itself, arguing that comparing rates of civilian and military domestic violence is difficult because of differences in the counting methodology. For instance, the military counts only spouse abuse rather than all domestic violence. It also reports on emotional and physical spouse abuse that required no medical treatment.

Civilian law enforcement personnel have no jurisdiction on military bases, while military authorities have wide discretionary powers in investigating cases of domestic violence and punishing abusive men. Legislation has been called for to change the way military protective orders are issued and enforced on military bases, and for the creation of uniform sentencing guidelines in penalizing military and civilian batterers.[70]

7. Marital Rape and Sexual Factors in Battering

Woman battering has been shown to commonly include not only physical abuse but sexual abuse by the male batterer. Many abused women submit to sexual relations with husbands or boyfriends as a means to avoid being beaten; others are victims of marital or date rape as part of the abusive treatment. Some are victimized sexually without other forms of domestic violence present. Not too surprisingly, sexual assaults among intimates are rarely acknowledged by victims or reported to law enforcement authorities as one of the most hidden forms of domestic violence. Even when reported, few intimate rapists or sexual assaultists are prosecuted or imprisoned. Despite laws against marital rape in every state, definitions of marital rape tend to be inconsistent both in legal terms and in general, compounding the problem and identification and treatment of victims. Related sexual issues such as date rape, pregnancy, sexual jealousy, and sexual intimacy are also part of the battered woman syndrome.

This chapter will address marital rape and other sexual factors that are often associated with the battering and violating of females by intimates.

Defining Marital Rape

What is marital rape? Does it differ from nonmarital rape? Or stranger rape? The answer is that rape is rape, regardless of the victim-offender relationship. The word "*rape*" itself is derived from the Latin word "*rapere*," which means "to steal, seize, or carry away."[1] Common law defines rape as the unlawful carnal knowledge of a woman by force and against her will. Sexual penetration, no matter how slight, was sufficient to constitute criminality, assuming the other elements were present. A resistance standard was instituted for the victim in order to distinguish forcible carnal knowledge (rape) from consensual carnal knowledge (fornication and adultery). Common law made both forms of carnal knowledge criminal acts, but if the act was forcible, the victim avoided punishment for adultery or fornication.[2]

According to legal theory, rape as

a crime exists only when there is concurrence of an unacceptable act and a criminal intent with respect to that act. The unacceptable act is called the actus reus; the criminal intent is called the mens rea. In traditional definition of rape, the actus reus is the unconsented-to sexual intercourse and the mens rea is the intention or knowledge of having the intercourse without the consent of the victim. Lack of consent of the victim is ultimately the characteristic that distinguishes rape. The concurrence of the act and the intent requires both that the victim in fact did not consent and that the perpetrator knew at the time that the victim did not consent.[3]

In accordance with both legal theory and common law tradition, the definition of rape is based upon "the victim's and offender's perception that the intercourse was not consensual."[4]

Herein lies part of the problem in recognizing and defining marital or conjugal rape. For many marital rape victims, marital rapists, and even experts, there remains confusion and stereotypes as to what constitutes rape in marriage. Kata Issari of the National Coalition Against Sexual Assault, illustrates this common perception of forced marital sex among victims: "They often don't define it as rape because of society's beliefs about what should go on in a marriage."[5] Drawing distinctions between marital rape and consensual sex also comes from rape professionals such as law professor Susan Estrich, who wrote: "When I talk about marital rape, I'm not talking about good marriages in which he may be more interested in sex than she is, or he pushes a little hard on Friday night."[6]

Even states took a while to recognize marital rape as a crime. Prior to 1975, most states had adopted a statutory definition of rape as the "act of sexual intercourse with a woman other than the perpetrator's wife committed without her lawful consent."[7] In 1975, Nebraska became the first state to outlaw marital rape. North Carolina was the last state to pass marital rape laws in 1993. However, the statutes vary from state to state in defining marital rape. In 20 states, including Oregon, Nebraska, and North Carolina, the penalties for marital rape mirror those for rape perpetrated by strangers. For the remaining 30 states, a spouse may be exempt from rape laws for various reasons, such as if the suspected rapist's wife does not suffer a serious injury.[8]

Most states now have laws that account for sexual assaults other than rape in and out of marriage in recognizing variations of assaultive behavior by intimates and loopholes in legislation.

The Extent of Marital Rape

Given the hidden nature of marital rape, it may be among the most difficult domestic crimes to accurately assess. Many rape experts believe marital rape may be the most underreported crime in the country, while one of the most widespread. According to *Rape in America*, a report issued by the National Victim Center (NVC) and the Crime Victims Research and Treatment Center (CVC), more than 61,000 women are raped by spouses or ex-spouses each year in the United States.[9] The CVC estimates that around 1.2 million women have ever been victims of spousal rape.[10] In a 1994 National Crime Victimization Survey, an estimated 36,000 rape and sexual assault victims of single-offender victimizations identified a spouse or ex-spouse as the one who assaulted them.[11]

Sexual assaults of all kinds against married women are staggering. It is estimated by the FBI that 25 million women are the victims of spousal sexual assaults in the United States annually.[12] One in every 10 wives have been sexually assaulted at least once by their husband, while between 50 and 87 percent of female victims of intimate rape report being sexually assaulted at least 20 times by their intimates.[13] In using a conservative definition of rape, Diana Russell found that marital rape occurred more than twice as often as rape committed by strangers.[14]

The Relationship Between Marital Rape and Wife Battering

There is a significant correlation between spousal rape and other physical violence perpetrated against women by their spouses. One study estimated that sexual assaults were reported by 33 to 46 percent of women who were physically battered by their intimates.[15] It is estimated that 1 in 3 rape victims are battered women and, among victims of rape over the age of 30, nearly 6 in 10 are battered women.[16] Russell reported that battered women stood a risk of being sexually assaulted by partners at a rate 3 to 5 times higher than nonbattered women.[17]

Lenore Walker found that 59 percent of her sample of abused women were forced to have sex with their husbands, compared to only 7 percent of women who were not abused.[18] Eighty-five percent of the abused women reported that the sex was unpleasant for the following reasons: (1) it was initiated in order to prevent abuse, (2) it occurred immediately after the violence to calm the abuser, (3) it took place after the batterer abused a child out of fear he would continue, and (4) to refuse sex meant the battered woman would not be given money for essentials, such as groceries or bills.

Other experts have strongly supported the relationship between marital rape and wife battering. Shelley Neiderback of the International Association of Trauma Counselors argued that "marital rape is another aspect of spouse battering. It is not about sex; it's about control, violence and humiliation."[19] Sociologist Kersti Yllo postulated that forced marital sex was a form of violent power and control rather than a means of sexual gratification.[20] In addressing spouse rape and motivations of spousal rapists, David Finkelhor stated: "These are brutal acts that are most often committed out of anger or power, with the idea to humiliate, demean or degrade the wife."[21]

Characteristics of Marital Rapists

Marital rapists cross all socioeconomic, racial, and ethnic lines as a reflection of the homogeneous nature of domestic violence and conjugal rape. They also share similar characteristics with nonmarital rapists. Yllo and Finkelhor identified 3 categories of marital rapists:

· Men motivated mostly by uncontrolled anger.
· Men who used rape as a means to gain power over their wives.
· Men obsessed with sex and who received pleasure from perverse and sadistic acts.[22]

The researchers found that nearly half the marital rapists studied fell into the uncontrolled anger category. These men typically raped their wives during or after physically assaulting them. The men who raped for power over their wives commonly only used the force necessary to coerce the victim into having sexual relations.

More than 50 types of rapists in general have been established by criminologists and sexual assault experts. In virtually all typologies, the act of rape is regarded not as an "aggressive expression of sexuality but rather as a sexual expression of aggression."[23] Most rapists tend to fall into one or more of the following categories:

- *The Sociopath Rapist.* The most common type of rapist. He is impulsive; motivated primarily by sex. The rape itself is a manifestation of deviant behavior.
- *The Situational Stress Rapist.* He is rarely violent or dangerous. The rape is usually due to situational stress, such as unemployment. He often has no history of violent behavior or sexual deviations.
- *The Masculinity Rapist.* A broad spectrum of rapists whose commonness is a real or perceived deficiency in their masculinity. The rape is usually planned and violent.
- *The Substance Abuse Rapist.* He is often under the influence of alcohol, drugs, or both. This plays a significant role in the rape, though usually in combination with other factors.
- *The Double-Standard Rapist.* He divides women into good ones who deserve to be treated with respect, and bad ones who do not deserve respect or consideration.
- *The Acquaintance Rapist.* He is acquainted with or may date his target, gaining her trust. He usually plans the rape, enjoys overpowering his victim, and has extreme self-confidence.
- *The Sadistic Rapist.* Representing only a small percentage of rapists but among the most terrifying and violent. He usually plans the rape, has a history of hostility and aggression toward women, and receives pleasure in ritualistic degradation of women.
- *The Unpredictable Rapist.* He is often psychotic and may give no indication based upon his history of his potential to rape.[24]

Within these categories, the rapist's interpretation of the sexual assault "may differ considerably depending on the individual. In almost all cases, the rapist who admits to sexual contact with the victim either defines his actions as rape or goes into a classic denial that a rape occurred."[25] This may be especially true for marital or date rapists under a power and control theory or stereotypical perception that consensual sex is implicit between intimates.

Theories on Men Who Rape

Theorists have sought to explain why men rape. Three of the more influential theoretical approaches of rape are: (1) interactionist theories, (2) psychoanalytic theories, and (3) opportunity structure theories.

Interactionist theories advance that "social interaction is meditated by signs and symbols, by eye contact, gestures and words."[26] This school of thought posits that rapists respond to the victim's actions and inactions. One such interactionist theory, for example, is the victim-precipitation theory. This theory postulates that the "rape victim is culpable to some degree due to the real or perceived communication between her and the rapist for consensual sexual relations."[27] Many intimate rapes may fall into this category from the perspective of the rapist. However, the burden of guilt still remains squarely with the rape perpetrator. As rape expert Menachem Amir asserted, the victim's behavior in any sexual assault is not as significant as the "offender's interpretation of her actions."[28]

Psychoanalytic theories view rapists as emotionally disturbed and "often with an intense hatred of women developed during childhood, triggering latent homosexual tendencies."[29] The rape is regarded as a reflection of this hatred and a strong need for the rapist to assure himself of his own masculinity.

Opportunity structure theories hold that rapists see women as "possessors of salable sexual properties."[30] Lorenne Clark and Debra Lewis noted: "When bargaining for sex, men reportedly use various forms of coercion. They may make promises they cannot or will not really fulfill. They may harass women or threaten them with physical harm."[31] This theoretical approach explains rape as a consequence of some men who lack the necessary social and economic means to attract women they desire. As a result, they must resort to sexual violence against such women to fulfill their desires.

Sexual Issues in the Battering of Women

Date Rape

Date rape of women and girls by intimates has been shown to be a major problem in this country and closely related to physical violence in dating relationships. Its characteristics are very similar to those found in marital rape, including an unwillingness to report the rape for reasons such as shame, denial, self-blame, fear of not being believed, fear of the date rapist, and confusion in defining what constitutes rape in dating relationships. The difficulty in recognizing date rape was illustrated in a recent study at the University of California in which more than half the female students interviewed believed that under some circumstances it was acceptable for a man to use physical aggression to get sexual favors from his date.[32] In another study done by *Ms.* magazine, nearly 3 in 4 rape victims, as legally defined, did not identify the rape as such.[33]

It is estimated that more than 50 percent of rapes are perpetrated against adolescent victims, with the "vast majority" occurring between acquaintances or those dating.[34] Many of these date rape victims are also victims of date abuse. Surveys reveal that violence in dating relationships is high. Approximately 1 in 3 females will be physically abused by boyfriends or ex-boyfriends before reaching the age of 18.[35] One study of 500 female adolescents found that nearly all had been victims of dating violence.[36]

Date rape in recent years has also been associated with drugs being used on the female victim as part of the assault. Drugs known as "date rape drugs" such as Rohypnol or "Roofies" and gamma hydroxy butyrate (GHB) or "Liquid X," have shown up on many college campuses.[37] These drugs can cause women to lose consciousness or become physically incapacitated, making them easy prey for date rapists. When taken with alcohol, the effects can be magnified and the vulnerability of victims increased.

Characteristics of date rape victims can be seen as follows:

- Most victims are single women between 15 and 25 years of age.
- One in 8 women is a victim of date rape.
- Two in 10 female college students are the victims of rape or attempted rape.
- Half of the females raped are victims of first dates, casual dates, or romantic acquaintances.
- Most nonstranger rapes occur in the evening and at night.
- Victims are less likely to take measures to protect themselves from rape by a date or acquaintance than a stranger.[38]

According to Christine Courtois, women sexually assaulted by dates are victims of "an endemic societal manifestation of the power imbalance between the sexes" whereby "men are conditioned into roles of power and domination ... and females ... are conditioned to be passive and dependent."[39] Sadly, this appears to be reflected in the data on date rape and domestic violence.

Pregnancy and Battering

Pregnant women are particularly at risk for battering by their husbands and boyfriends. Incidence levels of battered pregnant women reported in the literature have ranged from 8 to 15 percent of pregnant women in private and public clinics,[40] to anywhere from 17 to 26 percent of women who are pregnant and being abused.[41] The March of Dimes estimated that 25 to 45 percent of all battered women are victimized during pregnancy, increasing the risk of birth defects and low birth weight infants.[42] The abuser merely being told of the pregnancy itself has been shown to initiate spouse abuse and other family violence.[43]

Studies show that the number of episodes of battering is high during pregnancy; while the most severe wife abuse is often perpetrated on pregnant women.[44] One study found that 42 percent of the women reported being battered during pregnancy.[45] Walker[46] and Richard Gelles[47] reported a high degree of battering during first, second, and third pregnancies. In Walker's study, 50 percent of the batterers were reportedly initially pleased with the pregnancy, but it did not prevent the abuse from occurring. Researchers have "frequently noted the propensity of battering husbands to punch and kick their pregnant partners in the stomach, with resultant miscarriages and injuries to their reproductive organs."[48]

The battering of pregnant women has been found to often be related to one or more of the following factors:

• Added strain on the relationship and finances.
• Unplanned pregnancy.
• The number of children already in the family.
• Jealousy and resentment towards unborn child.
• Sexual problems.
• Substance abuse.
• Unemployment.
• Power and control.[49]

Battered women tend to be pregnant nearly twice as often as women who are not battered; are significantly more likely to have a pregnancy end in miscarriage or abortion, and have a greater likelihood of being pregnant at the time they are beaten than nonbattered women.[50]

Self-report data has revealed a significant relationship between domestic violence and abortion. In a study of the prevalence of battering among women seeking an abortion, Susan Glander found that nearly 4 in 10 women seeking elective pregnancy termination reported being abused by their partner.[51] White women were much more likely than nonwhite women to report a history of being abused. Women with histories of domestic violence were significantly less likely than their nonabused counterparts to inform their intimate of the pregnancy and have the partner's support or involvement in the decision to have an abortion.

Sexual Jealousy

Many abused women report that sexual problems such as impotency, frigidity, denial, and excessive demands often lead to arguments or confrontations erupting into physical violence.[52] In such instances, the batterer often doubts his own virility, is insecure, possessive, and questions his wife's fidelity, at times even casting doubt on the paternity of his children. As a consequence, many abusive men keep their wives isolated or severely curtail their time outside the home, or want detailed information on how it is spent. Because of the physical and sexual violence forced on them, many battered women feel alienated from their husbands or lovers and find consensual sexual intimacy difficult, both of which often perpetuate the violence.

Sexual jealousy can also be felt by the wife or girlfriend towards her significant other, which in turn may trigger give-and-take abuse and violence in the relationship.

Sexual Intimacy

Sex and intimacy are related to wife abuse in two important ways. One is the association between abuse and the victim's withdrawal from sexual intimacy. According to Maria Roy, this abuse and withdrawal commonly begins very early in the abusive relationship.[53] The women in her study expressed feelings of worthlessness and alienation from their abusive mates. This low self-esteem as a result of the battering made sexual intimacy hard for the woman to achieve. Roy cited that unfounded accusations by the husband of adultery and infidelity by the wife added to the sexual problems and domestic violence.

The second way in which sexual intimacy and battering are correlated is in the behavioral patterns of battered women and their inability to distinguish between sex and intimacy.[54] Experts have found that abused women usually have sexual relations with their abusive husbands for one or more of the following reasons:

• Seduction as an unrealistic sense of power.
• A means to keep the peace.
• Intense concentration on survival.
• Dependence on an abusive and sometimes loving man.
• Joy from an intense intimate relationship.
• To decrease the batterer's violence through a loving relationship.

Many such battered women have been victims of child sexual abuse. Walker forwarded that "it is quite possible that early exposure to sexual abuse, with or without accompanying physical violence, creates a dependency upon the positive aspects of the intense intimacy experienced prior to the beginning of the battering behavior and continuing during the third phase of loving-kindness."[55]

8. Battered Men

Few would dispute the statement that women are victims of far more severe abuse by their partners and, sometimes, deadly domestic violence. Most statistics confirm this, including crime data, victimization data, and hospital treatment data. However, there is growing evidence that women may be just as abusive in relationships as men, if not more so. Further, some women caught in the grips of back and forth intimate violence are resorting to intimate homicide, much as men are. This does not mean our focus must shift to battered and murdered men by intimates; rather the problem of abused men must be seriously explored within the context of domestic and family violence.

Extent of Male Battering

Just as it is difficult to assess the true incidence of battered women in this country, it is nearly impossible to know how many battered men there are. The task may be even more difficult as male victims of intimate violence are less likely to report it to authorities than female victims. What we do know suggests the problem of battered and beaten men is a serious one. Robert Langley and Richard Levy estimated that 12 million men in the United States are battered by spouses at some time during their marriage.[1] Suzanne Steinmetz estimated that nearly 300,000 men are victims of domestic violence every year in this country.[2] Steinmetz, M. Fields, and R. Kirchner further debated the issue of battered men and women.[3] A study of spouse abuse literature found that an estimated 2 million husbands had experienced at least one incident of severe spousal violence.[4]

Murray Straus approximated that nearly two-thirds of all married couples engage in some form of physical violence during their relationship, with one-fourth being of a serious nature.[5] R. Gelles found that 32 percent of the wives in his sample had been violent at some point, compared to 47 percent of the husbands.[6] In a study of college students, 10 percent of the mothers and 16.7 percent of the fathers were reported to have physically abused the other spouse during the students' high school senior year.[7] In an analysis of complaints by wives and husbands seeking divorce, G. Levinger found that while wives' complaints included physical or verbal spouse abuse, neglect, and mental cruelty; husbands tended to complain about emotional cruelty, neglect, sexual mismatching, and in-law intervention.[8]

According to the National Crime Victimization Survey (NCVS), between 1992 and 1996, men were victims of violent crimes committed by an intimate an average of approximately 150,000 times a year. Figure 8-1 illustrates this pattern of intimate victimization of males by females. Victimizations peaked in 1994 at more than 176,000. From 1995 to 1996, the number of male victimizations by intimates climbed more than 28 percent. By comparison, female victimizations by intimates, while greater overall, decreased from 1995 to 1996 by more than 12 percent.[9]

Are Female Intimates as Violent as Their Male Counterparts?

Just how violent are women in intimate relationships compared to men? The statistics suggest the disparity between men and women intimates with respect to domestic violence is great. But is it true? Are men really far more likely to inflict severe abuse on their intimates than women? Some of the data aforementioned calls this into question. At the very least, it appears that in relative terms violent females are gaining on violent males in intimate violence.[10] A recent article in the *U.S. News & World Report* noted that in Wisconsin, the "number of abusive men referred by the courts for counseling [had] doubled since 1989, while the number of abusive women referred for counseling increased 12-fold."[11] Other reports on violent intimates show similar indications of rising numbers of abusive women.[12]

Self-report surveys seem to support the notion that male and female intimate violence is fairly even in terms of both simple assaults and severe assaults.[13] This is not always reflected in victimization surveys and official data. Indeed, some data clearly suggest that the rate of severe intimate violence is actually higher among female perpetrators per 1,000 couples than male perpetrators.[14]

Figure 8-1
Male Violent Victimization by Intimates, 1992–1996

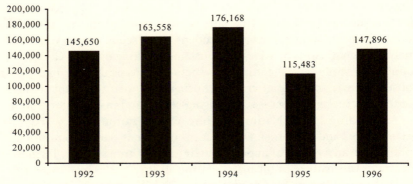

Source: Constructed from U.S. Department of Justice, Bureau of Justice Statistics Factbook, *Violence by Intimates* (Washington, D.C.: Government Printing Office, 1998), p. 37.

On the whole, most indicators show that men continue to perpetrate the greater amount of serious violence and injuries against female intimates than women to men. There can be no denying that many women are striking back, if not first, and sometimes fatally.

Male Intimate Fatalities

The relationship between domestic violence and intimate fatalities is well documented.[15] In most instances, it is the female intimate who becomes a homicide victim due to domestic violence.[16] However, men are also susceptible to dying at the hands of an intimate. Between 1976 and 1997, more than 20,650 men were victims of intimate murder by wives, ex-wives, girlfriends, and ex-girlfriends.[17] Nearly 6 percent of all male victims of homicide during the span were killed by an intimate.[18]

Studies illustrate the intimate nature of most homicides perpetrated by women. In G. Rasko's comprehensive examination of female homicides and attempted homicides in Hungary, it was found that 40 percent of the victims were husbands, common law husbands, or lovers.[19] J. Totman's study of female killers also revealed that husbands, live-in boyfriends or other intimates were the victims in 40 percent of the cases of homicidal women.[20] Another study of accused female murderers found that more than 4 in 10 of the women were charged with killing a husband or boyfriend.[21] In a study of violent female state prisoners, more than half those convicted of murder had killed an intimate or family member.[22]

Sociologists contend that spousal homicide is not an "isolated occurrence or outbreak, but rather is the culminating event in a pattern of interpersonal abuse, hatred and violence that stretches back well into the history of the parties involved."[23] Indeed, most women in prison for killing an intimate report often undergoing years of physical and mental abuse from the victim prior to the homicide.[24] A study of 30 female California state prison inmates convicted of killing their spouses found that nearly 3 in 10 women had been battered wives.[25] In a study of intimate murders in Kansas City, it was found that in 90 percent of the cases, the police had gone to the home on at least 1 occasion in the 2 years prior to the killing; and in 50 percent of the cases, police had been called to the residence on at least 5 occasions.[26]

Elissa Benedek described the typical pattern of a battered wife driven to kill her abusive husband:

> Such a woman often comes from a house where she has observed and experienced parental violence and sees violence as a norm in social interaction and as a solution for conflict. Marriage is frequently seen as an escape route, but her choice of husband is not intelligently determined. Thus, the potential offender often chooses a mate with a high penchant for violence. She has been beaten repeatedly and brutally for a period of years by a spouse or lover who may be drunk, sober, tired, depressed, elated, mentally ill, or just angry. Lacking educational and financial resources, she describes a feeling of being trapped. This feeling increases proportionately with the number of children she has. Community resources are disinterested, ineffective, or unavailable.... The battered wife has turned to social agencies, police, prosecutors, friends, ministers, and family, but they have not offered meaningful support or advice.... Abused women who have murdered their spouses reveal that they feel that homicide was the only alternative left to them.[27]

The battered woman murderess has been compared with the suicidal woman in that she is so consumed "with helplessness, hopelessness, despair, low self-esteem, and a distorted conception of reality, that she fails to think logically, to look beyond a horrible situation for which there seems to be no reasonable solution, and thus she seeks an unreasonable one."[28] Lenore Walker talked about the state of mind, before and after, of the battered woman turned killer of her intimate:

> Most women who killed their batterers have little memory of any cognitive processes other than an intense focus on their own survival. Although, retrospectively, it can be seen where her defenses against denial of her anger at being an abuse victim are unraveling, the women do not have any conscious awareness of those feelings. Their description of the final

incident indicates that they separate those angry feelings by the psychological process of a disassociative state and thus do not perceive them. This desperate attempt at remaining unaware of their own unacceptable feelings is a measure of just how dangerous they perceive their situation. They fear showing anger will cause their own death, and indeed it could, as batterers cannot tolerate the woman's expression of anger.[29]

Many abusive men turned murder victims of intimates were also *abused* men or children in a cycle of familial violence that often extends from spouse to spouse to children to parents and grandparents and to the outside world — in some instances turning deadly, be it in the family, school, or some other expression of pain, anger, and violence.[30]

9. Elderly Abuse

One of the groups most vulnerable to maltreatment within the family is the elderly. Yet the study of elderly abuse and neglect pales by comparison to domestic violence and child abuse. Why is that? Primarily it is a reflection of the greater visibility of younger people in society and more attention and importance placed on their health, welfare, and well being than their older counterparts. Sadly, many view the elderly as old, ill, frail, and sometimes mentally incompetent. The result is that abuse or neglect can go unrecognized, undiagnosed, or undetected as such by medical workers, friends, or even members of the victim's own family.

Many abused elderly are dependent upon their often overburdened, stressed out, under-appreciated abuser, financially and otherwise, and thus are even less likely to admit being victimized than the perpetrator is to acknowledge it. This only perpetuates the abuse that sometimes began years earlier with the elderly parent or grandparent as the abuser, continuing a cycle of family violence and mistreatment.

Entering a new century, the population of older Americans is expected to rise dramatically. This will leave millions susceptible to elderly victimization unless light is shed on the problem and the conditions creating familial elderly mistreatment. Only then can strategies be employed in identifying and responding effectively to this branch of family violence.

Elderly Crime Victimization

Much of the data on elderly crime victimization has focused on violent crimes such as rape, robbery and assault; personal theft; and household crimes including burglary, household larceny, and motor vehicle theft. Until recently, relatively little focus has been on elderly crime involving caretakers or relatives, per se. However, crime surveys on crimes against elderly people in general do allow us some context into the victimization of older Americans.

The National Crime Victimization Survey (NCVS) offers the most complete look at the types of offenses aforementioned affecting elderly victims. According to the NCVS, persons age 65 or older have the lowest overall crime rate in the nation as seen below:

Number of Victimizations
Per 1,000 Persons or Households[1]

Age	Violent crime	Personal theft	Household crime
12–24	64.6	112.7	309.3
25–49	27.2	71.2	200.2
50–64	8.5	38.3	133.0
65 or older	4.0	19.5	78.5

Crime rates for every category tend to decrease with age. The rate of violent crime is more than 16 times greater for persons under age 25 than for those age 65 and over, while the rate is more than 5 times as high for personal theft, and nearly 4 times as high for persons under 25 for household crime as persons over age 65. While persons 65 or older represent around 14 percent of those surveyed age 12 and over, they report under 2 percent of all victimizations.[2]

Elderly persons are also less likely to be murder victims, comprising around 5 percent of total people murdered in the United States.[3] With respect to violent crime victimization, the elderly appear to be most susceptible to criminality motivated by economic gain. Robberies represent almost 40 percent of the violent crimes against the elderly.[4]

DYNAMICS OF ELDERLY VICTIMIZATION

Elderly violent crime victims are more likely to suffer a serious injury than younger victims.[5] Around one-third of elderly victims are injured in a violent crime, nearly 1 in 10 suffering a serious injury; almost twice the percentage of persons under 65.[6] Nearly 1 in 5 elderly violent crime victims require medical care, with 14 percent needing hospital treatment.

Percent of Violent Crime Victims

Outcome	Under 65	65 or older
Injured	31%	33%
Serious	5	9
Minor	26	24
Received medical care	15	19
Hospital care	8	14

Table 9-1 shows the victim-offender relationship for violent crimes, for victims under age 65 and 65 or over. Senior citizen victims of violent crimes are more likely to be victimized by strangers than acquaintances or relatives. More than 8 in 10 robbery victimizations against persons age 65 and over are committed by strangers. Nevertheless, crimes of violence perpetrated by relatives represent around 8 percent of elderly violent victimizations. Thirteen percent of assaults against victims 65 years of age or over were committed by relatives.

Half of the violent crimes against the elderly occur in the victim's home or near home, with around 3 in 10 victimizations taking place on the street (see Table 9-2). Nearly 6 in 10 elderly victims of assaults are victimized at or near their residence. According to the Bureau of Justice Statistics' *Elderly Crime Victims*, "the vulnerability of the elderly to violent crime at or near their home may reflect their lifestyle. Often living alone and not working away from home, persons age 65 or older are also less likely than younger persons to go out after dark to social gatherings."[7] Indeed, public opinion surveys of persons age 50 and over indicate that around half are afraid to walk alone at night, even within their own neighborhood.[8]

As seen in Figure 9-1, nearly 4 in 10 elderly victims of violent crime are confronted by an armed assailant, whereas just over 6 in 10 victims face unarmed offenders. When accosted by an armed offender, more than 4 in 10 victims age 65 and over will be victimized by a perpetrator carrying a gun (Figure 9-2). Nearly 3 in 10 victimizations involve an offender using a knife or sharp instrument, while 3 in 10 senior citizens face violent offenders using blunt objects or other weapons.

PROFILING ELDERLY CRIME VICTIMS

Victimization data reflecting the demographic characteristics of elderly crime victims can be found in Table 9-3. Elderly men have higher

Table 9-1
Victim-Offender Relationship in Violent Crimes,
by Age of Victim

	Percent of violent crime victims whose offenders are:			
	Relatives	Acquaintances	Strangers	Relationship unknown
Crimes of violence				
Under 65	8%	33%	56%	3%
65 or older	8%	20%	64%	8%
Robbery				
Under 65	5%	17%	74%	4%
65 or older	3%	5%	83%	9%
Assault				
Under 65	9%	36%	52%	3%
65 or older	13%	32%	47%	8%

Source: Department of Justice, Bureau of Justice Statistics, *Elderly Crime Victims* (Washington, D.C.: Government Printing Office, 1994), p. 2.

Table 9-2
Places Where Elderly Violent
Victimizations Occur

	Place of occurrence					
	Total	At home	Near home	On the street	In public or business facility	Else-where
Crimes of violence						
Under 65	100%	14%	11%	39%	21%	15%
65 or older	100%	25%	25%	31%	9%	10%
Robbery						
Under 65	100%	13%	9%	52%	16%	10%
65 or older	100%	20%	21%	37%	13%	10%
Assault						
Under 65	100%	14%	12%	36%	21%	15%
65 or older	100%	27%	29%	27%	7%	10%

Source: Department of Justice, Bureau of Justice Statistics, *Elderly Crime Victims* (Washington, D.C.: Government Printing Office, 1994), p. 2.

Figure 9-1
Elderly Victims[a] of Violent Crime, by Armed or Unarmed Offender

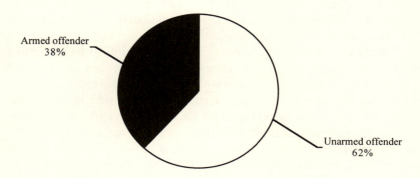

Armed offender
38%

Unarmed offender
62%

[a]Violent crime victims age 65 or older.

Source: Derived from Department of Justice, Bureau of Justice Statistics, *Elderly Crime Victims* (Washington, D.C.: Government Printing Office, 1994), p. 3.

Figure 9-2
Elderly Violent Crime Victims,[a] by Type of Weapon Used by Offender

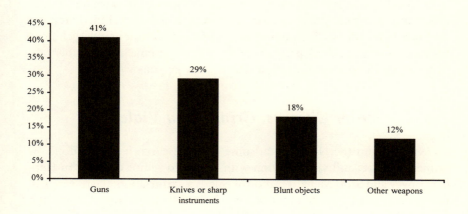

[a]Violent crime victims age 65 or older.

Source: Derived from Department of Justice, Bureau of Justice Statistics, *Elderly Crime Victims* (Washington, D.C.: Government Printing Office, 1994), p. 3.

victimization rates than elderly women. An exception to this is for personal larceny with contact (for example, purse snatching), where elderly women experience higher rates of victimization.[9] With respect to age, elderly victims age 65 to 74 have higher victimization rates than those age 75 and over for violent crimes, theft, and household crime.

Elderly blacks are more likely than elderly whites to be victims of crime overall. The rate of violent crime victimization for black persons age 65 or over is more than twice that of white persons 65 and older. However, elderly whites tend to have a higher victimization rate than elderly blacks for personal larceny not involving contact between the victim and offender.

Elderly violent crime victimization rates decrease the higher the income, but increase for theft victimization as income rises. Elderly persons with a family income of $25,000 or more have the highest victimization rates for household crime.

Separated or divorced elderly persons are more likely to be victims of every type of crime than persons age 65 or older who are never married, widowed, or married. The rate of violent crime victimization for married senior citizens is more than twice that of elderly persons who are never married.

Elderly residents living in urban areas have higher victimization rates for all kinds of crime than older people living in the suburbs or rural areas. The violent crime victimization rate for urban elderly is more than twice as high as that for suburban elderly and more than 3 times the rate of rural elderly citizens.

Elderly persons who rent have higher victimization rates for violent crime and theft than elderly persons who own their homes. Elderly renters are more than twice as likely to be victims of violent crime as elderly homeowners. However, elderly persons owing their own home have a higher rate of household crime victimization than elderly persons who rent.

Senior Citizens, Crime, and Violence

Aside from the NCVS data, some other research has been done on crime, violence, and victimization with regard to senior citizens. In Herbert Covey and Scott Menard's study of elderly victimization, the researchers proposed a need for examination of criminal victimization beyond the Federal Bureau of Investigation's (FBI) Crime Index offenses, consisting of major violent crimes (such as murder, forcible rape, robbery, and aggravated assault) and property crimes (including burglary, larceny-theft, motor vehicle theft, and arson).[10] Peter Yin[11] and Barry Lebowitz[12] found

Table 9-3
Characteristics of Elderly Crime Victims

| | Number of victimizations per 1,000 | | |
| Victim characteristics | Persons 65 or older | | Households headed by a person 65 or older |
	Violence	Theft	Household crime
Sex			
Male	4.9	19.8	82.2
Female	3.4	19.4	74.3
Age			
65 to 74	4.7	22.9	82.2
75 and over	3.0	14.2	74.3
Race			
White	3.6	19.5	70.9
Black	7.6	19.6	154.1
Family income			
Less than $7,500	12.0	29.1	76.3
$7,500-$14,999	8.4	30.4	70.2
$15,000-$24,999	6.5	40.3	81.3
$25,000 or more	6.1	60.8	96.0
Marital status			
Never married	3.0	18.2	77.6
Widowed	4.2	4.2	75.1
Married	7.6	26.3	71.1
Divorced/separated	11.3	35.4	110.4
Place of residence			
Urban	7.1	26.4	112.6
Suburban	2.9	19.6	61.2
Rural	2.2	11.4	64.5
Form of tenure			
Own	3.1	17.8	82.0
Rent	7.7	26.7	66.8

Source: Department of Justice, Bureau of Justice Statistics, *Elderly Crime Victims* (Washington, D.C.: Government Printing Office, 1994), p. 3.

that the elderly were more likely to fear crime than other age groups; while C. J. Wiltz reported that fear of criminality and crime victimization were important elements in many elderly citizens' lives.[13] Mary Hummert found that young and old people regarded the elderly as vulnerable to criminal victimization.[14]

Other studies such as by Jane Ollenberger[15] and John Linquist and Janice Duke[16] have supported NCVS data on the overall low rates of victimization among the elderly. Crimes such as robbery and vandalism have been found by criminologists to be among the more common crimes perpetrated against the elderly.[17] In a study of data from the FBI's National Incident-Based Reporting System, which provides more detailed crime and victim data than the FBI's *Uniform Crime Reports*, Kimberly McCabe and Sharon Gregory found that persons age 65 or older were more likely than younger persons to be victims of robbery, intimidation, vandalism, forgery, and fraud.[18]

Demographic studies on elderly victimization have found an at risk correlation with victimization based on gender and race. Jaber Gubrium found that elderly males were more likely than elderly females to be crime victims.[19] However, McCabe and Gregory found that while elderly males were more likely to be victims of proper crime than their female counterparts, elderly females were more likely than elderly males to be victims of crimes of violence.[20]

With respect to race and elderly victimization, Wiltz found a higher rate of criminal victimization among black elderly than white elderly.[21] However, McCabe and Gregory's research concluded that elderly whites were nearly twice as likely as elderly blacks to be crime victims.[22] Blacks age 65 and older were found to have higher victimization rates than whites age 65 or over for assaults and intimidations.

Defining Elderly Abuse

Elderly abuse, sometimes referred to as "granny bashing," generally encompasses similar definitional standards as wife abuse or child abuse. It relates to physical, emotional, and sexual abuse or neglect, as well as financial abuse and exploitation of a senior citizen, usually a person age 60 or over. The perpetrator is typically a child or grandchild of the abuse victim, but may be another relative or nonrelative as well. Some consider self-abuse or neglect by the elderly to also reflect elderly abuse.[23] This can often be attributed to a neglectful child or guardian, even if the maltreatment was through omission if not commission. David Finkelhor identified the three primary types of elderly abuse as *physical abuse, psychological abuse,* and *financial abuse.*[24] They are broken down as follows:

- *Physical abuse*: consisting of hitting, pushing, confinement of victim against his/her will, and sexual abuse.
- *Psychological abuse*: consisting of name calling, insults, threats, and ignoring victim.
- *Financial abuse*: consisting of illegal or unethical use of the elderly victim's money, property or other assets.

Most elderly victims of abuse and exploitation tend to experience more than one type of victimization.[25] They are also prone to being victimized by more than one perpetrator, both in and out of the family.

The Extent of Elderly Abuse

Elderly abuse and victimization is believed by many authorities to be the most underreported and consequential kind of family violence. It is estimated that only 1 case in every 14 is ever reported.[26] The reasons for this vary but include fear of, dependency on, and/or loyalty to the abuser; as well as shame, denial, confusion, senility, and other factors. This makes it nearly impossible to gain an accurate assessment of the magnitude of elderly abuse.

Some estimates and studies give rise to the severity of the problem. Approximately 1 million persons age 60 and older are believed to be victims of familial abuse in the United States annually.[27] A recent survey estimated that the majority of the projected 701,000 to 1,093,500 abused elderly in this country were victims of abuse by spouses.[28] In a survey of professionals who were aware of elderly abuse, including medical employees and law enforcement personnel, around 47 percent of those returning the questionnaire knew specifically of cases of abuse or neglect that had occurred within the past 12 to 16 months.[29] Nearly half of those who had worked with abused elderly reported seeing more than 5 cases of elderly victimization.

Who Are the Perpetrators of Elderly Abuse?

Elderly abusers can be anyone inside or outside the family and may involve multiple offenders. Most elderly victims are abused by caregivers or relatives. Adult children are believed to be the most frequent abusers, accounting for nearly 4 in 10 of reported cases of elderly abuse.[30] In their study of elderly victimization, McCabe and Gregory found that nearly 3 in 10 elderly victims of intimidation were abused by their children.[31] The researchers also found that more than 15 percent of offenders of elderly intimidation were grandchildren or other relatives.

Many elderly abuse victims are victimized by a spouse. One study found this to be a common problem in retirement communities.[32] Though there are no national statistics on the frequency of elderly spousal abuse, sociologists contend that the incidence of such abuses "are likely to grow as social-service resources dwindle and the country's population of people aged 65 and older grows to 35.3 million people — 12.8 percent of the U.S. population — by the year 2000."[33]

According to Marjorie Valbrun: "The idea of older people battering — sometimes even killing — other older people no longer surprises law enforcement authorities, who say they are encountering this kind of violence with growing frequency."[34] In most instances, the batterer and battered live together or are members of the same family. "Sometimes one is, or both of them are, sick and suffering. And almost always, the pressure of one taking care of the other has become too much."[35]

Characterizing Elderly Abuse Victims and Offenders

Elderly abuse victims are typically characterized by experts as being the following:

- Vulnerable.[36]
- Exploitable.
- Physically or cognitively impaired.
- Socially isolated.
- Dependent on a caretaker abuser.[37]

Most victims are abused "by those they live with, partly the result of the stress of caring for a person who is ill or disabled, who needs to be fed and toileted, and who provides little satisfying companionship."[38] Abusers of elderly often tend to have the following characteristics:

- A history of family violence.
- Mental illness.[39]

- Alcohol and/or drug addiction.
- Financial dependency on the elderly victim.[40]
- Stress.
- Prior victimization at the hands of the victim.[41]

Elderly abuse — whether physical, emotional, or financial — is usually a reflection of frustrations felt by the abuser (as well as the abused) due to the reversal of dependency roles, stresses related to the burdens placed on the caregiver, and financial needs or dependency by the offender or victim.[42] Also seen as a factor in elderly abuse is the older parent or grandparent's weakening of power and influence in decision making within the family.[43]

Elderly Abuse and Criminal Intent

Though many elderly citizens are the victims of criminality, abuse, and exploitation willfully with criminal intent in mind, most elderly victims of familial mistreatment are not harmed purposely. Rather the victimization is commonly a reflection of the stresses and strains which often accompany caring for aging relatives. The elderly person's physical and mental deterioration can be overwhelming, along with the necessary mental, physical and financial challenges of the caretaker or family in dealing with an elderly parent or grandparent. It is not surprising that in many instances these conflicting emotions and pressures result in abuse or neglect of the elderly. Sometimes the abuser is also elderly and suffering from similar problems as the victim, in addition to having to care for the person, increasing the risk for maltreatment.

Substance abuse is most often cited as the reason for elderly abuse, followed by the pressures put on caretakers and family in caring for the victim. Most experts focus on the burdens associated with elderly family members as the primary cause of abuse or neglect, and attributed the maltreatment to "bad situations, not bad people."[44] While mandatory reporting of elderly abuse by doctors and social service workers exists in some states, clearly what is needed is more voluntary reporting by those involved in elderly abuse. Also necessary is more effective diagnosis and medical treatment of abuse by professionals; along with greater access to social and counseling services by both the abused and abuser.

PART III

Child Maltreatment

10. Child Abuse
and Neglect

Child maltreatment in the form of familial child abuse and neglect is one of the more serious domestic issues of our time. It is estimated that as many as 4 million children are victims of child abuse or neglect each year in the United States.[1] Thousands of these victimizations result in severe injuries or fatalities.[2] Many do irreparable mental or physical, short- or long-term harm to the victim. There is indication that more and more children are being victimized. According to data from child protective services agencies, between 1990 and 1996 the number of victims of child maltreatment increased by 18 percent.[3] Recognizing and reporting child abuse and neglect continues to be the most important tool in detecting and combating child maltreatment.

This chapter will explore key aspects of child abuse and neglect in this country, including definitions, dimensions, and effects on the child.

Defining Child Abuse and Neglect

In defining child maltreatment, experts have focused on both broad parameters and specific types or subgroups of child abuse and neglect. C. Henry Kempe and colleagues' "battered child syndrome" identified physical injuries perpetrated on the child by caregivers.[4] Vincent Fontana's "maltreatment syndrome" included neglect in the definition of child abuse.[5] The American Bar Association Juvenile Justice Standards Project defined child abuse as a nonaccidental injury that "causes or creates a substantial risk of causing disfigurement, impairment of bodily functioning, or other serious physical injury."[6]

A group of professionals in child welfare defined "emotional neglect" as the "parent's refusal to recognize and take action to ameliorate a child's identified emotional disturbance."[7] David and Patricia Mrazek's definition of child sexual abuse is "the sexual misuse of a child for an adult's own gratification without proper concern for the child's psychosexual development."[8] K. T. Alvy termed child abuse and neglect as "collective abuse" or the "gamut of destructive collective attitudes towards children, such as racial and social class discrimination, and institutional abuse."[9]

The federal government's legal definition of child abuse and neglect comes under the Child Abuse Prevention and Treatment Act (Public Law 100-294). This included child physical and mental abuse, sexual abuse and exploitation, and neglect by a person responsible for the child's health and welfare. (See also Chapter 3.) The Child Abuse Amendments of 1984 (Public Law 98-457) expanded the definition of child abuse and neglect to include "the withholding of medical treatment to an infant with a life threatening health condition or complication."[10]

The National Association of Public Child Welfare Administrators' (NAPCWA) definition of child abuse and neglect further defined child maltreatment in a broad level as "any recent act or failure to act on the part of a parent or caretaker, which results in death or serious physical, sexual, or emotional harm or presents an imminent risk of serious harm to a person under age 18."[11]

Critics of the sometimes confusing, inconsistent, plethora of definitions of child abuse and neglect point out such problems as some are too narrow, others too inclusive, and the cross-cultural differences with respect to perceptions of child maltreatment and reporting of such. The lack of uniformity in definitions and the resulting inconsistencies in their application reflect "the manifold perspectives on these acts, and the inchoate state of conceptualization."[12]

Reports of Child Maltreatment

Much of what we know about the incidence of child maltreatment comes from reports of child abuse and neglect to child protective services agencies. In 1997, there were approximately 3.2 million reports of child maltreatment in the United States.[13] Of these, more than 1 million children were identified as substantiated, or indicated, abuse or neglect victims.

In 1996, for which the most detailed data on child maltreatment were available, child protective services agencies investigated over 2 million reports of alleged child maltreatment involving more than 3 million children.[14] The

Figure 10-1
Sources of Reports of
Child Maltreatment, 1996[a]

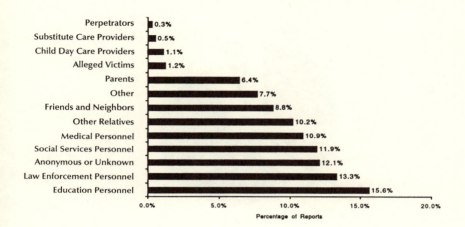

Perpetrators	0.3%
Substitute Care Providers	0.5%
Child Day Care Providers	1.1%
Alleged Victims	1.2%
Parents	6.4%
Other	7.7%
Friends and Neighbors	8.8%
Other Relatives	10.2%
Medical Personnel	10.9%
Social Services Personnel	11.9%
Anonymous or Unknown	12.1%
Law Enforcement Personnel	13.3%
Education Personnel	15.6%

Percentage of Reports

[a] There were a total of 1,490,340 reports from 42 states.

Source: U.S. Department of Health and Human Services, Children's Bureau, *Child Maltreatment 1996: Reports From the States to the National Child Abuse and Neglect Data System* (Washington, D.C.: Government Printing Office, 1998), p. 2-2.

national rate of children reported as maltreated was 44 per 1,000; an increase from 1990 when it was 41 children per 1,000.[15]

The sources of reports of maltreatment in 1996 can be seen in Figure 10-1. Professional reporters such as educators, law enforcement, social services, and medical personnel made up more than half the reports of alleged child abuse and neglect referred for investigation. Education personnel comprised the largest proportion of reports at nearly 16 percent, followed by law enforcement personnel at more than 13 percent. Parents, relatives, and victims of child maltreatment accounted for around 18 percent of the sources.

With respect to disposition, approximately 1.6 million investigations of child maltreatment were conducted in the United States in 1996. Figure 10-2 shows the percentage breakdown of investigated reports by disposition. More than 34 percent of the investigations resulted in a disposition of substantiated or indicated child maltreatment. In over half the investigations, the disposition was one in which the child maltreatment was not substantiated.

Figure 10-2
Investigated Reports, by Disposition, 1996[a]

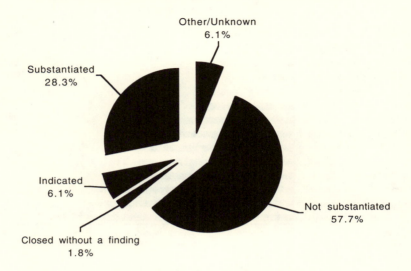

Other/Unknown
6.1%

Substantiated
28.3%

Indicated
6.1%

Not substantiated
57.7%

Closed without a finding
1.8%

[a]There were a total of 1,624,666 reports from 48 states.

Source: U.S. Department of Health and Human Services, Children's Bureau, *Child Maltreatment 1996: Reports from the States to the National Child Abuse and Neglect Data System* (Washington, D.C.: Government Printing Office, 1998), p. 2-3.

Based on data from the National Child Abuse and Neglect Data System's (NCANDS) Detailed Case Data Component (DCDC), more than 60 percent of all child maltreatment reports that were substantiated or indicated came from law enforcement, medical, social services, or education personnel sources.[16] Over half the law enforcement (61 percent) and medical personnel (56 percent) referrals were substantiated or indicated.

Types of Child Maltreatment

There are four primary types of child maltreatment: physical abuse, sexual abuse, emotional abuse, and neglect. The American Humane Association's recent Fact Sheet breaks these down as shown in Figure 10-3. In nearly 60 percent of the cases, the type of child maltreatment reported was neglect. Physical abuse accounted for more than 20 percent of the cases of maltreatment. Nearly 9 percent of child victims were sexually abused,

Figure 10-3
Types of Child Abuse and Neglect

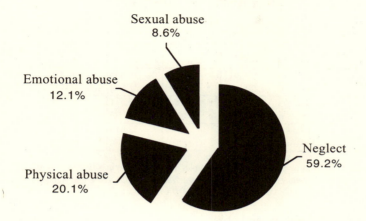

Source: *Child Abuse and Neglect Data: AHA Fact Sheet #1* (Englewood, CO: American Humane Association, 1994), p. 1.

while just over 12 percent suffered from emotional abuse. Data from the National Committee for Prevention of Child Abuse found that 45 percent of all reported child maltreatment involved neglect of the victim, with 27 percent of the cases concerning physical abuse, 17 percent child sexual abuse, and 7 percent emotional abuse of the child.[17]

Table 10-1 reflects the type of child maltreatment by sex of the perpetrator in 1996, according to the DCDC findings. Females were most likely to physically abuse, neglect, and emotionally maltreat children; while males were most likely to sexually abuse their children. In more than 55 percent of the reported physical abuse, nearly 72 percent of the neglect, over 78 percent of the medical neglect, and 57 percent of the emotional maltreatment cases, the perpetrator was female. Males were the perpetrators in more than 70 percent of child sexual abuse victimizations. In all, nearly 61 percent of the maltreatment was committed by females.

Children at Risk for Maltreatment

Studies have shown that some children are more at risk than others to be victims of child maltreatment. F. J. Bishop identified 6 groups of children that represent a "special" risk for child abuse or neglect victimization:

Table 10-1
Type of Child Maltreatment by
Sex of Perpetrator, 1996

Sex	Physical Abuse	Neglect	Medical Neglect	Sexual Abuse	Emotional Maltreatment	Totals
Male	17,590 (44.7%)	20,617 (28.1%)	1,893 (21.7%)	16,448 (71.5%)	2,586 (43.0%)	59,134 (39.3%)
Female	21,757 (55.3%)	52,675 (71.9%)	6,818 (78.3%)	6,571 (28.5%)	3,429 (57.0%)	91,250 (60.7%)
Totals	39,347 (100.0%)	73,292 (100.0%)	8,711 (100.0%)	23,019 (100.0%)	6,015 (100.0%)	150,384 (100.0%)

Source: U.S. Department of Health and Human Services, Children's Bureau, *Child Maltreatment 1996: Reports From the States to the National Child Abuse and Neglect Data System* (Washington, D.C.: Government Printing Office, 1998), p. 2-15.

- Congenitally malformed babies.
- Premature babies.
- Illegitimate children.
- Twins.
- Children conceived during the mother's depression.
- Children of mothers with frequent pregnancies and excessive work-loads.[18]

Richard Gelles compiled an "at risk" index that combined variables that produced the highest probability of injuring a child.[19]

A strong relationship has been shown between child maltreatment and unwanted pregnancies and pregnancy shortly after the birth of a previous child.[20] The size of the family has also been found to put children at risk for abuse or neglect. David Gil reported that child abuse victims were twice as likely to come from families with 4 or more children than was the case for the general population.[21] Studies conducted in the United States, New Zealand, and England lent support to this correlation, finding that the average family size for abusing families far exceeded the national average.[22]

Ray Helfer's psychodynamic model of child abuse posits that 3 conditions must be present for child abuse to take place: (1) a very special type of child, (2) a crisis or series of crises, and (3) the parental potential for maltreatment.[23] Blair and Rita Justice observed 2 types of "life" crises predisposing a child to abuse: (1) situational crises and (2) maturational crises. Situational crises consist of a "rapid series of situational events" which could be "compressed together."[24] Maturational crises include "marriage, pregnancy, a son or daughter leaving home, or retirement."[25]

In their study of the child's role in child abuse, J. Milowe and R. Lourie referred to "difficult" children whose irritable characteristics they first thought were due to child maltreatment. The researchers changed their opinion based on information from nurses who found themselves over-burdened in caring for the infants over an 8-hour shift. They commented on the "irritable cry, the difficulty in managing, and the unappealing nature of some of these children."[26] The study cited 2 children who had been abused in their separate homes presumably because of their "difficult" nature.[27]

Parental Character Traits

Parents who abuse or neglect their children are often characterized as being immature, impulsive, self-centered, dependent, rigid, and reject-ing. They typically lack "nurturing and coping skills, have a poor self-image, and a relatively low tolerance level. Violence is experienced and viewed as an option. Abusive parents tend to be socially isolated and distrustful of neighbors, possess a high level of stress, and exhibit a general pattern of social impoverishment."[28] Many perpetrators of child maltreatment find it difficult to be self-sufficient, or to be "counted on" by friends or neigh-bors.[29] Most abusive parents come from abusive families and tend to have a poor relationship with their own parents and spouses.[30] Substance abuse is a significant factor in child abuse and neglect.[31] (See also Chapter 14.)

Family Dynamics and Child Maltreatment

A typology of the typical abusive parent, abused child, and family dynamics was established by T. Solomon as follows:

Abusive Parent

- The vast majority are married and living together when abuse occurs.
- Average age of abusive father is 30 years old.
- Average age of abusive mother is 26 years old.
- The father is abusive slightly more than the mother.
- The mother is the more serious child abuser.
- The most common instrument for abuse is a hairbrush.

Abused Child

- Average age is under 4 years old.
- Most are under 2 years old.
- Average age of death due to abuse is less than 3 years old.
- Average time of exposure to maltreatment is 1 to 3 years.
- There is no sexual differentiation.

Family Dynamics

- Thirty to 60 percent of abusive parents were victims of child abuse.
- A high proportion of premarital conception.
- Married at a young age.
- Forced marriages.
- Unwanted pregnancies.
- Illegitimate pregnancies.
- Emotional problems in the marriage.
- Social and family isolation.
- Financial problems.[32]

A study by E. F. Lenoski shed additional light on the family dynamics of abusers.[33] In comparing 674 abusive parents against a control group of 500 nonabusers, Lenoski found that 65 percent of the abusers reported early exposure to family violence, compared to 43 percent of the nonabusers. Eighty percent of the child abusers claimed a religious affiliation, whereas 62 percent of the nonabusers did.

The Effects of Child Abuse

PHYSICAL DAMAGE

Physical damage is the greatest initial concern with respect to battered children. Because children have not fully developed, they are susceptible to a number of physical injuries such as fractures and internal injuries. Physical child abuse can also cause damage to the central nervous system, which can lead to mental retardation, cerebral palsy, seizures, hearing or visual damage, or learning difficulties.[34]

POOR PHYSICAL HEALTH

Children who are abused tend to be more susceptible to emotional distress and poorer health than other children.[35] In a study in Australia, abused children were found to be more than 5 times as likely as nonabused children to have significant illnesses in infancy.[36] Anemia and its consequences such as poor learning ability, apathy, and exhaustion have been shown to be common in maltreated children.[37] Other poor health problems related to child abuse include poor weight gain, insufficient protein intake, learning impairment, and below average height for age.[38]

PSYCHOLOGICAL DAMAGE

A number of studies have documented the relationship between child abuse and psychological damage. H. P. Martin and P. Beezley found that "four and a half years after their study, over half the children studied were sorrowful and displayed types of behavior that made parents, peers, and teachers reject them."[39] Characteristics noted among the children included withdrawal, low self-esteem, hypervigilance, school learning problems, pseudomature behavior, and psychiatric symptoms. A. H. Green made similar findings in the study and treatment of 20 abused children; additionally noting "impairment of ego functioning, traumatic reactions, with acute anxiety states, masochistic and self-destructive behavior, and lack of trust."[40] Most of the children had been victims of recurrent child abuse during the first 2 years of life. J. Roberts, M. M. Lynch, and P. Duff's study of long-term emotional and behavioral problems of abused children found evidence of social isolation, hostility, disruptive behavior, and violent tendencies.[41]

NEUROLOGICAL DAMAGE

Neurological damage has been observed in a high percentage of children who are severely abused. According to the Royal College of Psychiatrists: "If 75 young children per million of the total population are severely attacked each year, then 18–19 per million could suffer intellectual impairment each year, often to a profound degree."[42] H. Martin and associates found that 53 percent of the children sampled had some degree of neurological abnormality, while one-third were severely handicapped.[43] The researchers postulated that neurological dysfunction was closely associated with delayed development and a history of head trauma. In a 3-year study, C. W. Morse and colleagues found that 60 percent of the sample group of children were mentally retarded following the initial injury.[44] C. H. Kempe and associates reported brain damage in 25 of 45 fatal cases of child abuse.[45]

GROWTH PROBLEMS

Growth retardation has often been shown to be an effect of child abuse. A number of studies have reported poor physical growth and poor nutrition in roughly 25 to 35 percent of abused children at the time of identification.[46] Follow-up studies of battered children have supported a high rate of growth failure.[47] Research by H. Martin[48] and E. Elmer[49] found a significant difference in "intellectual prognosis when undernourished maltreated children were compared with well nourished maltreated children."[50] Such finds indicate that children who are "undernourished as well as abused have a much poorer prognosis in terms of mental function and neurological integrity."[51]

Dimensions of Child Maltreatment

CHILD NEGLECT

Although child physical abuse and sexual abuse draw much of the attention of researchers in the study of child maltreatment, the reality is that child neglect is the more common form of child victimization in the home. More than half of the substantiated reports of child maltreatment each year are for neglect, "which means that adults are not providing a safe environment with adequate shelter, clothing, food, and sanitation."[52] One expert notes painfully that of the roughly 1.5 million children in neglect cases every year, they are in child protective services agency files "because they were unwashed, unfed, untreated for illness, unwanted."[53]

Many children die each year in the United States as a result of neglect by the parents. According to Sandra Arbetter: "Women kill most often through severe neglect — like the mother in Memphis who left two toddlers in the car ... in 90-degree heat while she partied with friends. Temperatures in the car soared, and the children died."[54]

The National Incidence Study broke down neglect into three types: *physical*, *educational*, and *emotional*. Figure 10-4 illustrates the types, by percentage of reported cases, of neglect. Nearly 51 percent of the neglect cases involve physical neglect. More than 28 percent are for educational neglect, while in just over 20 percent of the cases parents emotionally neglect their children.

Child neglect can have a detrimental effect on the child victim in a number of ways. "Neglect can lead to malnutrition, lack of proper medical care, and [have] profound effects on the short- and long-term functioning of the body and development of the brain."[55] In fact, many child

Figure 10-4
Types of Child Neglect

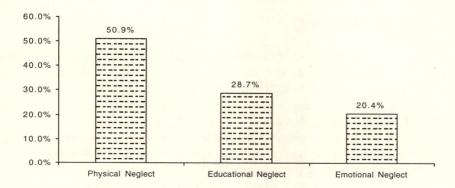

Source: *Child Abuse and Neglect: A Shared Community Concern* (Washington, D.C.: U.S Department of Health and Human Services, 1992), p. 4.

abuse experts believe that neglect may be more severe in its long-term implications on the child than physical or sexual abuse. In comparing the developmental consequences of child neglect, physical abuse, and sexual abuse, Penelope Trickett found that

> neglected children tended to be withdrawn and anti-social, not only with their parents but with other children.... Like abused children, neglected toddlers had learning delays, particularly in language skills. By elementary school, they had the lowest grades and test scores, the highest teacher ratings of learning problems, grade repeats, and school absences. More than that, they showed no signs of pulling ahead.[56]

The researcher found similar patterns when examining middle and high school students.

In a study of emotional neglect of children and the long-term impact, Byron Egeland, Martha Erickson, and colleagues identified 24 neglectful mothers out of their sample of 267 women, 19 of which were described as emotionally remote or "psychologically unavailable."[57] Their children, as opposed to others, were found to be "inattentive, uninvolved, overly passive, anxious, or impatient."[58] Erickson observed that unlike the episodic nature of physical and sexual abuse, "emotional neglect is chronic.... And if children are emotionally neglected in the first two years ... then there are going to be striking consequences."[59]

Experts believe that the greatest risk factor for child neglect is poverty.

Other risk factors include parents who are depressed, abuse drugs or alcohol, in bad relationships, too busy, or inattentive.

PARENTAL KIDNAPPING

Each year thousands of children are abducted by a parent, often as the consequences of a divorce, separation, or custody battle. Parental kidnapping, also referred to as "child snatching," has existed for many years, but only in recent memory has it become widely seen as another form of child maltreatment. Parental kidnapping by a noncustodial parent is believed to account for more than 100,000 child abductions a year in the United States.[60] Some experts suggest the figures will continue to rise, due largely to the soaring divorce rate in this country.[61] The American Bar Association estimates that 70 percent of children abducted by a noncustodial parent will never see their custodial parent again.[62]

Fathers are typically the kidnappers, as they abduct their children in order to "circumvent a legal system that in 92 percent of the cases grants custody of the child or children to the mother."[63] Tens of thousands of dollars are often spent by the custodial parent in an effort to locate and retrieve the child. Additionally, there is anguish, guilt, depression, anxiety, and other physical and mental stresses the parent must go through in both self-blame and wondering about the health and welfare of the missing child.

In many instances, the abducted child is returned home safely "only after the conflict is resolved satisfactorily for the parent kidnapper."[64] Because parental abductions are often still viewed by law enforcement authorities as a family matter, they are not always given the same intense efforts in locating the child as children who are abducted by strangers — estimated at upwards of 150,000 annually.[65] Even when it is given a top priority, locating children taken by a parent can be an almost impossible task, considering the size of the United States. Further, some abductors take children overseas, further complicating matters and lessening the chance the child will ever be reunited with the custodial parent.

Laws on parental kidnapping are not uniform from state to state, making the task of locating victims and prosecuting abducting parents that much more difficult. (See Chapter 19 for federal efforts in locating abducted children.)

Most experts agree that it is the emotional harm to the child, loss of parental unity, and family bonding that typically have the most long-term impact.

CHILD ABUSE AND NEGLECT IN THE ARMED SERVICES

Relatively little research has been done on child maltreatment in the armed services: the Air Force, Army, Navy, and Marine Corps. However, some data does indicate that child abuse and neglect is a serious problem in the military just as in civilian life. According to NCANDS data, there were 16,673 reports of alleged child maltreatment in the military in 1996.[66] In 48 percent of the investigations, there were dispositions of substantiated maltreatment of children. A breakdown of the type of child maltreatment victims found in the armed services follows:

- Forty-two percent were victims of neglect.
- Thirty-six percent were physical abuse victims.
- Fourteen percent were sexual abuse victims.
- Seventeen percent were victims of emotional maltreatment.

The proportion of child physical abuse victims was greater than the national proportion, while the proportion of neglect victims was lower than that of the general population.

Child maltreatment in the armed services has been associated with military life itself and circumstances within, including substance abuse, disciplinary infractions, reassignment, field training, payroll problems, living abroad, foreign spouses, and intracultural problems. John Miller reported that the most vulnerable population in the military for child maltreatment are young enlisted families who have been in the service for less than 3 years.[67] Within this group are "high-risk" families, as in civilian life, characterized by "inexperience, immaturity, lack of social skills, and inability to cope with life's stresses and problems."[68]

In a study of the types of child maltreatment in the armed services conducted at William Beaumont Army Medical Center in El Paso, Texas, it was found that 7 percent of the cases were "disciplinary abuse."[69] The term was first used in a study classifying types of child maltreatment among the civilian population, and descriptive of the typical pattern of the "military syndrome." The abusive parents were described as "rigid and unfeeling ... the homes were spotless ... abuse was centered upon any child who broke the rules and straps and sticks were used in place of hands."[70]

Although Family Advocacy Programs personnel in the armed services are required to report cases of child abuse and neglect to the child abuse registry in the state in which the victim lives, much like civilians, most child maltreatment in the military is believed to go unreported and, thus, remains a hidden tragedy.

11. Child Sexual Abuses

Child sexual abuse within the family is one of the most serious and widespread of all domestic crimes. The nature of familial sexual abuse and misuse of children includes incest, molestation, sodomy, forcible and statutory rape, child prostitution, and child pornography. The perpetrators are most often parents, but can be other siblings, uncles and aunts, grandparents, guardians, and other relatives. Although child sexual abuse tends to be typically associated with female victims, research shows that just as many male children are at risk for sexual victimization by family members.[1]

Child sex abuse victims range from "totally accidental victimization involving little victimogenesis to seductive sexual partners with extensive victimogenesis. In many instances, the child may consent to the sexual victimization unintentionally or unwittingly, or offer only passive resistance; in other cases of sex exploitation the victim and offender are in a symbiotic relationship or form a cooperative dyad."[2] In the worst case scenario, the sexually abused child "is completely powerless, vulnerable, and exploited by the powerful, non-vulnerable exploiter."[3]

The type of therapy for victims of child sexual abuse "seems to be related to where they are situated along the victim continuum in conjunction with such factors as the degree of physical force or violence used by the offender and the intensity of the victim-offender relationship prior to the sex offense."[4]

This chapter will define and examine the nature, scope, and implications of child sexual abuses.

Defining Child Sexual Abuse

Definitions of child sexual abuse generally refer to various types of sexual abuses and misuses perpetrated on minors by family members, or nonfamily members. Some definitions tend to be more specific or narrow in range, others all inclusive, along with the circumstances of such sexual abuse. The Child Abuse Prevention and Treatment Act (Public Law 100-294) defines child sexual abuse as

> (a) the employment, use, persuasion, inducement, enticement, or coercion of any child to engage in, or assist any other person to engage in, any sexually explicit conduct or simulation of such conduct for the purpose of producing any visual depiction of such conduct, or (b) the rape, molestation, prostitution, or other such form of sexual exploitation of children, or incest with children.[5]

Child sexual abuse and exploitation were defined in a report sponsored by the American Bar Association, the Legal Resource Center for Child Advocacy and Protection, the American Public Welfare Association, and the American Enterprise Institute. It defined child sexual abuse as "vaginal, anal, or oral intercourse; vaginal or anal penetrations; or other forms of contact for sexual purposes."[6] Child sexual exploitation was defined as "using a child in prostitution, pornography, or other sexually exploitative activities."[7]

The sexual abuse of children with respect to family or related dynamics typically falls under the following categories of offenders:

- *Familial Sexual Abuse.* The perpetrator is a member of the nuclear family such as a father or father substitute, mother or mother substitute, or a sibling.
- *Extended Familial Sexual Abuse.* The perpetrator is a nonnuclear family member such as a grandparent, uncle, aunt, or cousin.
- *Caretaker Sexual Abuse.* The perpetrator is a nonfamily member responsible for the child's welfare, such as a babysitter or day care worker.
- *Nonstranger Sexual Abuse.* The perpetrator is known by the child, such as an adult family friend or scout leader.
- *Peer Sexual Abuse.* The perpetrator is another child, nonfamily member, known by the victim.
- *Ritualistic or Satanic Sexual Abuse.* The perpetrator practices rituals or Satanism as part of abuse.[8]

The Scope of Child Sexual Abuse

There is no national consensus on the extent of child sexual abuse in this country. However most experts believe the incidence is significant. Estimates of child sexual abuse in large urban areas have been placed at 4,000 cases annually,[9] with 5,000 cases of father-daughter incest in the

United States each year,[10] and between 200,000 and 500,000 cases of sexual abuse perpetrated on girls 4 to 14 years of age.[11] In one large city with advanced services for child sex victims, nearly 1 in 4 of all sexual assaults were on children younger than the age of 14.[12]

In its annual 50 state survey, the National Committee for Prevention of Child Abuse found that approximately 17 percent of all child abuse and neglect cases involve sexual abuse.[13] The National Child Abuse and Neglect Data System (NCANDS) recently estimated that nearly 130,000 reports of child sexual abuse were substantiated after investigation that year.[14] Child protective services reported that an estimated 80,000 cases of child sexual abuse were confirmed in 1997, representing about 8 percent of all cases of child abuse.[15] In a study of child sexual abuse, David Finkelhor found that as many as 52 percent of the women and 9 percent of the men sampled had been sexually abused as children.[16]

Most experts agree that much of the child sexual abuse in this country goes unreported, indicating its magnitude.[17]

Risk Factors of Child Sexual Abuse

All children are at risk for sexual abuse and exploitation. However, studies show that some children are particularly susceptible for victimization, including the following factors:

- Being a female.
- Where there is a family cycle of sexual and/or physical abuse.
- In the absence of parents or guardians.
- Being a member of a stepfamily.
- Being the oldest child.
- Where there is familial alcohol or drug abuse.
- Being in an unstable family.
- Where there is poor or no family bonding.
- When there is mental manipulation or exploitation.
- In the absence of a supportive family.[18]

The American Humane Association (AHA) found the average age of sexually abused children to be 9.3 years.[19] Nearly 8 in 10 studied were females. The AHA reported that the sexual abuse of girls seemed to increase proportionately with chronological age. The National Incidence Study found that the incidence rate of child sexual abuse was highest among girls ages 12 to 17.[20] According to the Child Victimization Study, reported sexual abuse cases involved primarily male offenders and female victims, and were more likely to occur in middle class families than child physical abuse and neglect cases.[21]

Characterizing Child Sexual Abuse

There are a number of features that characterize child sexual abuse. Most relate to other aspects of family violence, including wife battering, marital rape, physical child abuse, child neglect, child emotional abuse, sibling abuse, substance abuse, and intergenerational abuse. Victims of child sexual abuse are often victims of one or more other family abuses.[22] Studies show that victims of intrafamilial sexual abuse are at greater risk for repeated sexual victimization than those abused by nonfamily members.[23] Some data indicate that sexually abused daughters may unconsciously "seek abusive environments in which they are subsequently victimized (through rape or spousal abuse) and are frequently unable to protect their children from being abused."[24]

Transgenerational sexual abuse is believed by some sociologists to be a learned behavior, which could result in an "escalating geometric progression of abuse in subsequent generations as some abused children in turn abuse their own children."[25]

Characteristics of Child Sexual Abuse Perpetrators

ADULT PERPETRATORS

Child sexual abuse is typically perpetrated by adults, often family members or family acquaintances. According to data from NCANDS Summary Data Component, more than 7 in 10 perpetrators of reported child sexual abuse are male.[26] Researchers have sought to isolate characteristics and behavioral patterns of child sex abusers. In a comprehensive study of child sex offenders, P. Gebhard and colleagues found that the offenders' "uncommon behavior" was motivated by "abnormal and/or pathological desires."[27] Other research has found that by comparison to the general population, child sex offenders are more likely to be "of subnormal intelligence than superior intelligence."[28] Subnormal intelligence has been shown to be more prevalent in sex offenders convicted of "incestuous relations, statutory rape, and bestiality than offenders convicted of exhibitory acts, forcible rape, and disseminating obscene materials."[29] There is evidence that some child sexual abusers may be driven in part by recurring sexual fantasies.[30]

The majority of child sex offenders tend to be young, single, and familiar with their victims, if not family members. Some studies have found child sex offenders to be disproportionately undereducated, and socially and economically disadvantaged.[31]

CHILD PERPETRATORS

The number of child sex abuse victims being abused by other children is on the rise in society. Many of these abuses are taking place in the home, committed by siblings. Note the authors of one book examining child sexual abuse: "It is increasingly recognized that there are many adolescents who abuse younger children both inside and outside their families. Because such cases are less likely to come to agency attention and because more information is greatly needed, it is important for research to include such abuse within their purview."[32]

A study of sexually abusive children by the state of Washington's Department of Social and Health Services established the following findings:

• Sixty-four percent were victims of sexual abuse.
• Half the offenders and victims lived in the same home.
• Fifty percent of the sexual abusers had 2 to 5 victims.
• Twenty-six percent of the offenders were preadolescent children.
• Nearly half the child aggressors were ages 13 to 14.[33]

According to the National Adolescent Perpetrator Network, approximately 50 percent of the sexual abuse of boys and 15 to 20 percent of the sexual abuse of girls was committed by other children.[34]

Such research as aforementioned further underscores the seriousness of child sexual abuse and its relationship to family violence.

The Effects of Child Sexual Abuse

The short- and long-term effects of sexual abuse perpetrated on children can be devastating. The normal, healthy development having been compromised, the child sexual abuse victim is typically "unable to cope emotionally, intellectually, and/or physically with sexual stimulation and responsiveness, regardless of whether the child finds the experience emotionally satisfying, erotically pleasurable, or negative in some fashion."[35]

In one study it was reported that the psychological scarring and stress of child sexual abuse and exploitation can often lead to alcohol and drug abuse in order to "deaden memories and desensitize present experiences."[36] Other research has produced similar findings in the "social maturation and psychological effects of victims of incest and child pornography. Most child sexual abuse victims experience feelings of guilt, betrayal, rage, worthlessness, and withdrawal — all of which have been shown to manifest themselves in both inwardly self-destructive behavior and outwardly socially aberrant behavior."[37]

The physical effects of child sexual abuse have been well documented in the literature, and include "lacerations to the genitals, sexually transmitted diseases, pregnancy, internal injuries, broken bones, and even death."[38] (See also Chapter 10 on for more about the effects of child abuse and neglect.)

The risk of HIV infection and sexual dysfunction are also prominent among victims of child sexual abuse. Furthermore, studies show there is a strong relationship between being a sex offender and a victim of child sexual abuse.[39]

12. Incest and Other Child Sexual Victimization

The sexual abuse and exploitation of children by other family members occurs far more often than the statistics indicate. Much of this is in the form of incestuous relations. Though incest is strictly prohibited in most modern societies, it is still practiced in many families. Uncovering its existence has proven difficult, as incest is one of the most closely guarded secrets of domestic crimes.

Other forms of child sexual victimization often involving relatives and acquaintances of the family or victim include pedophilia, child prostitution, child pornography, and ritualistic or satanic abuse. These sexual abuses and exploitation of children can do equal harm to the victim and are important to study in relation to the overall impact of familial violence on the family and society.

This chapter will explore the dynamics of incest and the sexual maltreatment and exploitation of children.

What Is Incest?

Defining precisely what constitutes incest today has been examined by many scholars in the sexual victimization of children. Definitions have broadened over the years as society itself has changed, along with family dynamics, sexual practices and prohibitions. The word *incest* itself comes from the Latin term *incestum*, which means unchaste and low.[1] Incest is most commonly defined as "sexual intercourse between relatives within the prohibited degrees of relationship defined by the law."[2] Similarly, the dictionary defines incest as "sexual intercourse between people regarded too closely related to marry each other."[3] Definitions of incest can vary from state to state. In some states, incest is recognized as "sexual intercourse between blood relatives; other states define it as *any* sexual act between various combinations of 'legal' relatives (such as a stepfather and stepdaughter)."[4]

Many professionals and sex abuse experts have broadened the definition of incest and incestuous relations to include "the often complex interrelationships between family members and the range of incestuous sexual contact including sexual intercourse, sodomy, oral sex, fondling, masturbation, exhibitionism, voyeurism, or any other actual or attempted sexual contact between a family member (biological or nonbiological) and a child (age 17 and under)."[5] The perpetrators of incest can be anyone in the immediate or natural family, extended family, or nonnatural family, family friends or acquaintances. Incestuous men and women may be the birth parents, adoptive parents, foster parents, stepparents, or legal guardians.

The Prevalence of Incest

Although there are no reliable figures on the extent of incest nationwide, given its secretive nature and reluctance of victims to report, most researchers and criminologists agree that incest directly affects a significant amount of the population. Estimates of incest in the United States have ranged from tens of thousands per year to over a million cases annually.[6] One study estimated that between 11 and 33 million people are involved in incestuous relationships in this country.[7]

As many as 1 in 3 people may be incest victims before reaching the age of 18.[8] In a report from the Family Violence Research Program at the University of New Hampshire, it was estimated that between 5 and 15 percent of all females under the age of 17 are victims of familial sexual abuse in the United States.[9] Mary Donaldson, a social worker, estimated that as many as 28 percent of all females in this country are victims of incest or other types of sexual abuse and exploitation.[10] Some figures report that as many as 1 in 10 females in the United States may be affected by incest.[11]

Despite these figures, most incest goes unreported. David Finkelhor estimated that 75 to 90 percent of all incest cases are not reported.[12] One expert contended: "The family as a whole supports actively or passively their own incestuous equilibrium."[13]

The Nature of Incest

Incest is not related to race, ethnicity, religion, class, income, or other such variables. Notes Susan Forward, a clinical social worker: "We know that incest cuts across every social, economic, and educational barrier."[14] As a result, "victims come from all walks of life and share a common bond of betrayal and exploitation by those often closest to them."[15] Incest victims can be any age, however studies show that incestuous relationships often begin when the victim is between 6 and 11 years of age, and last for at least 2 years.[16]

Typically, the active aggressor in an incestuous relationship is a male, while the passive victim is most often a female. It is estimated that in 90 to 97 percent of all incest cases the child molester is male, while more than 85 percent of reported incest victims are female.[17] H. Stoenner found the ratio of reported incest to be 10 girl victims for every 1 boy victim.[18]

It is estimated that 78 percent of all incest reported today involves father-daughter, 18 percent sibling-sibling, 1 percent mother-son, and the remainder accounting for other incest such as mother-daughter, grandfather-granddaughter, and multiple incestuous relationships.[19] According to Rita Justice and Blair Justice: "The typical [incestuous] father is white and middle class, has a high school education and often some college, and holds a white-collar job or skilled trade. He's most often in his late thirties, married more than ten years. His wife is slightly younger than he is."[20]

The incestuous father is also characterized as follows:

- The median age of the molester is 35.
- He is in a state of reassessing his life.
- Suffers from depression.
- Experiences spousal rejection.
- Has diminished potency.[21]

The typical daughter victim of incest can be seen below:

- The median age is 8½, with most victims between the ages of 5 and 16.
- She is usually entering adolescence.
- She is most often the oldest daughter.[22]

The following is a typology of other patterns of incestuous relations:

Type of Incest	Motivations (Individual Psychopathology)
Father-Son	Homosexual conflict
Sibling (older)-Sibling	Expression of unconscious conflict
Mother-Son	Substitute gratification for absent father
Mother-Daughter	Psychosis/infantilism
Grandfather-Granddaughter	Assertion of manhood[23]

Incestuous Men

FATHER-DAUGHTER INCEST

It is estimated that as much as three-quarters of the total incest in the United States involves men molesting their own daughters.[24] The sexual molestation of daughters can begin in infancy and continue well into adulthood. Incestuous fathers tend to be mostly between the ages of 30 and 50, with the average molester in his mid 30s. The majority of men who sexually abuse their daughters have "introverted personalities, an intrafamily background, and are socially isolated. Many are gradually heading towards incestuous contact with their daughters. In some cases, the wife may unwittingly aid and abet in the incestuous behavior by arranging situations that isolate the father and daughter from others."[25]

In one of the most comprehensive studies to date of men who sexually molest their daughters, Finkelhor and Linda Williams established 5 categories of incestuous fathers:

- *Sexually preoccupied*: men who have a conscious or obsessive sexual interest in their daughters.
- *Adolescent regressive*: men who become sexually attracted to their daughters as they reach puberty.
- *Instrumental self-gratifiers*: fathers who regard their daughters in nonerotic terms and feel guilt over the incestuous relations.
- *Emotionally dependent*: fathers who are emotionally in need, depressed, and/or lonely.
- *Angry retaliators*: men who sexually molest their daughters out of anger towards them or their mother who may have neglected or deserted them.[26]

Adolescent regressives made up the largest percentage of incestuous fathers, representing approximately 33 percent of the sample, followed by *sexually preoccupied* men who comprised more than 25 percent of the father moles-ters. The *angry retaliators* constituted around 10 percent of the incestuous fathers and were also the most likely to have criminal records involving rape or assault.[27]

The researchers also found that alcohol or drugs were a factor in the incest for 43 percent of the molesters, while marital discord was present in 43 percent of the incestuous relationships. Seventy percent of the moles-ters reported being victims of child sexual abuse.[28]

A high rate of father-daughter incest involves stepfathers and step-daughters.[29] A typical scenario is "a man who has married a woman with a daughter by a previous marriage. His sexual attraction to the daughter as a sex object may continue for years, though he may also view her as a child dependent."[30]

FATHER-SON INCEST

The incidence of father-son incest is very rare. When it does occur, experts believe it to be a reflection of "interactional family disturbances and intrapsychic conflicts of the incestuous father."[31] Studies show that father-son incest commonly involves a combination of individual and family pathologies.[32] Recently, a case of parricide in which two teenage boys were convicted of killing their parents drew national attention. The boys claimed the killings were the result of years of incestuous relations with their father.[33]

Incestuous Women

Mothers who sexually molest their children represent less than 2 per-cent of all incest cases.[34] However, many believe there may be a much higher incidence of incest perpetrated by mothers than is reported. In a study of incest survivors, Ruth Matthews found that one-third said they had been sexually molested by their mothers, though *true* female pedo-philes accounted for only around 5 percent of the sample.[35] Approximately 80 percent of the women and men victims of incest interviewed by Kathy Evert, a therapist, reported being molested by their mothers in what was "the most closely guarded secret of their lives."[36] According to Nicholas Groth, incestuous mothers may not be identified as such due to the rela-tive ease in which they can molest their children under the guise of nor-mal child care.[37]

Matthews divided female sex offenders into 4 primary types:

- *Teacher-lover* — older women who have sexual relations with a young adult.
- *Experimenter-exploiter* — females from rigid families where sex education is proscribed.
- *Predisposed women* — those with a predisposition to sexually molest children because of their own history of sexual and physical victimization.
- *Male-coerced females* — women who sexually molest children because men force them to.[38]

The researcher found the *teacher-lover* the most likely to go undetected because the "behavior is usually socially sanctioned."[39] *Male-coerced* molesters, like *predisposed* molesters, were found to have a history of child abuse as victims. Many are married to child molesters "who were the first to molest their own children, long before the wife became aware of it and an active participant in incest."[40]

MOTHER-SON INCEST

Studies reveal that in mother-son incest, the woman is often severely disturbed.[41] However, in both Evert's and Matthews's studies only a fraction of the molesters were found to be severely psychotic.[42] In mother-son incestuous relationships, the father is usually absent and the mother seeks sexual gratification from her son. Some sociologists believe that a mother sexually active with her adolescent son may be more socially acceptable than a father engaging in sexual relations with his daughter. Usually only the most blatant examples of mother-son incest result in societal condemnation or legal action.

Even in situations when the father is present, and in which the mother may be forced to molest a child, some cases have found the mother to initiate the incest herself. In one study, the incestuous mother candidly admitted: "Having sex with my son was more enjoyable than with my husband."[43] Matthews found that most of the molesting mothers had an adult partner living with them during the time the molestation took place.[44]

Some mothers who are incestuous with their sons are physically or sexually abusive toward their daughters. In Evert's study, the female perpetrators in mother-son incest often "abused their daughters violently, beat and terrorized them, and raped them with objects. But they treated their sons like substitute lovers."[45]

MOTHER-DAUGHTER INCEST

Mother-daughter incest is even more rare than mother-son incest. Not much is known about the motivating factors of this type of incest. The mother is usually extremely disturbed and exhibits infantile and/or psychotic tendencies. "By turning to her daughter for emotional nurturance, she may effect a complete role reversal in their relationship."[46]

R. Medlicott cited a case of mother-daughter incest in which the mother slept with her daughter to avoid the father, at which time the mother initiated sexual contact with the daughter.[47] In a study of the homosexual tendencies of three incestuous mothers, R. Lidz and T. Lidz found that the incestuous relationships involved sexual molestation while the daughter was asleep, touching and anal contact, and aloofness. All three incest victims suffered from schizophrenia in adulthood.[48]

In an article, "Incest: A Chilling Report," Heidi Vanderbilt described incestuous women molesting their daughters in which they "wash, fondle, lick, and kiss the child's breasts and genitals, penetrate vagina and anus with tongue, fingers, and other objects: dildos, buttonhooks, screwdrivers — one even forced goldfish into her daughter."[49] One survivor of mother-daughter incest spoke frighteningly: "My mom would play with my breasts and nipples and insert things into my vagina to see if I was normal."[50]

Sibling-Sibling Incest

Although much of the literature on incest focuses on adult-child incestuous relations, evidence suggests that incest between siblings may be far more prevalent. Some studies have found that brother-sister incest may be 5 times as common as incestuous relations between a father and daughter.[51] Yet sibling incest is largely hidden, ignored, or misdiagnosed.

In brother-sister incest, the sister oftentimes had prior sexual experiences (in many cases with an incestuous father). The youngest female sibling is especially at risk to be molested by an older sibling. In *The Victimization and Exploitation of Women and Children*, it is pointed out that, "the brother may have coerced the sister into sexual relations after having assumed a father role in the family (usually after the biological father has abandoned the family). The idolizing sister may succumb to her brother's request while experiencing little guilt at the time."[52]

Grandfather-Granddaughter Incest

The characteristics of grandfather-granddaughter incest are similar to those in father-daughter incest. This is particularly true when the grandfather is young. However, when the grandfather is older, the incest is more often initiated to "bolster the molester's ego and help him reassert his manhood and self-esteem which have decreased due to his natural physical deterioration."[53]

Evidence also exists to support the belief that incest can be trigenerational, or involving a grandfather who may have molested his daughter first before moving on to his granddaughter.[54] In many cases, the grandfather was sexually molested as well during childhood. One study found that grandfather-granddaughter incest represented nine to eleven percent of all cases of incest.[55]

Multiple Incest

Incest involving multiple combinations of family members also occurs, even though it is relatively rare. K. C. Meiselman found that 30 percent of her sample had either been actively involved in incestuous relations with more than one family member or was aware of other incest within the family.[56] This suggests that "once the taboo is broken in a family, it may become more acceptable amongst family members, thereby increasing the chances of its spreading beyond the initial incestuous relationship."[57]

Incest and Victim Compliance

The victim's role in incest has been debated in the literature with respect to compliance, provocation, and degree of culpability. Some researchers such as L. Bender and A. Blau[58] have accused children as young as four years of age of "unusual attractiveness, seduction, and outright instigation of incest in the home."[59] Marshall Schechter and Leo Roberge posited that the physiological and social changes experienced by female victims of incest during their adolescent years results in an increased sexual drive which "produces an acceptance of the incestuous relationship if not at times seductive partner whose tenuous oedipal resolution make her especially vulnerable."[60]

Most behavior scientists who study victim-compliance in an incestuous relationship believe that only a small percentage actively "solicit or encourage incestuous contact with adults."[61] Contrarily, many dismiss any such consensual incestuous relations altogether, placing blame solely on the shoulders of the molester. One social worker insisted: "It is always the responsibility of the adult to control any destructive interaction, no matter what the child's behavior is."[62]

The Effects of Incest

For most incest victims, the effects of incest can be traumatic. In young children, incest can result in a range of physical and psychological problems, including "internal bleeding, injuries to the vagina, anus, and stomach; bed wetting, nightmares, suicide, running away, and precociousness."[63] Adolescent incest victims have been associated with sexual promiscuity, child prostitution and child pornography, substance abuse, sexually transmitted diseases, and emotional dysfunction.[64]

Adult incest survivors are also susceptible to long-term effects of sexual abuse. Many suffer from flashbacks, sexual issues, prostitution, pornography, social and mental disorders, and physical traumas. A strong relationship has also been established between victims of incest and a cycle of incestuous relations, as well as child abuse, family violence, and criminality.[65]

What most incest victims share in common are feelings of "shame, denial, self-blame, anger, guilt and, most of all, distrust."[66]

Pedophilia

Pedophilia, or child molestation, is a term used to describe "occasions in which a child is the favored sexual object of an adult."[67] This form of child sexual abuse is the most common and usually consists of "nonviolent sexual contact with a child including genital viewing or fondling, orogenital contact, penetration, and any other immoral or indecent behavior involving sexual activities between an adult and child."[68]

It is estimated that more than 2 million children are victimized by child molesters every year.[69] An 18-month study of child molestation cases reported to child protective services agencies produced the following results:

- Child molestation is the most prevalent form of child maltreatment.
- The median age of sexually molested children is 11.
- Younger children, including infants, are also at risk for molestation.
- Female victims outnumber male victims by 10 to 1.
- The molesters are male in 97 percent of the cases.
- In 3 out of 4 cases, the molester is known to the victim or family.
- The median age of the molester is 31.
- In over 40 percent of the cases, the molestation occurs over a period of time.

- Six in 10 children are victims by force or threat of force.
- Two-thirds of molested children suffer from some identifiable emotional trauma.
- More than 1 in 10 become severely disturbed.[70]

Studies have characterized the pedophile or pedophiliac as "passive, immature, and insecure regarding his inability to engage in normal adult heterosexual relations."[71] J. M. Reinhardt found that some young or middle-aged pedophiles turned to children only after failing to achieve sexual gratification with adults.[72] Older pedophiles, usually over 50, have been shown to molest children as a result of "diminishing physical and mental abilities brought about by the aging process."[73]

Ritualistic Sexual Abuse

A disturbing form of child sexual abuse that appears to be on the rise is ritualistic or satanic sexual abuse. This abuse of children is typically related to religious, supernatural, or "black magic" practices.[74] An estimated 1 to 5 percent of all child sexual abuse cases may involve some form of ritualism or Satanism.[75] Three types of ritualistic child abuse have been established:

- *Cult-based*— where the sexual abuse is secondary to a larger goal.
- *Pseudo-ritualistic*— with sexual abuse as the primary goal.
- *Psychopathological*— where there is a single abuser.[76]

Perpetrators of ritulalistic abuse include family members, organized groups, national and international organizations with local affiliations, and mentally unbalanced abusers. Drugs and alcohol often play a large role in ritualistic sexual abuse of children. This type of maltreatment also typically includes other forms of sexual abuse such as necrophilia and bestiality.[77]

Many groups that engage in ritualistic or satanic sexual abuse are highly structured and may involve the child victim's own parents or siblings, as well as their "cult parents" in the victim's indoctrination. "Children may be taken from natural parents and placed in the care of other group members as a means of ensuring continued group involvement by natural parents."[78]

Presently there are no formal national networks exploring ritualistic sexual abuse. The Resource and Educational Network on Ritualistic Abuse (RENRA) in Los Angeles offers information gathering and sharing.[79]

Child Prostitution

Child prostitution is another form of child sexual abuse often rooted in familial dynamics. It is estimated that anywhere from tens of thousands to well over a million girls and boys are actively involved in the sex-for-sale business.[80] Many are runaways or throwaways, having left home due to sexual, physical, or emotional abuse; substance abuse by parents, siblings, or their own drug or alcohol abuse; or other negative factors that effectively forced them out on the streets.[81]

Some teenage prostitutes are recruited into prostitution by their own parents or other family members.[82] "In 4 out of every 100 cases of girls entering prostitution, the 'pimp' or influencing person was a relative."[83] This person may be a mother, father, sister, brother, uncle, or other relative. In some cases, it is another prostitute in the family that lures the teenager into prostitution.[84]

By its very nature, the lucrative sex trade industry draws some parents into it, who in turn exploit their own progeny. These children "have been coerced into sexual servitude. Some, abducted by con men, are raped and psychologically pummeled into submission…. But not all pimps are gangsters. Often it is the father who sits in the backup car or mother who negotiates the deal for her daughter."[85] (See also Chapter 15.)

Child Pornography

Similar to child prostitution, child pornography is another form of sexual misuse and exploitation of children that sometimes involves family members. Child pornography is a multibillion dollar business. Eighty-five percent of worldwide sales of child pornography takes place in the United States.[86] Child pornographers, including fathers and mothers of targeted children, recruit often willing participants from a pool of vulnerable child victims such as relatives, runaways, throwaways, drug addicted teenagers, and neighborhood youths.[87] In many instances, children coerced into pornography are victims of other sexual abuse, physical abuse, neglect, substance abuse, and other maltreatment.[88] Some are already being sexually exploited as prostitutes or by pedophiles.[89] The men who support child pornography "do so to rationalize and seek justification for their perverted and deviant mentality."[90]

13. Sibling Abuse and Parent Abuse

Domestic crimes and family violence go beyond spousal violence and parental abuse and neglect of children. Many times it is the minor children themselves who are abusing their brothers and sisters after often being abused by parents or witnessing abuse and violence. Other times children are abusing their parents or grandparents, reflecting the cycle of family violence and its rippling effect on everyone within the family unit. Child violence towards family members is typically a reflection of the same dynamics of domestic violence and child abuse: drug or alcohol problems, family tensions and stress, uncontrolled anger, a history of physical or sexual maltreatment, and mental illness.

In this chapter we will examine the emerging issue of child perpetrated abuses on siblings and parents.

Sibling Violence

Sibling abuse, or violence directed towards one's sibling, is believed to be the most underreported branch of family violence. Many believe that sibling abuse may be the most frequent type of abusive behavior in the home. However, violence between siblings, such as wrestling, fighting, arguing, and name calling, is typically seen as normal, acceptable, and even healthy. In the book *Sibling Abuse: Hidden Physical, Emotional, and Sexual Trauma*, the author notes that "sibling abuse has been ignored in part because the abusive behavior of one sibling toward another is often excused as normal behavior. Sibling rivalry must be distinguished from sibling abuse."[1]

Experts are now beginning to recognize the harm that can come from sibling abuse, which is often a symptom of other family violence such as spouse abuse, child abuse, and sexual abuse in the home, including sexual abuse of children by their brothers or sisters. According to Sandra Arbetter:

> Sibling sexual abuse is an underreported phenomenon, partly because parents resist recognizing it and partly because there's confusion about where normal sex play ends and incest begins. Sex play usually occurs between children who are close in age, and before puberty. If there is an age difference of even a few years, there is an imbalance of power and the younger child is being coerced.[2]

Most sibling sexual abuse is perpetrated by a male child, 8 to 16 years of age, in which a younger child, usually his sister, is sexually molested.[3] The sibling sexual abuser has often been a victim of sexual abuse.[4]

THE INCIDENCE OF SIBLING ABUSE

It is impossible to know the extent of sibling abuse in this country, as the vast majority goes unreported or unacknowledged. However, it is estimated that millions of children are at risk of being abused or battered by siblings each year.[5] The National Crime Victimization Survey reported that there were 138,887 single-offender crimes of violence victimizations committed by brothers or sisters in 1994.[6] More than 7,000 multiple-offender victimizations of violent crimes were perpetrated by siblings that year.[7]

Official data also indicate a problem that appears to be getting worse. As shown in Figure 13-1, between 1988 and 1997, the number of persons under 18 arrested for offenses against family and children rose nearly 150 percent. The increase was over 150 percent for males under 18 arrested for family and children offenses.[8] This compares to an increase of more than 109 percent for persons of all ages in arrests during the 10 year span.[9]

The rise in juvenile assaultive crimes can be seen in other data as well. Arrest statistics for juvenile aggravated assaults and other assaults from 1988 to 1997 also show a significant rise (see Figure 13-2). Arrests for aggravated assaults grew by more than 51 percent, while arrests for other assaults rose 84 percent over the 10 year period. These offenses, which may include assaults against family, are indicative of the correlation between overall juvenile violence and family violence involving perpetrators under the age of 18.

The first major empirical study on sibling violence was conducted by

Figure 13-1
Juvenile Arrest Trends for Offenses Against
Women and Children, 1988–1997

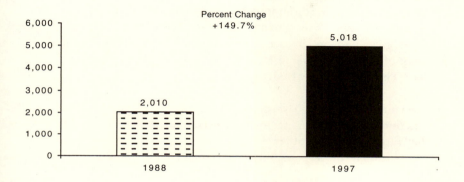

Source: U.S. Department of Justice, Federal Bureau of Investigation, *Crime in the United States: Uniform Crime Reports 1997* (Washington, D.C.: Government Printing Office, 1998), p. 226.

Figure 13-2
Juvenile Arrest Trends for Assaults,
1988–1997

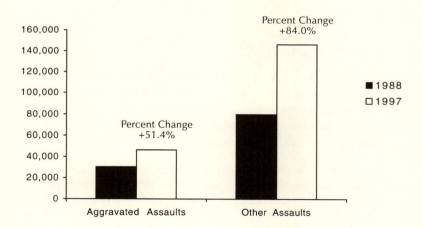

Source: U.S. Department of Justice, Federal Bureau of Investigation, *Crime in the United States: Uniform Crime Reports 1997* (Washington, D.C.: Government Printing Office, 1998), p. 226.

Suzanne Steinmetz in the late 1970s. In a study of students at a large university in the United States, Steinmetz found that virtually all the respondents reported using verbal aggression against siblings, while 7 in 10 used physical violence to resolve sibling conflicts.[10]

In a second study, the researcher examined physical violence between 88 pairs of siblings from randomly selected families with 2 or more children between 3 and 17 years of age. Steinmetz found that 70 percent of the siblings age 8 and under used physical violence to resolve conflicts, 68 percent of the pairs ages 9 to 14, and 63 percent of the siblings age 14 and older.[11] The conflicts involved:

- The youngest group: possessions, such as toys.
- The middle group: infringement of personal space, touching, or looking "funny" at one another.
- The oldest group: responsibilities and social obligations.

Murray Straus and colleagues' study of family violence found further evidence of the magnitude of sibling abuse. In 75 percent of the families surveyed with children between the ages of 3 and 17, there was some form of violence reported among siblings.[12] In extrapolating the data nationwide, the researchers estimated that 138,000 children had actually used a violent weapon on a sibling during the survey year. The data approximated that based on "ever happened," a staggering 8.3 million children in the United States have been "beaten up" by a sibling, while 2.3 million have on one occasion or another used a knife or gun on a brother or sister.[13]

THE EFFECTS OF SIBLING ABUSE

Sibling abuse can have a number of devastating effects on the victim including physical, sexual, and psychological. These include everything from serious injuries to the body, sexual dysfunction, and mental illness. The psychological impact may be the worst of all. According to Ellen Whippie and Sara Finton, sibling abuse could result in

> severe psychological effects in the child subjected to the abuse. It is typically perpetrated by an older sibling, which may be in the form of taunting, insults, isolation, physical violence, intimidation and other forms of psychological cruelty. These situations may be ignored by the parent or exacerbated by similar treatment. The abused child then becomes impaired in aspects of cognitive functioning, language development or motor coordinations, and may have nightmares or be extremely active or shy.[14]

In most cases of sibling abuse, neglect or failure to recognize sibling maltreatment on the part of the parents can actually lead to, increase, or promote sibling abuse. An example of such physical and psychological abuse perpetrated on one sibling by another can be seen in the following case study:

> "I begged my parents not to go out and let my sister, Lila, baby-sit," says Sam, now 17. "She'd sit on me and put a pillow over my face and punch my head. She'd tickle me until I wet my pants, and then threaten to tell everyone at school about it. Once she pointed my father's gun at me and said she'd kill me if I didn't do what she asked."[15]

Most victims of sibling abuse can recover from its devastating psychological effects with intensive therapy involving the entire family. According to one expert, with such therapy 95 percent of sibling sexual abusers will not engage in further sibling maltreatment.[16] But getting to the root of the problem can often be an arduous task, as sibling abuse tends to be only a part of a larger problem of violence within the family. Sadly, this can often go unchecked, damaging everyone in its path.

Parent Abuse

A disturbing phenomenon in the study of family violence is children abusing parents. This is seen as a reflection of family dysfunction including domestic violence, child abuse, sibling abuse, substance abuse, broken homes, and other family stresses. Unrecognized until recently, the "battered parent syndrome," is said to be "the next larger of family violence to be exposed."[17] In addressing the seriousness of parent abuse, Richard Gelles pointed out: "If we were talking about some communicable disease, we'd be talking in terms of an epidemic."[18]

It is estimated that 2.5 million parents in the United States are struck by their children, mostly teenagers, every year.[19] Of these assaults, approximately 900,000 parents are victims of severe violence, including victimization by a knife or gun. Murray Straus and colleagues found that almost 1 in 10 parent victims reported being physically assaulted by a child during the survey year.[20]

Parent battering is being viewed as "the next logical progression in the study of family pathologies."[21] In a study of 15 teenage psychiatric patients, Carol Warren found 3 primary reasons for adolescent children's violence against parents:

- Violence as a response to alcohol use by the victim.
- Violence in response to goals being blocked.
- Violence as a resource.[22]

Other studies describe the parent batterer as the recipient of poor models of social behavior and extremely stressful social circumstances, "either or both of which cause children to strike out as they have been told or in the only way they can."[23] Some research has pointed out the direct correlation between parent abuse and child abuse. One study found that "parents who are not violent toward their children stand only a 1 in 400 chance of being on the receiving end. But if a parent is violent toward the child, the probability of attack goes up to 200 out of 400."[24]

The characteristics of the typical parent abuser and parent victim are as follows:

- Teenage sons are the most frequent parent abusers.
- Most victims of parent abuse are mothers.
- Battered parents tend to feel embarrassment, guilt, shame, and failure as parents to the perpetrator.
- Middle-aged victims tend to be the most reluctant to seek help, often out of fear.
- To keep the family unit intact, parent victims and their child batterers often hide behind a wall of secrecy and denial.[25]

Teenage substance abuse is believed to be a strong factor in parent battering, often clouding the offender's perceptions of right and wrong (see also Chapter 14). Lack of parental authority and/or discipline are also viewed as symptoms of parent abuse by children. Don Cuvo, a therapist, notes: "A family is not a democracy. Youngsters need firm structure. They may object verbally, but that's what they want. And parents aren't providing it."[26] Child psychiatrist Rudolf Dreikers asserted that with parent support and encouragement, children will not resort to violence against parents or one another.[27]

Grandparent Abuse

Along with the battering of parents, many grandparents are also being abused and neglected by their adult children and juvenile grandchildren. Referred to by some as "granny bashing," the battering of elderly parents and grandparents is believed to be the most neglected form of family violence. It is estimated that upwards of 1 million senior citizens are victims of familial abuse each year in the United States.[28] The relative ease in masking grandparent abuse due to fear, isolation, illness, and often misdiagnosis of the victim's injuries or maltreatment makes it difficult to assess its magnitude and severity as part of the overall picture of family violence.

Grandparent abuse can be physical, sexual, or emotional and is typically a reflection of "frustration due to the reversal of dependency roles, stress, socioeconomics, and weakening of the grandparents' power and influence in family decision making."[29] It has also been documented, in an ironic sad twist of fate, that "many victimized grandparents [and elderly parents] are in fact the recipients of the same brand of violence they once exhibited over their children — which the children not only return, but also extend to their own children in what becomes a cycle of violence."[30] See Chapters 9 and 15 for more discussion on elderly abuse and a familial cycle of abuse, respectively.

PART IV

Symptoms of Domestic Crimes

14. Substance Abuse, Intimate Abuse, and Family Abuses

There has been a clear relationship established between alcohol, drugs, and violence in the family, or between intimates.[1] Substance abuse is not the cause of intimate abuse or child abuse, per se. However, it does appear to play a significant role in the onset of physical and sexual violence in the family, or among intimate partners or ex-intimates, often in combination with other factors such as stress, depression, unemployment, and a cycle of interpersonal violence or criminality. Understanding more about this association between drugs, alcohol, and domestic crime may allow us to establish better means to control, if not eliminate, both familial or intimate violence and substance abuse.

This chapter will explore the often complex interrelationship of substance abuse, patterns of drugs and drinking in society, and domestic violence, family offenses, and child maltreatment.

Alcohol and Drug Use in Society

The use of alcohol or drugs in the home or by intimates is reflected in their use in society at large. One need only look at the magnitude of alcohol and drug use in the United States to recognize the severity of the problem and its implications on the individual, family, and intimates. The Substance Abuse and Mental Health Services Administration's (SAMHSA) recent National Household Survey on Drug Abuse (NHSDA) estimated

151

Table 14-1

Estimated Prevalence of Drug and Alcohol Use During Lifetime, by Type of Drug, United States, Selected Years 1985–1996

Type of drug	Percent Reporting Use During Lifetime									
	1985 (N=8,021)	1988 (N=8,814)	1990 (N=9,259)	1991 (N=32,594)	1992 (N=28,832)	1993 (N=26,489)	1994 (N=17,809)	1995 (N=17,747)	1996 (N=18,269)
Any illicit drug[a]	34.4%	34.0%	34.2%	34.1%	33.3%	34.2%	34.4%	34.2%	34.8%
Marijuana and hashish	29.4%	30.6%	30.5%	30.5%	30.2%	31.0%	31.1%	31.0%	32.0%
Cocaine	11.2%	10.6%	11.2%	11.5%	10.9%	11.3%	10.4%	10.3%	10.3%
Crack	NA	1.3%	1.5%	2.1%	1.5%	1.9%	1.9%	1.8%	2.2%
Inhalants	7.9%	6.4%	5.7%	6.1%	5.3%	5.9%	5.8%	5.7%	5.6%
Hallucinogens	6.9%	7.6%	7.9%	8.4%	8.3%	9.0%	8.7%	9.5%	9.7%
Heroin	0.9%	0.9%	0.8%	1.2%	0.8%	1.0%	1.0%	1.2%	1.1%
Nonmedical use of any psychotherapeutic[b]	15.3%	11.2%	11.3%	11.9%	11.0%	10.5%	10.0%	10.1%	9.5%
Stimulants	7.3%	5.7%	5.5%	5.6%	5.0%	4.8%	4.6%	4.9%	4.7%
Sedatives	4.8%	2.6%	2.8%	3.2%	2.6%	2.6%	2.6%	2.7%	2.3%
Tranquilizers	7.6%	4.4%	4.0%	5.1%	4.7%	4.2%	4.0%	3.9%	3.6%
Analgesics	7.6%	5.8%	6.3%	6.8%	6.1%	6.4%	6.0%	6.1%	5.5%
Any illicit drug other than marijuana[c]	22.4%	19.3%	19.5%	19.8%	18.9%	19.7%	18.8%	19.1%	18.9%
Alcohol	84.9%	84.0%	82.2%	83.6%	81.9%	82.6%	84.2%	82.3%	82.6%

[a]Includes use at least once of marijuana or hashish, cocaine (including crack), inhalants, hallucinogens (including PCP and LSD), heroin, or any prescription-type psychotherapeutic used nonmedically.

[b]Inclues nonmedical use of any prescription-type stimulant, sedative, tranquilizer, or analgesic; does not include over-the-counter drugs.

[c]Includes use at least once of any of these listed drugs, regardless of marijuana use; marijuana users who also have used any of the other listed drugs are included.

Source: Derived from U.S. Department of Health and Human Services, Substance Abuse and Mental Health Services Administration, *National Household Survey on Drug Abuse: Main Findings 1996* (Washington, D.C.: Government Printing Office, 1998), p. 29.

that 72 million persons aged 12 and over in the United States reported using an illicit drug at least once over their lifetime.[2] This represented more than 34 percent of the population in that age range. Nearly 11 percent reported using an illegal drug within the past year, and 6 percent in the past month. In a High School Senior Survey conducted by the National Institute on Drug Abuse (NIDA), over 48 percent of high school seniors reported ever using an illicit drug, 39 percent said they had used an illegal drug during the past year, and almost 24 percent reported use of an illicit drug within the last month.[3] In 1994 alone, the SAMHSA Drug Abuse Warning Network reported more than half a million drug-related episodes in hospital emergency departments across the nation.[4]

Table 14-1 shows the estimated prevalence of drug and alcohol use during a lifetime in selected years between 1985 and 1996. Approximately one-third of those surveyed had ever used an illicit drug in each year. In 1996, nearly 35 percent of Americans had used an illegal drug at some time in their life, a slightly higher percentage than every other year in the survey. More than 3 in 10 had ever used marijuana or hashish, while nearly 2 in 10 had ever used any illicit drug other than marijuana. Over 1 in 10 reported ever using cocaine, and around 1 in 10 a hallucinogen or psychotherapeutic drug. Alcohol was by far the most ever used drug. Almost 83 percent of respondents reported using alcohol during their lifetime.

Demographic data on the estimated prevalence and most recent use of alcohol and marijuana in the United States in 1996 can be seen in Table 14-2. Nearly 65 percent of Americans age 12 and over had used alcohol within the last year and 51 percent in the past 30 days. Males, whites, and persons age 18 to 34 were most likely to have ever used alcohol, or used within the last year, or past 30 days. Regionally, those in the Northeast and North Central states had the highest percentage of ever used within the past year and during the last 30 days. The characteristics of alcohol users indicate the widespread use of alcohol across demographics. For instance, more than 6 in 10 females and over half of blacks and Hispanics had used alcohol during the last year, while more than 4 in 10 in these groups had used alcohol during the past 30 days.

Marijuana use showed more variance among groups, but still reflected a high incidence overall. Nearly 4 in 10 males and 3 in 10 females had ever used marijuana, and whites were more likely than blacks or Hispanics to have used marijuana during their lifetime. However, blacks were more likely than whites or Hispanics to have used marijuana within the past year or last 30 days.

The use of marijuana tended to vary with age and most recent use. Persons between the ages of 26 and 34 had the highest prevalence of ever

Table 14-2
Estimated Prevalence and Most Recent Use of Alcohol and Marijuana, by Sex, Race, Ethnicity, Age, and Region, United States, 1996

| | Alcohol | | | Marijuana | | |
| | | Most recent use | | | Most recent use | |
	Ever used	Within last year	Within last 30 days	Ever used	Within last year	Within last 30 days
Total (N=18,269)	82.6%	64.9%	51.0%	32.0%	8.6%	4.7%
Sex						
Male	86.6%	70.0%	58.9%	37.0%	11.4%	6.5%
Female	78.8%	60.2%	43.6%	27.5%	6.0%	3.1%
Race, ethnicity						
White	86.2%	68.0%	54.2%	34.4%	8.6%	4.6%
Black	72.8%	52.9%	41.9%	29.6%	11.1%	6.6%
Hispanic	71.7%	58.6%	43.1%	22.0%	7.0%	3.7%
Age						
12 to 17 years	38.8%	32.7%	18.8%	16.8%	13.0%	7.1%
18 to 25 years	83.8%	75.3%	60.0%	44.0%	23.8%	13.2%
26 to 34 years	90.3%	77.2%	61.6%	50.5%	11.3%	6.3%
35 years and older	87.8%	64.9%	51.7%	27.0%	3.8%	2.0%
Region						
Northeast	86.5%	69.5%	55.0%	31.4%	7.5%	3.7%
North Central	86.6%	71.4%	54.4%	32.6%	9.4%	5.5%
South	78.8%	59.3%	47.1%	29.3%	8.2%	4.3%
West	80.6%	62.4%	49.8%	36.4%	9.3%	5.4%

Source: Derived from U.S. Department of Health and Human Services, Substance Abuse and Mental Health Services Administration, *National Household Survey on Drug Abuse: Population Estimates 1996* (Rockville, MD: U.S. Department of Health and Human Services, 1997), pp. 23-27, 83-87.

having used marijuana, those ages 18 to 25 within the last year, and persons 12 to 17 in the last 30 days. Regional use of marijuana was fairly evenly distributed for each type of most recent use, although those living in the West were most likely to have ever used marijuana.

THE WORKPLACE AND SUBSTANCE ABUSE

The problem of alcohol and drug abuse in this country is also reflected in the workplace, which often begins in the home and can lead to other abuses in the family or a relationship. As seen in Table 14-3, among full-time workers age 18 to 49 in the United States in 1994, around 8 percent reported illicit drug use or heavy alcohol use during the past month. Nearly twice as many male workers reported illicit drug use as female workers, and more than 3 times as many reported heavy alcohol use. Illicit drug use within the past month occurred most often among workers who were white, 18 to 25 years old, with less than a high school education, earning less than $9,000 a year in personal income, and living in the South. Heavy alcohol use was most often a problem with full-time workers who were white or Hispanic, 18 to 25 years of age, with less than a high school education, earning $9,000 to $19,999 per year, and living in the North Central States. Ten percent of full-time workers who heavily used alcohol were high school graduates.

Occupational categories of full-time workers who used illicit drugs, or were heavy alcohol users during the past month are shown in Table 14-4. Illicit drug use was most likely to occur among workers in construction. The percentage of construction workers' illegal drug use was more than twice that of full-time workers overall. Other occupations exceeding the total percentage included sales; food preparation, wait staff, and bartenders; machine operators and inspectors; and handlers, helpers, and laborers.

Heavy alcohol use was also highest among full-time construction workers and more than twice the percentage of total workers. Also reflecting double digit percentages of heavy alcohol use were handlers, helpers, and laborers; machine operators and inspectors; transportation and material moving; precision production and repair; and food preparation, wait staff, and bartenders.

CRIMINAL JUSTICE SYSTEM INVOLVEMENT AND ILLICIT DRUG USE OR ALCOHOL ABUSE

The relationship between drug or alcohol abuse, criminality, and involvement in the criminal justice system has been well documented.[5] This correlation is also commonly reflected in domestic crimes such as spouse violence and child abuse.[6] According to the Federal Bureau of Investigation's *Uniform Crime Reports*, there were more than 2.6 million arrests in the United States in 1997 for drug or alcohol-related crimes.[7] As shown in Figure 14-1, arrest trends for drug and alcohol-related offenses reveal that arrests for drug abuse violations increased by more than 48 percent between 1988 and 1997. While arrests for driving under the influence and

Table 14-3
Full-time Workers Age 18 to 49 Reporting
Illicit Drug or Heavy Alcohol Use During Past Month,
by Demographic Characteristics, United States, 1994

	Total[a]	Illicit drug use[b]	Heavy alcohol use[c]
Total	100.0%	7.6%	8.4%
Sex			
Male	58.9%	9.3%	11.9%
Female	41.1%	5.2%	3.3%
Race, ethnicity			
White	78.5%	8.3%	8.9%
Black	11.5%	6.5%	5.2%
Hispanic	10.0%	5.6%	8.8%
Age			
18 to 25 years	16.3%	12.4%	13.6%
26 to 34 years	31.8%	8.6%	8.9%
35 to 49 years	51.9%	5.4%	6.3%
Education			
Less than high school	11.6%	9.7%	13.2%
High school graduate	33.3%	8.3%	10.0%
Some college	24.9%	7.5%	8.3%
College graduate	30.1%	6.1%	4.7%
Personal income			
Less than $9,000	8.9%	13.3%	9.4%
$9,000 to $19,999	28.8%	9.6%	10.5%
$20,000 to $39,999	39.6%	6.1%	7.1%
$40,000 to $74,999	19.5%	4.3%	7.9%
$75,000 and over	3.2%	12.1%	5.7%
Region			
Northeast	17.9%	7.6%	8.1%
North Central	23.8%	7.4%	11.1%
South	36.4%	8.2%	8.4%
West	21.9%	6.7%	5.6%

[a] Detail may not add to 100 because of missing data on the demographic variables and rounding.

[b] Illicit drug use was defined as any nonmedical use of marijuana, cocaine, crack cocaine, hallucinogens, tranquilizers, stimulants, analgesics, and opiates in the past 30 days. The use of over-the-counter drugs was not included.

[c] Heavy alcohol use was defined as having five or more drinks on five or more occasions in the past 30 days.

Source: Derived from John P. Hoffman, Cindy Larison, and Allen Sanderson, *An Analysis of Worker Drug Use and Workplace Policies and Programs*, Substance Abuse and Mental Health Services Administration, Analytic Series: A-2 (Rockville, MD: U.S. Department of Health and Human Services, 1997), p. 54.

Table 14-4
Full-time Workers Age 18 to 49 Reporting
Illicit Drug or Heavy Alcohol Use During Past Month,
by Occupational Category, United States, 1994

Occupational category	Illicit drug use[a]	Heavy alcohol use[b]
Total	7.6%	8.4%
Executive, administrative, and managerial	5.5%	6.5%
Professional specialty	5.1%	4.3%
Technicians and related support	5.5%	6.2%
Sales	11.4%	8.3%
Administrative support	5.9%	3.5%
Protective service	3.2%	6.3%
Food preparation, waitstaff, and bartenders	11.2%	12.2%
Other service	5.6%	5.1%
Precision production and repair	7.9%	13.1%
Construction	15.6%	17.6%
Extractive and precision production	8.6%	12.9%
Machine operators and inspectors	10.5%	13.5%
Transportation and material moving	5.3%	13.1%
Handlers, helpers, and laborers	10.6%	15.7%

[a]Illicit drug use was defined as any nonmedical use of marijuana, cocaine, crack cocaine, hallucinogens, tranquilizers, stimulants, analgesics, and opiates in the past 30 days. The use of over-the-counter drugs was not included.

[b]Heavy alcohol use was defined as having five or more drinks on five or more occasions in the past 30 days.

Source: Derived from John P. Hoffman, Cindy Larison, and Allen Sanderson, *An Analysis of Worker Drug Use and Workplace Policies and Programs*, Substance Abuse and Mental Health Services Administration, Analytic Series: A-2 (Rockville, MD: U.S. Department of Health and Human Services, 1997), p. 27.

drunkenness decreased by about 20 percent, they rose nearly 2 percent for liquor law violations during the period.

A breakdown of criminal arrests and criminal activity by reported illicit drug users age 18 or older in the United States during the past year between 1991 and 1993 is provided in Table 14-5. Just over 10 percent of the males and 4 percent of the females who had used any illicit drug in the past year had criminal arrests. Most involved driving under the influence charges. Men were nearly 4 times as likely to be arrested for drunk driving as women. Both males and females were next most likely to be arrested for violent offenses such as aggravated assaults, other assaults, forcible rape, and murder/homicide. Around 8 percent of men and just over 2 percent of women were on probation or parole at the time of arrest.

Among the criminal activities resulting in arrest for persons using

Figure 14-1
Arrest Trends for Drug- and
Alcohol-Related Offenses, 1988–1997

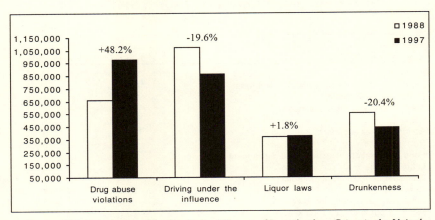

Source: U.S. Department of Justice, Federal Bureau of Investigation, *Crime in the United States: Uniform Crime Reports 1997* (Washington, D.C.: Government Printing Office, 1998), p. 226.

illicit drugs during the past year, more than 56 percent of males and over 37 percent of females were engaged in some offense. Driving under the influence constituted the greatest criminal activities for both sexes, followed by violent crime and property crime. Drug sales accounted for male illegal drug users' next most frequent criminal activity, compared to other alcohol or drug offenses for female illicit drug users.

More than 1 in 5 males and less than 1 in 10 females involved in criminal arrests reported problem drug use in the past year, including dependency, frequent or daily drug use, and IV drug use. This resulted in increased criminal activity. Nearly 62 percent of the males and more than 43 percent of the females reporting problem drug use perpetrated any offense, such as driving under the influence and violent crimes.

Intimate Abuse and Substance Abuse

Intimates who use alcohol or drugs are more likely to engage in domestic violence than those who do not. Studies show that substance abuse can often lead to intimate abuse, or intensify or prolong abuse already occurring.[8] For years researchers have linked alcohol abuse and drug abuse to violent behavior, including criminal assaults, forcible rape, and other crimes of violence.[9] Some experts have even suggested that alcohol, for example, may have a psycho-pharmacological effect on violent individuals, which can increase excitability and raise one's courage level or act as a disinhibitor.[10]

Surveys of jail and prison inmates incarcerated for violent offenses committed against an intimate indicate that alcohol use and abuse, in particular, or in combination with drug use, is a significant factor in violent relationships. According to the Bureau of Justice Statistics *Violence by Intimates*, more than 3 in 10 jail and prison inmates were drinking only when committing their intimate offense.[11] Around 8 percent of jail inmates and about 4 percent of prison inmates were using drugs only at the time of offense. More than 20 percent of prisoners were drinking and using drugs during the intimate offense, compared to 13 percent of jail inmates.

About half of prison and jail inmates surveyed reported drinking beer or liquor when committing a violent intimate crime. Of inmates who had been drinking before the offense against an intimate, a high percentage had been drinking for hours, as seen below:

Number of hours drinking before crime	*Percent of violent intimate offenders*
1 hour or less	9.4%
2 hours	14.4%
3 hours	11.1%
4 hours	7.3%
5 hours	8.9%
6–12 hours	20.9%
More than 12 hours	28.1%

Nearly half of state prisoners and over one-third of convicted jail inmates had been drinking alcohol for 6 or more hours prior to committing the violent offense against a spouse, ex-spouse, or other intimate. Almost 3 in 10 prison inmates had been drinking for more than 12 hours before perpetrating the intimate offense.

Among convicted jail inmates of crimes against an intimate partner, around 4 in 10 reported drinking the equivalent of about a 6-pack of beer before committing the crime; while around 1 in 5 reported consuming the equivalent of 2 dozen beers or more prior to perpetrating the violent intimate offense.

The correlation between alcohol and/or drug use by violent intimates

Table 14-5

Estimated Percent of Persons 18 and Older Reporting Involvement in the Criminal Justice System or Criminal Activities, by Illicit Drug Use in the Past Year, United States, 1991–1993

| | Percent reporting use during past year | | | | | | | | | | | |
| | Any illicit drug use[a] | | No illicit drug use | | Cocaine use[b] | | No cocaine use | | Problem drug use[c] | | No problem drug use | |
	Male	Female	Male	Female	Male	Female	Male	Female	Male	Female	Male	Female
Criminal arrests												
Any offense	10.1%	4.0%	1.4%	0.2%	17.7%	11.1%	2.0%	0.4%	20.6%	8.4%	2.1%	0.4%
Violent offense[d]	2.8%	1.1%	0.4%	0.1%	5.2%	3.2%	0.6%	0.1%	6.8%	2.4%	0.6%	0.1%
Property offense[e]	2.6%	1.0%	0.2%	0.1%	5.3%	2.5%	0.4%	0.2%	5.9%	3.1%	0.4%	0.2%
Driving under influence	5.5%	1.5%	0.9%	0.1%	9.6%	4.2%	1.3%	0.2%	11.4%	2.0%	1.3%	0.2%
Drug sales or possession	2.6%	0.6%	0.1%	b	7.3%	3.0%	0.2%	b	7.3%	2.9%	0.2%	b
On probation or parole	7.9%	2.3%	1.2%	0.3%	15.1%	7.3%	1.6%	0.4%	19.3%	7.1%	1.6%	0.4%
Criminal activities												
Any offense	56.1%	37.6%	13.7%	5.5%	71.7%	59.5%	17.7%	7.6%	61.7%	43.1%	18.4%	7.9%
Violent crime[f]	18.7%	10.5%	3.7%	1.4%	27.3%	17.7%	5.0%	2.0%	29.1%	17.6%	5.1%	2.0%
Property crime[g]	14.1%	10.1%	2.2%	1.2%	21.4%	16.6%	3.2%	1.8%	21.8%	15.1%	3.3%	1.8%
Driving under influence of alcohol or drugs	42.3%	25.6%	8.9%	3.1%	56.6%	44.8%	11.9%	4.5%	43.5%	29.0%	12.7%	4.8%
Drug sales	7.1%	2.3%	0.1%	b	16.9%	6.4%	0.5%	0.1%	18.0%	7.5%	0.6%	0.1%
Other alcohol or drug offense	6.4%	4.8%	0.4%	0.2%	9.3%	8.3%	0.9%	0.5%	7.3%	7.0%	1.0%	0.5%
Property damage	7.0%	3.3%	0.9%	0.2%	10.8%	7.0%	1.4%	0.4%	13.3%	6.5%	1.4%	0.4%

[a]Includes use, at least once, of marijuana, cocaine (including crack), inhalants, hallucinogens, heroin, and nonmedical use of psychotherapeutics.

[b]Includes crack.

[c]Includes respondents who reported any of the following in the previous 12 months: dependence on any illicit drug; receipt of treatment for drug use; frequent drug use (daily or more frequent use of marijuana, or weekly or more frequent use of psychotherapeutics, hallucinogens, inhalants, or cocaine); use of any heroin; or injection drug use.

[d]Includes aggravated assault, other assault, robbery, forcible rape, and murder/homicide/manslaughter.

[e]Includes larceny, theft, burglary, breaking and entering, and motor vehicle theft.

[f]Includes using weapons or force to steal from a person, hitting someone or getting into a physical fight, and seriously injuring someone.

[g]Includes stealing, car theft, and breaking into a house or building.

Source: Adapted from U.S. Department of Health and Human Services, Substance Abuse and Mental Health Services Administration, *Substance Use Among Women in the United States*, Analytic Series: A-3 (Rockville, MD: U.S. Department of Health and Human Services, 1997), pp. 8–16, 8–17.

is shown in victimization surveys in which battered women have reported similar rates of alcohol and drug abuse by abusive partners.[12]

Child Abuse and Substance Abuse

The evidence of an interrelationship between child abuse and substance abuse by perpetrators of child maltreatment may be even stronger than when speaking of violence between domestic partners, drugs, and alcohol. The number of parents who abuse drugs and alcohol alone is staggering. According to the NIDA, an estimated 12.8 million children under 18 years of age live with a parent who has used 1 or more illicit drugs within the past year, including marijuana, cocaine, heroin, and nonmedical use of prescription drugs such as tranquilizers and stimulants.[13] A high incidence of alcohol use by parents was also found. It was estimated that 5.2 million parents were daily or almost daily alcohol users, including 14 percent of fathers and 3.8 percent of mothers.[14] More than 5 million parents were classified as "binge drinkers," which consisted of 5 or more alcoholic drinks on at least 3 occasions in the past month. Fathers were more than 3 times as likely to be binge drinkers as mothers.

CHILD MALTREATMENT AND PARENTAL ALCOHOL USE

A number of studies have linked alcohol abusing parents to child maltreatment. Michael Martin and James Walters found a relationship between alcoholic fathers and child sexual abuse.[15] David Gil reported that in 13 percent of child abuse cases, the offender was intoxicated at the time of the abuse.[16] R. Famularo and colleagues found that nearly 4 in 10 parents who lost their children due to child abuse or neglect were alcoholics.[17] The Children of Alcoholics Foundation estimated that 40 percent of all child maltreatment cases involved alcohol use by the perpetrators.[18]

A high incidence of alcohol abuse or alcoholism among child abusing parents was also noted by B. Miketic[19] and Z. Popisil, K. Turcin, and R. Turcin.[20] In a study of the prevalence of alcohol-related child abuse at a large clinic, D. W. Behling found the following:

- Fifty-seven percent of the abused or neglected children had at least one grandparent who was an alcoholic or abused alcohol.
- Sixty-five percent of the suspected child abusers or neglecters were alcoholics or abused alcohol.

- Eighty-eight percent of the previously abused parents were abused by an alcoholic or alcohol-abusing parent.
- Eighty-four percent of the abused or neglected child victims had at least 1 parent that was an alcoholic or abused alcohol.[21]

Inmate data supports the correlation between alcohol use and child maltreatment. In a survey of inmates in state correctional facilities, nearly 4 in 10 child victimizers reported using alcohol at the time they committed the violent offense.[22] The number of hours drinking prior to the crime tended to be related to the child victimization, as seen below:

Number of hours drinking before crime	Percent of violent child offenders
1 hour or less	8.6%
2 hours	12.3%
3 hours	10.7%
4 hours	11.9%
5 hours	7.9%
6 or more hours	48.6%

Nearly half the inmates reported that they had been drinking alcohol for 6 or more hours prior to committing the crime of violence against a child.[23] More than one-third of the child victimizers had been drinking anywhere from 2 to 4 hours preceding the crime.

Child Maltreatment and Parental Drug Abuse

Drug use by child abusers has also been shown to be a significant factor in child abuse and neglect.[24] This has been especially true for child sexual abuse and child homicide. A study on adult deviant populations found a relationship between adult drug addiction and sexual abuse of children.[25] Patricia Mrazek posited that the "organicity associated with drug induced psychosis and other forms of toxicity may ... act as a trigger for incestuous relationships."[26] Homicidal fathers have been associated with a history of child abuse and substance abuse.[27]

Prisoner surveys reveal that around 1 in 10 of inmates who used drugs at the time of their violent crime had victimized a child.[28] About 13 percent of the inmates reported using alcohol and drugs during the commission of violent offenses against children.

Other studies have examined the effects of alcohol or drug use in abusive parents. One survey found that excessive drug or alcohol intake was a potential source of parental stress, accounting for 14 percent of the cases of child abuse or neglect.[29] Brandt Steele reported that "the chronic use of alcohol and the taking of hallucinogenic drugs can cause severe distortions of mental functioning with delusional thinking and the lowering of the threshold for the release of violence in many forms, including child abuse, homicide, and suicide."[30] In a study of incestuous fathers, David Finkelhor and Linda Williams found that alcohol or drugs played a role in 43 percent of the cases.[31] Alcohol and/or drug abuse resulting in child maltreatment has been commonly associated with such factors as depression, social stresses, unemployment, marital conflict, parental background, psychological maladjustment, and inadequate access to essential resources or services.[32]

Some research has found that child abuse tends to occur more frequently when the child uses alcohol or drugs.[33] Children born out of wedlock "in a transient commune-type of domestic situation (the 'flower children' of the drug culture) are often victims of habitual addiction or sustained overdoses of depressant drugs administered to keep them docile and tranquilized, often resulting in brain damage."[34]

PARENTAL SUBSTANCE ABUSERS AND CHILDREN AT RISK FOR MALTREATMENT

Although substance abusing parents and abused children come from every walk of life, studies have been able to target parents and children particularly at risk for the cycle of alcohol or drug abuse and mistreatment of children. The NHSDA recent findings reveal that:

- Of the nearly 13 million children living with a parent who used an illicit drug in the past year, approximately 6 million live with parents who reported using an illegal drug in the past month.
- Twenty percent of children of parents who used illicit drugs in the past year or past month are under the age of 3.
- Marijuana is the most popular illicit drug used by parents.
- The prevalence rate for daily or almost daily alcohol use by parents over the past year nearly doubled that of marijuana using parents.
- Nearly 2 million parents reported using cocaine or crack within the past 30 days.
- Prevalence rates of drug use are generally higher among younger parents than older parents.
- Parents with children living at home tend to use illegal drugs less often than do persons aged 15 to 44 without children in the household.

- The prevalence of illegal drug use by parents is similar demographically to drug use in the population as a whole.
- The rates of illicit drug use in the past month are more than 3 times as high for unemployed parents as those employed.
- The prevalence rate for illicit drug use in the past month by parents below the poverty line is more than 2 times that of illicit drug-using parents living above the poverty line.
- Three-quarters of parents who used illicit drugs in the last month have incomes above the poverty line.
- One-fourth of parents using illegal drugs during the past month have incomes more than 3 times above the poverty line.[35]

The study on drug and alcohol abuse among parents concluded that "where substance abuse is serious enough to affect parental functioning, some of these children may suffer deleterious social and emotional effects. In addition, some of the children in substance-abusing families will have been exposed to alcohol or other drugs prenatally."[36] According to an expert on child abuse, parental substance abuse "undermines adults' ability to function in many areas, including parenting, work, and personal life.... These parents can be unstable; sometimes substance abuse is a destructive anesthetic for them."[37]

SUBSTANCE ABUSING MOTHERS

Mothers who abuse alcohol and/or drugs put their children at an even greater risk for child abuse and neglect, as well as other hazards. Recent data on women and alcohol or drug use has found that:

- Sixty percent of adult females are drinkers and 5 percent are heavy drinkers.
- One out of 3 members of Alcoholics Anonymous is a female.
- Female alcoholics drink on average 11 times more often than nonalcoholic drinkers.
- Women frequently combine alcohol abuse with abuse of illicit drugs.
- Adult female addicts are older than adult male addicts, usually starting to use drugs in their mid–20s.
- Women addicts are more likely to have children and to be divorced, separated, or widowed than men addicts.
- Many pregnant IV drug users have infants who are born addicted.
- Female addicts tend to have more family-related problems than male addicts.

- Female drug addicts are often high school dropouts and have poor work histories.
- Most women prisoners have used drugs; around 4 in 10 were daily users before being incarcerated.
- A high percentage of drug-involved female offenders have children.
- Female substance abuse is more indicative of some pathology than male substance abuse.[38]

Studies on child-abusive and neglectful mothers, and substance abuse, indicate a strong correlation.[39] Martin and Walters associated child abandonment with the mother's alcoholism.[40] Another study warned of the perils of the widespread use of tranquilizers by tense young mothers: "The benzodiazepine tranquilizers can have an 'alcohol-like' effect in reducing higher cortical control, thereby reducing anxiety, but increasing the risk of explosions of temper."[41]

Women who are pregnant can abuse their unborn child in various ways. The NIDA estimated that around 19 percent of pregnant women in the United States used alcohol, while 1 in 5 pregnant women smoked cigarettes.[42] Just under 6 percent of women used any illicit drug during pregnancy, and about 10 percent had medical use of a psychotherapeutic drug such as amphetamines or sedatives. Many such alcohol or drug-using women risk exposing their child to such things as fetal alcohol syndrome (FAS) — one of the leading causes of birth defects — drug addiction, and even the AIDS virus.[43] The latter is particularly true for IV drug using mothers.[44]

Other Family Violence and Substance Abuse

The relationship between substance abuse and other types of family violence such as elderly abuse, sibling abuse, and parental abuse has also been documented.[45] One study, for example, found that a primary reason for child violence against parents is a response to the parent victim's use of alcohol.[46] In a 1997 Gallup Poll, 3 in 10 respondents reported drinking as having ever been a cause of trouble in the family.[47] The National Institute on Alcohol Abuse and Alcoholism reported to Congress that alcohol "often plays a major role in such violent events as motor vehicle accidents ... crime; suicide; and family abuse."[48]

Other studies have associated drug use or a combination of drug and alcohol use with patterns of abuse and violence towards family members.[49] Substance abuse has also been linked to ritualistic abuse, often involving family members as victims and perpetrators.[50]

The Cycle of Substance Abuse and Family Violence

Some findings have shown a familial cycle of substance abuse, which is also interrelated with other intergenerational abusive practices within the family and by family members against others.[51] For example, state prisoner surveys of child victimizers show a correlation between substance abuse by inmates when committing their crime and inmates with parents or family members who abused drugs or alcohol and/or had criminal backgrounds.[52] Similar inferences can be made with inmate data on intimate offenders and substance abuse. (See also Chapter 15.)

15. Cycle of Family Violence and Other Crimes

There has been much debate over the years with respect to a cycle of family violence and abusive behavior, as well as other forms of criminality. This notion suggests that violent and deviant behavior may have an intrafamilial, intergenerational base, or is passed on from generation to generation either through learned behavior or genetic transmission. Critics have argued against such correlations or explanations of violence, preferring to relate it more to the individual, social structure, or socioeconomic factors. However, the literature is replete with findings that indicate a strong relationship between abusive or violent childhoods, family violence, and assaultive or violent tendencies in both childhood and adulthood. This school of thought posits that the key to reducing, if not eliminating, violence in society may be in breaking the cycle of child abuse and other family or intimate-related violence.

This chapter will address the association between intergenerational violence and maltreatment in the home and violence and other offenses elsewhere.

Child Abuse and Family Violence

There is little doubt among most experts in child abuse and family violence that a correlation exists between being the victim or witness to familial abuses or violence and becoming a perpetrator of such. Murray Straus contended that abusive parents learned this behavior from their own parents,[1] while G. V. Laury suggested that child abusers may have

167

been the victims of child abuse and unwittingly imitated their parents.[2] Vincent Fontana advanced that the background of abusive parents was unloving, cruel, and brutal[3]; whereas T. C. Gibbons and A. Walker argued that it was indifference, hostility, and rejection in childhood that produced cruel parents.[4]

Christopher Ounsted and associates found that abusing parents came from families where violence has existed for generations.[5] According to Mia Pringle, most, if not all, violent parents were themselves victimized as children through an uncaring or abusive upbringing. She held that such parental hostility perpetrates itself from generation to generation in what she described as "quite literally a very vicious cycle."[6]

Other researchers have associated child sexual abuse with perpetrating sexual abuse and sexual crimes in adulthood, including pedophilia and rape.[7] One study found that 75 percent of parents who sexually abused their children were themselves victims of child sexual abuse.[8] Another study noted the trigenerational characteristics of incestuous behavior.[9] Child victims of sexual abuse have also been found to sexually abuse other children or become involved in prostitution or promiscuity.[10]

Child neglect has also been shown to be intergenerational. C. Henry Kempe found that neglected children tend to marry and conceive children earlier in life, then repeat the mistakes of their parents.[11] In Norman Polansky and colleagues' study of neglectful families, the researchers documented a "generation-to-generation transference of a lifestyle of neglect that comes from the sharing and passing on of family misfortunes."[12]

Inmate data supports the cycle of child abuse. About 3 in 10 child victimizers in prison reported being victims of childhood physical or sexual abuse.[13] Inmates imprisoned for committing violent crimes against children were more than twice as likely to have themselves experienced physical or sexual abuse as prisoners serving time for violent crimes against adult victims.[14]

Other forms of intergenerational violence have also been associated with parental mistreatment of children, such as parent battering. For instance, in a study of violence in the family, Suzanne Steinmetz advanced that abusive parents stood a 200 out of 400 chance of in turn being abused by their children, compared to only a 1 in 400 chance that nonabusive parents would become abuse victims.[15] This is supported by other research that links elderly abuse to prior child abuse by the elderly victims.[16]

The cycle of child and family violence theory may be "explained by the fact that abused children become 'needy' adults who want infants for gratification, or by a feeling that beatings are a necessary and proper part of child rearing, or by a self-protective identification with the aggressive, more powerful adult."[17] The primary weakness of this theory is that most victims of child abuse do not become abusive parents, while many child abusers were not abused as children. Further, as Monica Holmes pointed out:

> While there is general agreement that abusive parents were themselves treated with hostility and lacked nurturant care in childhood, there is virtually no empirical substantiation of the often repeated view that abusive parents were actually abused as children.... In the absence of normative data, it is impossible to determine the extent to which a childhood characterized by hostility and lack of nurturance is particularly characteristic of abusive parents.[18]

L. DeMause contended, with respect to the drawbacks of generation-to-generation violence, that it "is highly plausible that parents and their children share the same social norms, and that these common norms may be what mediate the relation between being abused as a child and becoming an abusing parent."[19] This view argues, in effect, that abusing a child "produces a pathology in that child that may manifest itself in part in the child becoming an [abusive] parent."[20]

Intimate Violence and Family Violence

The intergenerational theory of child abuse and other family violence also applies to intimate violence in its dynamics. Many batterers and battered victims come from violent families in which there was spouse abuse, child abuse, or other forms of violence.[21] Some studies have found that half the men who beat women were themselves beaten or witnessed their mothers or other family members being beaten.[22] In Bonnie Carlson's study, around 1 in 3 abused women came from families where wife abuse had taken place.[23] J. Gayford found that nearly one-fourth of the battered women sampled had come from abusive homes.[24]

Inmate data shows a strong relationship between battered women prisoners and a history of intimate violence, often perpetrated by their victims. More than 43 percent of incarcerated women report experiencing physical or sexual abuse from intimates or family members.[25] A high percentage of these women were in prison for intimate or child abuse offenses.[26] Many male intimate victimizers behind bars also have a history of victimization. For nearly 3 in 4 male inmates physically or sexually abused prior to incarceration, the offender was an intimate, parent, or other relative.[27]

Violent Crimes

The cycle of violence theory has also proven to have a strong basis concerning crimes of violence such as murder, forcible rape, and aggravated assault. Studies show that most violent offenders came from violent backgrounds that include child abuse and other types of family violence.[28] Violent offenders are more likely to come from abusive or neglectful families than families where there is no child abuse or neglect. In Cathy Widom's study of where child abuse or neglect victimization increased the probability of arrest and criminality of victims, "the research clearly revealed that a childhood history of physical abuse predisposes the survivor to violence in later years and that victims of neglect are at increased risk to engage in later violent criminal behavior as well."[29]

Prisoner studies support the association between child abuse or family violence and juvenile or adult violent criminality. In a study of chronic offenders incarcerated, Joan Petersilia, Peter Greenwood, and Marvin Lavin found that a greater proportion of intensive offenders (career criminals) were violent and had violent backgrounds.[30] A survey of state prison inmates revealed that more than 4 in 10 female inmates and more than 1 in 10 male inmates had experienced physical or sexual abuse prior to incarceration.[31] Nearly half the women prisoners reported being abused by an intimate and almost 40 percent by a parent or guardian. Seven in 10 men in prison reported being abused by a relative, with nearly 6 in 10 having been the victims of physical or sexual abuse by a parent or guardian.

The intergenerational theory on violent criminality has also been examined as to genetic predisposition to commit violent acts. A seemingly prime example of such a possibility was studied by this author in *The Sex Slave Murders*.[32] An executed double murderer had a son who became a convicted serial killer. Was it a case of genetic transmission of homicidal tendencies? In fact, coincidentally, the father and son never even met. However, there was evidence of a family history of dysfunction, violence, and aggressive behavior. Most criminologists, this one included, dismiss the hereditary hypothesis of generation-to-generation violence, and instead focus on the socialization process of violent offenders and individual motivating factors.

Juvenile Delinquency

Child abuse and neglect has been closely associated with juvenile delinquency, and vice versa, in a cycle of violence. According to Martin Haskell and Lewis Yablonsky, juvenile correctional facilities are filled with

adolescent victims of family pathology and abuse.[33] Brandt Steele cited
research in which 82 percent of the sample group of juvenile offenders had
been victims of child abuse or neglect.[34] Forty-three percent of the juveniles actually recalled being knocked unconscious by a parent. D. Lewis and
J. H. Pincus found that violent adolescents had been victims of, and wit-
nesses to, severe physical abuse.[35] In studying 653 delinquents, D. E. Adams,
H. A. Ishizuka, and K. S. Ishizuka found that 43 percent of the delinquents
had ever been victims of abuse, neglect, or abandonment.[36]

The "bad seed" theory of juvenile delinquency or "violence breeds violence" concept of violent or deviant tendencies passing from generation to
generation was proposed by W. McCord.[37] H. E. Simmons asserted that "a
brutal parent tends to produce a brutal child."[38] In a study of chronically
violent juvenile offenders, Jeanne Cyriaque found that "violence-domi-
nated lifestyles [of] ... sexually and physically abusing families, particularly
characterize juvenile murderers and sex offenders."[39] Sheldon and Eleanor
Glueck held that parents of delinquents have consistently been described
as possessing characteristics of delinquency and emotional disturbances.[40]

E. Y. Deykin[41] and M. F. Shore[42] found a correlation between extreme
physical disciplinary abuse in the home and aggressive, destructive delinquency. In relating juvenile delinquency to child abuse, James Garbarino
argued that "many abused children and youth attempt to avoid or escape
their parents. In doing so, they are likely to become involved in a variety
of delinquent behaviors related to their status (unsupervised, uncared for
minors), as well as their personal history (inadequate learning of social
skills)."[43] The significant link between child maltreatment and juvenile
delinquency prompted B. D. Schmitt and C. H. Kempe to strongly suggest
that stopping child abuse will prevent delinquency.[44]

In spite of the considerable body of literature supporting the association of child abuse and juvenile delinquency, some critics have questioned
its validity, pointing out the delinquent children who come from loving,
nonabusive, nonviolent households. Moreover, according to Robert Weinback and colleagues:

> We would be both naive and grandiose if we were to assert that we can
> document a relationship of cause and effect when we attempt to associ-
> ate delinquency and child abuse.... Furthermore ... we cannot assume
> that all child abuse, as defined by rigid and perhaps culturally biased
> definitions, is motivated by sadism, frustration, or ignorance of human
> development.[45]

Most experts see child maltreatment as an almost intrinsic variable
in the dynamics that reflect a high proportion of juvenile delinquency.

Runaways

It is estimated that anywhere from several hundred thousand to as many as 2 million children run away or are thrown out of the home each year.[46] The correlation between runaways and child abuse has been well documented.[47] Most runaway youth have experienced one form of child abuse or another, including physical, sexual, and emotional. The National Network of Runaway and Youth Services estimated that 7 in 10 runaways in youth shelters have been physically abused or sexually molested.[48] Another study found that at least 90 percent of girl runaway prostitutes were victims of severe child maltreatment, including "lots of incest, lots of alcoholism, lots of physical assault, lots of sexual battering."[49]

In a study of runaway and nonrunaway children by the Children's Hospital of Los Angeles, it was found that runaways were 4 times as likely as nonrunaways to have been sexually abused and develop emotional problems.[50] Widom found that, in general, children who were abuse or neglect victims were significantly more likely to run away from home than children who were not abused or neglected.[51] Child sexual abuse victims were more than 3 times as likely to become runaways as the control group.

Other studies on runaway and homeless children have found the following disturbing characteristics:

- Half of all runaways were victims of sexual or physical abuse at home.
- Twenty-five percent of female runaways had been raped.
- Thirty-six percent had been pregnant.
- Sixty percent of runaways had parents who were alcoholics, drug abusers, or criminal offenders.
- Twenty-five percent were born to mothers under the age of 17.
- Seventy percent abuse alcohol and/or drugs.
- Most come from dysfunctional families.
- Eighty percent of runaway and homeless youth have severe emotional or behavioral problems.[52]

Most runaway children will face further abuse and victimization on the streets as addicts, homeless, and/or prostitutes, and be put at risk for violence, exploitation, and HIV infection, among other perils.[53] Studies show that the cycle of abuse and violence from child maltreatment to runaway often leads to delinquency and other criminality.[54]

Prostitution

It has long been established that there is a significant correlation between child intrafamilial sexual abuse and prostitution.[55] The research supports this contention. According to the Huckleberry House Project, 90 percent of girl prostitutes had been sexually molested.[56] Around two-thirds of the prostitutes in Mimi Silbert's study were victims of incest and child abuse.[57] Some studies have found that as many as 8 in 10 female prostitutes were sexually abused or rape victims before the age of 14 — often by a parent/guardian, other family member, or someone close to the family.[58] Researchers have also shown a link between child sexual maltreatment, child prostitution, and child pornography.[59]

A relationship between prostitution and child physical abuse has also been documented. In Maura Crowley's study of prostitutes, more than two-thirds reported being physically abused at home.[60] A similar finding was made by the Huckleberry House study.[61] A study of adult female prostitutes found that the majority had been victims of physical abuse by parents, relatives, lovers, pimps, and johns.[62] In a national study of male prostitutes, the researchers found that most had been physically, sexually, or emotionally abused.[63]

Most persons who enter prostitution began as runaways escaping abusive environments in a pattern of violence, exploitation, and criminality. One study found that two-thirds of teenage prostitutes were runaways.[64] Some suggest the numbers of runaway prostitutes are much higher.[65] In a 50-state survey of juvenile prostitution, it was found that the majority of prostitutes had run away from home.[66] According to an expert on child sexual exploitation, most runaways turned prostitutes "have experienced a major trauma: incest, domestic violence, rape, or parental abandonment."[67]

Child neglect, parental absence, and/or family dysfunction also appear to be strong factors in prostitution. In Crowley's study, 85 percent of the prostitutes reported the absence of at least one parent in the household.[68] Seven in 10 prostitutes in the Huckleberry House Project came from homes with one or both parents absent.[69] A similar finding came from Jennifer James's study of prostitutes.[70]

Diana Gray reported that 75 percent of the prostitutes interviewed described their relationships with parents as being "poor" or "very bad."[71] The Huckleberry House study found that few prostitutes had positive, attentive, or caring relationships with their parents.[72]

A relationship has also been demonstrated between child abuse, substance abuse, and prostitution.[73] Most prostitutes use or abuse alcohol and/or drugs.[74] Many began drinking or using drugs while living at home in order to "deaden memories" associated with sexual or physical maltreatment they endured.[75]

As part of the typical hazards of prostitution life, including substance abuse, sexually transmitted diseases, and customer violence, many prostitute victims of child maltreatment are battered women as well. Most are involved in an intimate relationship with pimps, some of whom are violent and abusive in perpetuating the unending cycle of violence the prostitute becomes immersed in. (See also Chapter 6.)

PART V

Explaining Family Violence and Child Maltreatment

16. Causes of Domestic Violence and Child Abuse

Criminologists, sociologists, family violence experts, and others have long sought to explain violence and abuse in the family through various causal and theoretical concepts. W. Goode held that "one reason intimates commit violence against one another is that they are in each other's presence a lot, and few others can anger one so much as those who are close."[1] R. Chester and J. Streather found the assaultive nature of male spouse aggression to be the primary cause of marital unhappiness, discord, and divorce.[2] Some researchers such as L. Eron[3] and L. Kopernik[4] have noted the feeling of rejection present in aggressive, abusive children in many families due to the birth of another child, parental neglect or indifference, or separation from parents.

Family crimes such as domestic violence and child abuse have commonly been associated with a number of causal factors and determinants. These include:

- Social and economic elements such as poverty, class, and education.
- A history of child abuse, neglect, or sexual abuse.
- A cycle of familial violence or criminality.
- Substance abuse.
- Mental illness.
- Depression.
- Stress.
- Sexual problems in the marriage.
- Illegitimate, unwanted, or special needs children.
- Predisposing familial violent personality characteristics in abusers or abused.

Theories of family violence, domestic violence, or child abuse largely focus on these interconnecting themes in trying to understand and identify domestic criminality and its participants.

This chapter will explore influential theories and concepts on family violence, domestic violence, and child abuse and neglect.

Family Violence

Most theories on family violence generally fall into 1 of 3 categories: (1) psychiatric-psychological theories, (2) social-structural theories, and (3) social-cultural theories.

PSYCHIATRIC-PSYCHOLOGICAL THEORIES

Psychiatric-psychological theories of family violence tend to focus on the perpetrator's or victim's personality traits as they relate to violence and abuse in the home. This approach often associates family violence with mental illness and/or substance abuse.[5] Some studies have found a relationship between family violence and mental disorders such as depression, schizophrenia, and psychosis.[6] Others have found a correlation between violence in families and neurotic and psychotic tendencies[7]; while other research has linked some family offenses such as incest and infanticide to severely mentally disturbed mothers.[8]

Many researchers have established a correlation between psychological disorders, substance abuse, and familial violence. For example, in a study of family violence, Brandt Steele related the chronic use of alcohol or hallucinogenic drugs with severe mental dysfunction and delusions causing the substance abuser to act violently towards family members.[9] (See also Chapter 14.)

SOCIAL-STRUCTURAL THEORIES

Social-structural theories view family violence as a reflection of "the external and environmental variables that affect family life and focus on the individual daily interactions that are most susceptible to familial violence."[10] Communication, stress, and intergenerational violence are seen as indicative of familial violence under this school of thought.[11] The socialization of aggression is examined in the social-structural theory of family violence. It postulates that children are more aggressive when punished more severely by parents, perpetrating a cycle of violence.[12] In Murray

Straus's general systems theory, family violence is explored in relation to family group characteristics such as beliefs, values, organization, and position within the social structure.[13] Other theories applying social structure and social-psychological concepts of family violence include the exchange theory[14] and learning theory.[15]

SOCIAL-CULTURAL THEORIES

Social-cultural theories tend to explore family violence in terms of "socially structured inequality and cultural norms concerning violence, abuse, and family relations."[16] David Gil studied the societal power struggles and the effect on family violence.[17] D. Abrahamsen reported on cultural values and attitudes that sanctioned violence as a way of life[18]; while D. Owens and M. Straus advanced that cultural and social theories are interrelated with respect to family violence.[19] Prominent social-cultural theories include the structural-functional theory[20] and the subculture-of-violence theory.[21]

Domestic or Spousal Violence

Theories examining domestic or spousal violence, in particular, include (1) personality theories, (2) social-structural theory, (3) societal structure theory, and (4) power and control theory.

PERSONALITY THEORIES

The Abusive Partner

Personality theories of domestic violence draw on personality traits of the abusive partner and the abuse victim in explaining the dynamics that create abusive situations. One of the more significant personality characteristics associated with wife abuse is the abuser's "strict adherence to a traditional male role."[22] His compulsive masculinity, also known as "machismo," is an attempt to maintain complete dominance over his wife victim.[23] There are many male batterers whose personalities include feelings of helplessness and dependency. The violent husband has been at times characterized as a "little boy wanting to be grown up and superior, as he'd been taught he should be, yet was not in fact; requiring those around him to join in his pretense if he were to survive emotionally, and his family survive physically."[24]

Abusive spouses have been described as "intractable" or "treatable" depending upon how they perceive the spousal violence. "The intractable abuser finds no fault in his abusive action, whereas the treatable husband experiences guilt and remorse after the violence. In the latter instance, it is possible that with counseling the offender can learn nonviolent means of coping."[25] Other characteristics associated with batterers include an inability to communicate verbally, anger, insecurity, split personality, and moodiness.[26]

The Abused Partner

Abused women typically tend to follow stereotypical attitudes with respect to appropriate masculine and feminine behavioral patterns. According to one expert on domestic violence: "The victims may exemplify society's old image of ideal womanhood: submissive, religious, non-assertive, accepting of whatever the husband's life brings.... The husband comes first for these women, who perceive themselves as having little control over many areas of their own lives."[27] Battered women often see themselves and all women as inferior to men, "have a tendency to cope with anger either by denying it or turning it inward, and suffer from depression, psychosomatic illnesses, and feelings of guilt."[28] (See Chapter 6 for discussion on the cycle theory of domestic violence.)

SOCIAL-STRUCTURAL THEORY

Richard Gelles posited that violence is a direct response to certain structural and situational stimuli.[29] In order for violence to occur, two conditions must be met: (1) structural or situational stress must be present, and (2) the potential batterer must have been socialized to view violence as an appropriate response to certain situations, such as frustration. Within social-structural theory the assumption is made that "less educated, lower income, lower occupational status families are more likely to encounter both structural and situational stress; and that individuals in different socioeconomic groups are socialized differently in their acceptance of violence."[30]

There have been criticisms leveled at social-structural theory. One is that it fails to account for the reality that wife abuse can occur even without the abuser coming from an abusive family, or otherwise being socialized to regard violence as acceptable behavior. Another shortcoming is that many studies indicate that domestic violence may be equally as prevalent among higher educated or higher income levels, but is more easily hidden due to greater resources and more incentive for such victims of abuse to keep it in the family.

SOCIETAL STRUCTURE THEORY

According to researchers, there are certain societal values in American culture which tend to support the institution of domestic violence. Straus described nine "specific ways in which the male-dominated structure of the society and of the family create and maintain a high level of marital violence,"[31] as follows:

- Compulsive masculinity.
- The defense of male authority.
- Economic constraints and discrimination.
- The single-parent household myth.
- The preeminence for women of the wife role.
- The woman's negative self-image.
- The conception of women as children.
- The difficulties of child care.
- The male orientation of the criminal justice system.[32]

Lee Bowker advanced that "these values and norms bind women into a position in which they are easily victimized and at the same time that they encourage men to flex their muscles."[33] Robert Whitehurst combines structural and cultural theories in proposing that "cultural elements supporting male dominance will continue in the face of an increase in structural factors favoring equality of the sexes; the result is an increase in the level of domestic battering."[34]

POWER AND CONTROL THEORY

The "power and control" theory of domestic violence was established by Ellen Pence in describing the dynamics existing in a violent relationship between intimates.[35] The theory contends that violence is used by a person to maintain power and control over another or others. The use of violence in the domestic arena "is reinforced when it works every time it is used."[36] Widely accepted by professionals who work with abuse victims and perpetrators, the power and control hypothesis challenges conventional theories on intimate violence such as a cycle of family violence, substance abuse, stress, poverty, and other causes related to individual characteristics, family history, and socioeconomic factors. Pence maintains that "the use of force is always a choice, and that in our society it is a choice that can be made in order to meet one's needs with little or no consequence."[37]

In order to gain and retain power and control, a number of techniques are used by an abuser in "a deliberate and systematic manner."[38] These include the following:

- Physical violence.
- Intimidation.
- Threats and coercion.
- Isolation.
- Sexual abuse.
- Emotional abuse.
- Economic abuse.
- Using the children.
- Male privilege.
- Minimizing or denying.
- Blaming the victim.

Child Abuse

The causes of child abuse and neglect have been explored extensively in the literature. Among the most influential explanations for child abuse are the following eight theories: (1) psychodynamic theory, (2) personality or character trait theory, (3) social learning theory, (4) family structure theory, (5) environmental stress theory, (6) social-psychological theory, (7) mental illness theory, and (8) psychosocial systems theory.

PSYCHODYNAMIC THEORY

The psychodynamic theory grew out of work of the earliest pioneers in addressing and identifying the battered child, relying on psychodynamic determinants in explaining child abuse. C. Henry Kempe saw the lack of being mothered and nurtured as the essential dynamic for the potential to abuse a child.[39] As a consequence, in adulthood the abuser could not mother and nurture her own child. In combination with this inability to nurture is an interplay of other dynamics including isolation, lack of trust, a nonsupportive spousal relationship, and excessive child expectations. Kempe found that two other factors needed to be present for abuse to occur: (1) a special child (such as mentally retarded) and (2) a crisis (creating stress).

The primary feature of the psychodynamic model is that it "assigns a secondary role to everything except the individual's internal psychology."[40] Other features include role reversal, parental background, and the perpetrator's own history of child abuse victimization. The main criticisms of the theory relate to the degree of mothering required to prevent abuse, as it varies from mother to mother, and that there are no specific guidelines to that effect.

PERSONALITY OR CHARACTER TRAIT THEORY

The personality or character trait theory differs from the psychodynamic theory of child abuse in that it takes less into consideration the factors that underlie the traits of the child abuser. There is also a greater inclination with the personality theory to describe the abuser with characteristics such as immature, impulse-ridden, self-centered, chronically aggressive, highly frustrated, and suspicious.[41]

E. J. Merrill broke down abusive parents into three groups in relation to their psychological traits: (1) chronically aggressive, (2) rigid and compulsive, lacking warmth and reason, and (3) those who demonstrate a high degree of passivity and dependence.[42] Merrill also noted a fourth group, characterized by extreme frustration which often manifested itself in child abuse. This group of abusers consisted primarily of young, unemployed fathers.

The personality or character trait theory is limited in that while it describes personality features of abusers, the theory still does not explain why abuse occurs, particularly considering that many nonabusers have the same or similar character traits. However, these limitations are "reduced when the personality factors are put in perspective within the larger context of environmental influences and the role children may play in the abuse."[43]

SOCIAL LEARNING THEORY

The social learning theory of child abuse focuses on the failure of child abusers to acquire the skills needed to function adequately in the home and society. This theory advances that abusers lack social skills, get little satisfaction from the parental role, are often ignorant in child development, and have unrealistic behavioral expectations for their young children.[44] Such parents further tend to have mistaken notions of child rearing, do not know how to encourage and guide their children at various ages, and are inclined to physically discipline them, having received similar treatment during their own childhood.[45]

Though the social learning theory has its limitations in explaining child abuse, it nevertheless is significant in the formulation of intervention and treatment strategies. The theory requires the monitoring of specific behavior by the parent and child that leads to abuse, the idea being that "if the immediate antecedents of abusive behavior are identified, steps can be taken to control, if not prevent abuse."[46] This model is also helpful in teaching parents child rearing skills and modifying their expectations of what parent and child behavior should be.

FAMILY STRUCTURE THEORY

The dynamics that form the family structure theory on child abuse concern "alliances, enmeshments, coalitions, and disengagements among family members."[47] While familial theories and family systems models have yet to examine directly the problem of child abuse, they offer potential in both explaining child maltreatment and designing therapeutic interventions. Related to the family structure model and coalitions are the strong findings that illegitimate and unwanted children are at high risk for abuse.[48] Similarly, scapegoating by parents is also a behavioral pattern often cited as leading to child abuse that is applicable to this theory.[49]

ENVIRONMENTAL STRESS THEORY

The leading advocate of the environmental stress theory is David Gil, who found child abuse to be a multidimensional concern and emphasized stress as the primary cause.[50] Gil asserted that were it not for chance environmental factors such as poverty, poor education, and occupational stress, child abuse would not be in existence. According to the researcher, economic stresses on the poor weakened their self-control, leading them to abuse their own children. He argued that child abuse could be all but eliminated if programs were created to end poverty, educate people, improve their skills, and change disciplinary patterns.

The major shortcoming of the environmental and economic stress theory is that it inaccurately dismisses child abuse perpetrated at the higher social and economic levels. Furthermore, the theory fails to take into account the reality that the majority of people living under economic constraints do not abuse their children. J. J. Spinetta and D. Rigler support this contention in their study of child abusing parents, in arguing that "while eliminating stress factors and battering conditions may reduce child abuse, there remains the problem, insoluble at the demographic level, of why some parents abuse their children while others under the same stress factors do not."[51]

SOCIAL-PSYCHOLOGICAL THEORY

A social-psychological theory of child abuse was formulated by Richard Gelles.[52] This theory posits that frustration and stress are strongly related to child abuse, with the stress a product of one or more factors such as unemployment, marital problems, too many or unwanted children, and social isolation. In conjunction with other factors (for instance, community norms and social class influence), Gelles postulated that these stresses lead to "psychotic states, personality and character traits, and poor control and neurological disorders, which contribute to the potential for abuse."[53] The final "chain of events" described as necessary for abuse to occur are "immediate precipitating situations," such as the child's misbehavior, which could result in a single or repeated episode of physical violence or psychological abuse.

The implications of Gelles's theory is that intervention strategies that offer treatment for psychopathic disorders of abusing parents are rarely successful, with the only other strategy being removal of the child from an abusive home. The weaknesses of this model lie in its confusing use of such terms as psychopath, sociopath, and psychological states and disorders. Additionally, the social-psychological theory fails to recognize the importance of the symbiotic interaction between spouses, and between parents and children in abusive or violent families.

MENTAL ILLNESS THEORY

Mental illness theories of child abuse have long since related it to mental disorders such as psychosis and neurosis, as well as character defects. In fact, most research has found that abusive parents suffering from hallucinations, delusions, or other mental illnesses are rare.[54] Although the literature does not widely reflect mental disorders when explaining child abuse, there are frequent references to terminology characterizing mental illness. Before Kempe's "battered child syndrome" was brought to light, P. V. Wooley and W. A. Evans studied twelve infants with multiple fractures and found that they came from households that had a high rate of neurotic and psychotic behavior.[55]

Since then, mental retardation and organic brain disturbances have been related with cases of abuse.[56] Incestuous mothers have been characterized as severely disturbed.[57] S. Zalba reported that child maltreatment was perpetrated by parents possessing a number of mental problems, including impulse-ridden character disorder and violent and/or episodic schizophrenia.[58] Other research has found that the limbic system in the brain may be disturbed in some excessively aggressive people with violent tendencies.[59]

PSYCHOSOCIAL SYSTEMS THEORY

The psychosocial systems theory was established by Blair Justice and Rita Justice in an effort to bridge the gap existing in other child abuse theories. This theory focuses on the shifting symbiosis at work in the family system in which there is abuse, as well as the larger system of family environment and culture.[60] The larger system is described in terms of host(s), environment, agent, and vector as follows:

- Host(s): represents the parent(s).
- Environment: represents the physical and social influences and stresses.
- Agent: represents the child and behavior he/she embodies.
- Vector: represents expected patterns of interaction between individuals in a society.

In the psychosocial system there is a "continual interaction and feedback between any two points as well as among all the variables taken as a whole, including subsystems such as a biological element."[61] An example of this was described by F. J. Bishop, who contended that the host's child-rearing abilities are "determined by her own genetic endowment modified positively or negatively by her own parenting experience; her adaptation to it; her present emotional and physical health, as well as current socioeconomic and interpersonal stresses."[62] Thus, the variables at any point in this system are multiple and interactive. In spite of subsystems, the Justice's consider the psychological and social variables as the most significant characteristics of the model.

PART VI

Incarcerated Offenders and Intrafamilial Violence

17. Inmates and Intimate Violence

The relationship between prisoners and domestic crimes such as intimate and family violence is significant. Studies reveal that a high percentage of jail and prison inmates are incarcerated for interpersonal offenses, including intimate violence and familial offenses.[1] Most such offenders have a history of family violence or child maltreatment as perpetrators or victims, come from broken homes or families where there is a pattern of criminal behavior, and have used or abused alcohol and/or drugs, often during the course of their crimes.[2] Many battered women in prison were convicted of crimes involving self-defense from abusive husbands, crimes of child abuse and neglect, and offenses they were forced to commit by their batterers.[3] The majority of prisoners have left children behind — which is child abuse and neglect in itself.[4] Many such children are more or less left to fend for themselves, or placed at risk to be abused by others or on the streets.

This chapter will examine the characteristics and dynamics of persons confined to jail and prison correctional facilities with respect to domestic criminality and violence between intimates.

Jail Inmates and Intimate Violence

There is a high incidence of intimate violence among jail inmates' offenses for which they were convicted. According to the Bureau of Justice Statistics (BJS) Survey of Inmates in Local Jails, 1995, nearly 1 in 4 inmates in jail in the United States committed their offense against a spouse,

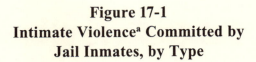

Figure 17-1
Intimate Violence[a] Committed by
Jail Inmates, by Type

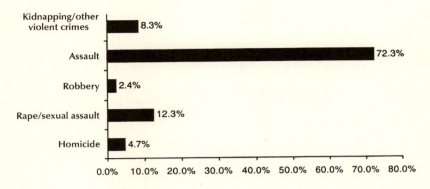

[a] Intimates include current and ex-spouses, boyfriends, and girlfriends.

Source: Constructed from U.S. Department of Justice, Bureau of Justice Statistics Factbook, *Violence by Intimates* (Washington, D.C.: Government Printing Office, 1998), p. 25.

ex-spouse, girlfriend, boyfriend, or former intimate.[5] Another nearly 1 in 10 inmates were convicted of violence against other relatives. Figure 17-1 shows a breakdown of the intimate violence offenses perpetrated by jail inmates. More than 72 percent of the inmates were convicted of assault, while over 12 percent committed rapes or sexual assaults. Less than 5 percent were in jail for murder, and just over 2 percent for robbery.

As shown in Table 17-1, more than half of all convicted jail inmates serving time for intimate violence in 1995 had a history of being placed under a restraining or protection order. When such an order had been placed, the spouse was the victim of the violence in more than 39 percent of the cases while girlfriends, boyfriends, or ex-spouses accounted for nearly 61 percent of the victimizations. Around 40 percent of the restraining or protection orders were taken out by spouses with more than 42 percent taken out by other intimates. When there was no history of restraining or protection orders, the spouse was the victim of intimate violence around one-third of the time with the victim a boyfriend, girlfriend, or ex-spouse in about two-thirds of the cases.

Approximately 4 in 10 inmates sentenced to jail for violence against an intimate in 1995 had been on probation, parole, had a restraining order against them, or another criminal justice status such as alcohol or drug diversion program or electronic monitoring.[6] For those inmates who had been on parole or probation when perpetrating their offenses, about 1 in 4 had a restraining order against them.

It is estimated that more than three-quarters of local jail inmates convicted of violence against intimates had prior convictions, with more than half the convictions for crimes of violence.[7]

Prison Inmates and Intimate Violence

Prisoners convicted of violent crimes against intimates represented only about 7 percent of the total violent offenders in prison in the United States, according to the BJS Survey of Inmates of State Correctional Facilities, 1991.[8] However, such prisoners were more likely than other violent inmates to be serving time for homicide.[9] As seen in Figure 17-2, more than 4 in 10 state prisoners convicted of intimate violence had murdered their victim. Nearly 3 in 10 offenses were assaults, while more than 2 in 10 inmates had raped or sexually assaulted an intimate.

PROFILE OF PRISONERS CONVICTED OF INTIMATE VIOLENT CRIMES

Female violent prisoners tend to have committed more crimes against an intimate than male violent prisoners. The BJS data shows that around 3 times as many women are in prison for intimate crimes as men.[10] Demographic characteristics of state inmates convicted of violent crimes are shown in Table 17-2. When the victim was an intimate, nearly 9 in 10 offenders in state prisons were male and just over 1 in 10 female. However, the percentage of female prisoners when the victim was an intimate was more than 3 times higher than when the victim was not an intimate.

Prisoners serving time for intimate violence were most likely to be white, over the age of 24, and high school graduates. Though white inmates comprised nearly 47 percent of the offenders of violent crimes against intimates, nearly 41 percent of the inmates were black, well above their proportion of the population. About 1 in 10 prisoners convicted of intimate violence were Hispanic, with less than 3 percent other minorities. Nearly 1 in 4 prisoners who victimized intimates had an education level of from 9th to 11th grade.

USE OF WEAPONS BY CONVICTED PRISONERS OF INTIMATE VIOLENCE

Around 3 in 10 prisoners who committed a crime against a spouse, ex-spouse, or other intimate were armed with a gun during the offense.[11]

Table 17-1
Convicted Jail Inmates' Intimate Violence,
by Victim and Orders of Protection

Convicted Intimate Violent Offenders in Local Jails: 100%

Previously placed under a restraining or protection order: 50.9%		No history of restraining or protection orders: 49.1%	
Person who took out the restraining or protection order		**Victim of intimate violence**	
Spouse	39.9%	Spouse	33.9%
Boyfriend, girlfriend, or ex-spouse	42.4%	Boyfriend, girlfriend, or ex-spouse	66.1%
Other relatives or acquaintances	17.7%		
Victim of intimate violence			
Spouse	39.3%		
Boyfriend, girlfriend, or ex-spouse	60.7%		

Source: Adapted from U.S. Department of Justice, Bureau of Justice Statistics Factbook, *Violence by Intimates* (Washington, D.C.: Government Printing Office, 1998), p. 25.

Figure 17-2
Intimate Violence[a] Committed
by State Prison Inmates, by Type

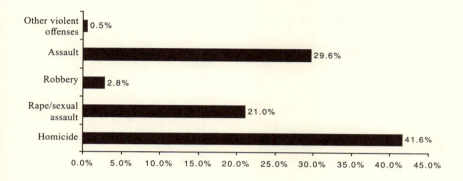

[a] Intimates include current and ex-spouses, boyfriends, and girlfriends.

Source: Constructed from U.S. Department of Justice, Bureau of Justice Statistics Factbook, *Violence by Intimates* (Washington, D.C.: Government Printing Office, 1998), p. 28.

Males are more likely to be victims of intimates with guns than females. A study found 29 percent of the male victims and 17 percent of the female victims reported that the intimate offender had used a weapon.[12] Male victims of intimate violence with a weapon were more likely to be assaulted with a sharp or blunt object, whereas female victims of an armed intimate partner were equally likely to be victims of a firearm, knife, or an object.

TYPES OF VICTIM INJURIES FROM INTIMATE VIOLENCE BY INMATES

Figure 17-3 shows the type of injuries suffered by victims of intimate violence in which the offender was sentenced to state prison. Nearly 8 in 10 inmates serving time as a result of intimate violence murdered or injured their victim. More than 47 percent of the intimate violence led to the victim's death, while nearly 13 percent were raped or sexually assaulted. Bruises or cuts accounted for around 8 percent of the victimizations, followed by stab wounds at 5 percent. Considering all victims of crimes of violence committed by prison inmates, the rate of death or injury was higher among intimates than any other type of violent crime.[13]

Table 17-2
Profile of Violent State Prison Inmates,
by Type of Victim

Characteristic of violent offenders in State prisons	When the victim was an intimate[a]	When the victim was not an intimate
Male	89.6%	96.8%
Female	10.4%	3.2%
White	46.8%	36.9%
Black	40.8%	46.5%
Hispanic	9.5%	13.9%
Other	2.9%	2.6%
Age 24 or younger	9.8%	19.5%
25-34	41.1%	44.9%
35 or older	49.1%	35.6%
8th grade or less	14.6%	14.3%
9th-11th grade	24.3%	24.9%
High school graduate	45.2%	49.3%
Some college	15.9%	11.4%

[a] Intimates include current and former spouses, boyfriends, and girlfriends.

Source: Adapted from U.S. Department of Justice, Bureau of Justice Statistics Factbook, *Violence by Intimates* (Washington, D.C.: Government Printing Office, 1998), p. 28.

Length of Sentence for Violent Inmates

Intimate killers tend to receive longer prison sentences for violent offenses than violent offenders serving time for offenses against strangers, other relatives, friends, or acquaintances. As seen in Table 17-3, the median sentence for state prisoners convicted of assaulting a spouse was 4 years longer than for assaultive inmates of other types of intimates or strangers, and 5 times longer than the sentence for inmates who assaulted other relatives, friends, or acquaintances.

Prisoners convicted of spousal homicide had a longer median sentence than every other violent prisoner who committed homicide, except for strangers. One-third of violent prisoners with spouse victims received a life sentence, while nearly 48 percent were convicted of homicide. Almost

Figure 17-3
Types of Victim Injuries in Intimate[a] Violence by State Prisoners

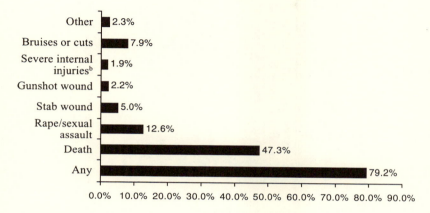

[a]Intimates include current and former spouses, boyfriends, and girlfriends.
[b]Injuries include broken bones, lost teeth, and being knocked unconscious.

Source: Constructed from U.S. Department of Justice, Bureau of Justice Statistics Factbook, *Violence by Intimates* (Washington, D.C.: Government Printing Office, 1998), p. 29.

30 percent of those imprisoned for intimate violence were serving a life sentence, and were convicted of murder.

Battered Women Prison Inmates

Many women in prison for crimes against intimates were battered by the victims of their offenses, or otherwise have a history of domestic violence victimization. In a study of 30 female prison inmates convicted of murdering their husbands, 28 reported being beaten by their victims.[14] Another study of female spouse killers found that in 90 percent of the cases the police had been called to the house for domestic violence at least once in the 2 years prior to the killing; and in 50 percent of the cases the police had gone to the home on at least 5 instances.[15] Studies show that though abused women tend to have a less extensive criminal history than other incarcerated offenders, they reflect a high percentage of female inmates.[16] Only 2 in 10 battered women charged with killing an intimate are acquitted, while others are either convicted or plea bargain, avoiding a trial.[17]

Table 17-3

Median Sentence for Violent State Prisoners, by Relationship to Victim

Offense	All violent offenders	Victim's relation to the prisoner				
		Spouse	Ex-spouse nonmarital intimate	Other relative	Friend/ acquaintance	Stranger
Median sentence						
All violent offenses	180 mo.	180 mo.	180 mo.	144 mo.	180 mo.	168 mo.
Homicide	264 mo.	300 mo.	240 mo.	240 mo.	264 mo.	300 mo.
Assault	120 mo.	168 mo.	120 mo.	108 mo.	108 mo.	120 mo.
Percent of prisoners						
With a life sentence	16.6%	32.5%	14.9%	10.3%	18.4%	18.3%
Having a life sentence, were convicted of homicide	46.8%	47.9%	29.7%	35.4%	41.2%	52.5%

Source: Constructed from U.S. Department of Justice, Bureau of Justice Statistics Factbook, *Violence by Intimates* (Washington, D.C.: Government Printing Office, 1998), p. 29.

Experts contend that women convicted of violent offenses are more likely to receive stiffer sentences than men convicted of "masculine" offenses such as robbery and homicide.[18] In testimony of battered women offenders before the Committee on Domestic Violence and Incarcerated Women, the average sentence was 15 years.[19] This finding was supported in another study which found that men who murdered their mates, often in self-defense, served 15 years in prison on average[20]; and Charles Ewing's study on convicted battered women killers, of which nearly half received sentences of more than 10 years.[21] Around 2 in 10 of the women received life sentences.

Race has been shown to be a factor in battered women convicted of killing an intimate. One study found that while women of color comprised one-third of the sample, they made up only 25 percent of the women found not guilty.[22] Black women, in particular, who killed an intimate mate in self-defense were 2 times as likely to be convicted and imprisoned as a white woman who killed an intimate.

Substance Abuse and Inmate Intimate Offenders

There is a strong correlation between alcohol or drug use and intimate violence committed by convicted inmates. As illustrated in Figures 17-4 and 17-5, more than half of all jail and prison inmates convicted of violent offenses were drinking alcohol or using drugs at the time of the offense. Among jail inmates, more than 56 percent were drinking or using drugs when committing the intimate crime, while over 55 percent of the state prisoners were. Around one-third of the prison and jail inmates were drinking only during their intimate crime, with under 8 percent of jail inmates and less than 4 percent of prison inmates using drugs only at the time of the offense. About 1 in 5 state prisoners used a combination of alcohol and drugs, compared to just over 1 in 10 inmates in jail.

Other data reflect the high percentage of inmates using drugs or alcohol before or during the commission of their crimes. Jail and prison inmate surveys have revealed that:

- Almost 8 out of 10 prison inmates had ever used drugs.
- More than 4 out of 10 male jail inmates and 2 in 10 female jail inmates were under the influence of alcohol at the time of their offense.
- Around half of all inmates used drugs in the month before the offense.

Figure 17-4
Jail Intimate Offenders'
Drinking and Drug Use Patterns

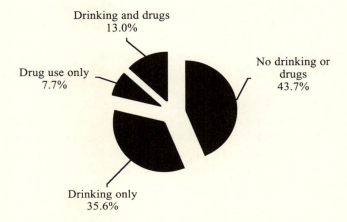

Drinking and drugs
13.0%

Drug use only
7.7%

No drinking or
drugs
43.7%

Drinking only
35.6%

Source: Derived from U.S. Department of Justice, Bureau of Justice Statistics Factbook, *Violence by Intimates* (Washington, D.C.: Government Printing Office, 1998), p. 26.

- Nearly one-third of inmates perpetrated their offense under the influence of drugs.
- Female inmates were more likely than male inmates to have used drugs daily in the month before the current offense.
- More than 2 in 10 male jail inmates and 1 in 10 female jail inmates had ever been an alcoholic.
- More than half the inmates younger than 35 had used drugs in the month before the offense.[23]

Family Violence

Inmates convicted of violent crimes against family members other than an intimate are also well represented in jails and prisons across the United States.[24] Most have been incarcerated for assaultive crimes, including physical and sexual assaults. Jail inmate data, as seen in Figure 17-6, reveal that more than 52 percent of the inmates serving time for a violent crime against a relative were convicted of rape or sexual assault, while over 34 percent committed assault against a relative. Only 2 percent of the inmates were in jail for familial homicide, less than 4 percent robbery, and just over 7 percent for other violent offenses.

Figure 17-5
State Prison Intimate Offenders'
Drinking and Drug Use Patterns

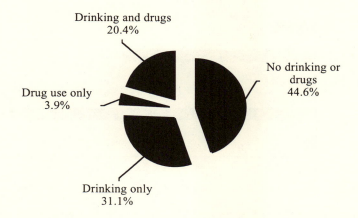

Drinking and drugs
20.4%

No drinking or
drugs
44.6%

Drug use only
3.9%

Drinking only
31.1%

Source: Derived from U.S. Department of Justice, Bureau of Justice Statistics Factbook, *Violence by Intimates* (Washington, D.C.: Government Printing Office, 1998), p. 26.

Among state prisoners convicted of crimes of violence against relatives, more than 6 in 10 were serving time for rape or sexual assault, according to prisoner surveys (see Figure 17-7). More than 8 times as many prison inmates as jail inmates were likely to be serving time for killing a family member. Nearly 17 percent of violent state offenders incarcerated for family violence had committed a homicide. One in 10 inmates in state prisons for violent family offenses were convicted of assaults, less than 2 percent robberies, and under 6 percent other violent crimes.

Figure 17-8 shows the type of injuries inflicted on relatives by prison inmates convicted of familial crimes of violence. More than 19 percent of the victims were raped or sexually assaulted by the inmate, while over 18 percent were killed. Less than 3 percent, respectively, were victims of such offenses as bruises or cuts, gunshot wounds, severe internal injuries, or other injuries committed by the inmate relative of the victim.

The median sentence for state prison inmates sentenced for violent offenses against relatives other than intimates was 144 months. For homicide, the median sentence was 240 months. Around 1 in 10 prisoners with a violent offense against a relative were serving life sentences, while more than 35 percent of these prisoners were convicted of homicide (see Table 17-3).

Figure 17-6
Jail Inmates' Violent Offenses
Against Relatives, by Type

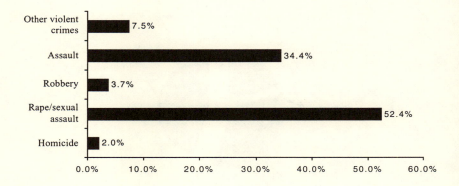

Source: Adapted from U.S. Department of Justice, Bureau of Justice Statistics Factbook, *Violence by Intimates* (Washington, D.C.: Government Printing Office, 1998), p. 25.

Figure 17-7
State Prison Inmates' Violent Offenses
Against Relatives, by Type

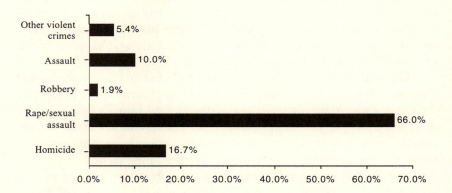

Source: Adapted from U.S. Department of Justice, Bureau of Justice Statistics Factbook, *Violence by Intimates* (Washington, D.C.: Government Printing Office, 1998), p. 25.

Figure 17-8
Types of Victim Injuries in State Prisoners' Violence Against Relatives

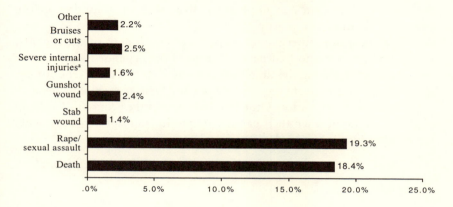

[a]Injuries include broken bones, lost teeth, and being rendered unconscious.

Source: Adapted from U.S. Department of Justice, Bureau of Justice Statistics Factbook, *Violence by Intimates* (Washington, D.C.: Government Printing Office, 1998), p. 29.

Family Dynamics and Prisoners

A high percentage of inmates involved in domestic and family violence come from families in which there was abuse, violence, and criminality; substance abuse, broken homes, and other negative dynamics.[25] Studies show that more than half of all state prison inmates grew up in single-parent homes or were raised by relatives.[26] Most inmates who committed family offenses such as spouse abuse and child abuse were themselves victims of family violence or child sexual abuse.[27] Many prisoners also come from families where other members were incarcerated. One study found that 40 percent of prison inmates had a member of the immediate family who had served time behind bars.[28] In another study, almost 47 percent of female prisoners and nearly 37 percent of male prisoners reported having a family member who had been incarcerated.[29]

The majority of jail and prison inmates convicted of family crimes and other offenses have children, most of whom had been dependents prior to confinement.[30] It is estimated that there are 25,700 female prisoners alone with more than 56,000 children under 18 years of age.[31] A Law Enforcement Assistance Administration (LEAA) survey reported that 6 in 10 inmates had dependents.[32] The Justice Department found that more than half of prisoners had children, the majority under the age of 18.[33] Another study found that nearly 8 out of 10 female inmates and more than 6 in 10 male inmates have children.[34] Two-thirds of these children are younger than 18 and more than 7 in 10 prisoners lived with their children before their incarceration.

In associating imprisonment with impoverishment of dependents, the LEAA survey found that nearly 4 in 10 of the dependents of inmates were on welfare during the time the survey was conducted.[35] The survey, however, did not indicate the number of child welfare recipients prior to the prisoners' incarceration. Other studies support the economic hardship placed on children when their parents are put in jail or prison, representing another form of child abuse and neglect.[36]

18. Prisoners and Child Abuse

Similar to prisoners incarcerated for offenses against intimates, the prevalence of jail and prison inmates whose crimes were against their own children or other children they knew is high. Prison surveys reveal that one-third of child victimizers in prison committed familial child abuse or child sexual abuse crimes.[1] Most inmates convicted of murdering a young child were related to the victim,[2] while around 1 in 5 of all child murderers was a family member.[3] The majority of violent inmate child victimizers were themselves victims of physical or sexual abuse[4]; and alcohol and/or drugs were often a factor in their offenses against child victims.[5] Despite the growing number of inmates convicted of crimes against persons under the age of 18, the reality is that most such child predators are not behind bars. Instead, they are out in society free to abuse or violate children, many their own, often hidden from official view. Some are eventually detected, prosecuted, and imprisoned.

This chapter will explore the characteristics of prisoners who have been sent to prison as child abusers and victimizers.

Inmate Child Victimizers

Tens of thousands of inmates in state prisons across the country committed their offenses against child victims. According to offenders in the 1991 Survey of Inmates in State Correctional Facilities, the most current detailed inmate data available, an estimated 61,000 state prisoners were serving sentences for violent crimes against victims under the age of 18.[6]

This represented nearly 19 percent of all violent prison inmates. Table 18-1 distributes offenses involving victims under the age of 18 for which state prisoners were convicted. In almost 94 percent of the cases, the child victimizers committed violent offenses. More than two-thirds of the crimes against children were rapes or sexual assaults. Nearly 9 percent of the inmates were convicted of homicide against a child victim, while more than 9 percent had committed assaults against minors. Less than 3 percent of these were for child abuse. However, child abusers are often classified as having committed other types of violent crimes such as rape or aggravated assault.[7] Robberies comprised just under 6 percent of the convictions against child victims, with kidnapping at slightly more than 2 percent of the offenses, and nonviolent offenses at around 6 percent of the child victimizations.

Table 18-2 reflects violent child victimizers in state prisons by the victim's age. Most prisoners convicted of violent crimes against children committed their offenses against victims age 12 or under. More than 55 percent of the violent offenders of children were serving time for crimes involving children under the age of 13. The victim was younger than 12 in more than 90 percent of the child abuse convictions and in over 60 percent of those incarcerated for negligent manslaughter, forcible sodomy, lewd acts with children, statutory rape, and other violent assaults. The distribution of offenses against child victims shows that in more than 3 out of 4 convictions involving children age 12 and younger and more than 6 in 10 with victims age 13 to 17, the prisoner was serving time for rape and sexual assault offenses. Older children were slightly more likely to be murder victims of inmates than younger children, representing around 10 percent and 9 percent of all child victimizations, respectively. Similar percentages can be seen for assaults of children.

Most inmates' crimes of violence against children occurred in the victim's or offender's home. Imprisoned child victimizers surveyed indicate that more than 3 out of every 4 violent offenses were perpetrated in the victim's or victimizer's home.[8] Around 4 in 10 children were victimized in their own home. Sexual assaults comprised the greatest incidence of violent child victimizations to occur in either the offender's or victim's home. Over half of all child abuse offenders committed their violent crimes in their own residence.[9]

Inmate Child Abusers

Prisoners doing time for child abuse offenses constitute only around 1 in 500 inmates in state prisons in the United States and under 3 percent

Table 18-1
Offense Distribution of State Prisoners
with Crime Victims Under Age 18

Offense	Child victimizers		Percent of all prisoners serving time for crimes against children
	Number	Percent	
All offenses[a]	65,163	100.0%	9.2%
Violent offenses	61,037	93.7%	18.6%
Homicide	5,792	8.9%	6.6%
Murder	4,677	7.2%	6.3%
Negligent manslaughter	1,115	1.7%	8.7%
Kidnapping	1,508	2.3%	18.0%
Rape and sexual assault	43,552	66.8%	65.5%
Forcible rape	8,908	13.7%	39.1%
Forcible sodomy	1,741	2.7%	85.5%
Statutory rape	1,102	1.7%	94.8%
Lewd acts with children	10,799	16.6%	100.0%
Other sexual assault	21,002	32.2%	70.7%
Robbery	3,772	5.8%	3.6%
Assault	6,058	9.3%	10.2%
Aggravated assault	3,933	6.0%	7.1%
Child abuse	1,717	2.6%	100.0%
Simple assault	408	0.6%	20.3%
Other violent	355	0.5%	16.0%
Nonviolent offenses	4,126	6.3%	1.1%

[a] Detail may not add to totals because of rounding.

Source: Adapted from U.S. Department of Justice, Bureau of Justice Statistics, *Child Victimizers: Violent Offenders and Their Victims* (Washington, D.C.: Government Printing Office, 1996), p. 1; BJS Survey of Inmates in State Correctional Facilities, 1991.

of those incarcerated for crimes against child victims.[10] Nevertheless, child abusers are well represented among prisoners according to self-report and victimization surveys[11]; as well as studies that have found that a high percentage of offenders convicted of crimes against children — such as sex offenses — often committed similar crimes against their own children.[12] Additionally, as definitions of child abuse vary in criminal data on offenders, many such inmates serving time for assaults, sexual assaults, and other crimes actually victimized their own offspring or child relatives.[13]

Table 18-2
Violent Child Victimizers in State Prisons,
by Age of Victim

		Prisoners serving time for crimes against children			Distribution of offenses Percent of violent offenders with victims --	
Violent offense	All	Victims age 12 or younger	Victim age 13 to 17	Percent with victims age 12 or younger	Age 12 or less	Ages 13-17
Total[a]	60,285	33,287	26,998	55.2%	100.0%	100.0%
Homicide	5,792	3,006	2,787	51.9%	9.0%	10.3%
Murder	4,677	2,279	2,399	48.7%	6.8%	8.9%
Negligent manslaughter	1,115	727	388	65.2%	2.2%	1.4%
Kidnapping	1,508	682	826	45.2%	2.0%	3.1%
Rape and sexual assault	42,993	25,102	17,892	58.4%	75.4%	66.3%
Forcible rape	8,908	3,893	5,015	43.7%	11.7%	18.6%
Forcible sodomy	1,729	1,039	690	60.1%	3.1%	2.6%
Statutory rape	984	611	373	62.1%	1.8%	1.4%
Lewd acts with children	10,370	7,175	3,195	69.2%	21.6%	11.8%
Other sexual assault	21,002	12,384	8,619	59.0%	37.2%	31.9%
Robbery	3,656	1,051	2,605	28.7%	3.2%	9.6%
Assault	6,035	3,215	2,818	53.3%	9.7%	10.4%
Aggravated assault	3,933	1,623	2,309	41.3%	4.9%	8.6%
Child abuse	1,694	1,513	181	89.3%	4.5%	0.7%
Simple assault	408	79	328	19.4%	0.2%	1.2%
Other violent	301	231	70	76.7%	0.7%	0.3%

[a] Excludes 752 cases for which the specific age of the victim was not reported. Detail may not add to total because of rounding.

Source: Adapted from U.S. Department of Justice, Bureau of Justice Statistics, *Child Victimizers: Violent Offenders and Their Victims* (Washington, D.C.: Government Printing Office, 1996), p. 2; BJS Survey of Inmates in State Correctional Facilities, 1991.

More than 4 in 10 prison inmates with child victims reported that they were related to the victim, while for 3 in 4 of such offenders and around one-third of all child victimizers, the victim was their own child or stepchild.[14] Most inmates sentenced for child abuse victimized young children. In almost 9 out of 10 convictions for child abuse, the victim was under the age of 13. This percentage was significantly higher than all other child victimizers' offenses against children age 12 or younger (see Table 18-2).

The victim-offender relationship among inmates imprisoned for violence against children can be seen in Table 18-3. Around one-third of prisoners serving time for a violent crime against children victimized their own child. Nearly one-fourth of the homicides of child victimizers were against

Table 18-3
Victim-Offender Relationship Among Prisoners
Serving Time for Violence Against Children

Single-victim incident	Number of State prison Inmates	Percent of State prison inmates serving time for a violent crime, by relationship to their child victim				
		Stranger	Own child[a]	Other family	Acquaintance	Intimate[b]
Total	42,616	14.6%	32.1%	11.1%	38.4%	3.8%
Homicide	3,545	29.5%	23.3%	8.2%	37.4%	1.6%
Murder	2,906	29.1%	23.3%	9.3%	38.3%	0%
Negligent manslaughter	639	31.5%	23.3%	2.8%	33.7%	8.7%
Kidnapping	1,153	55.5%	7.1%	7.5%	16.8%	13.1%
Rape and sexual assault	32,923	9.9%	33.4%	12.5%	40.1%	4.1%
Forcible rape	7,099	11.9%	36.2%	8.9%	36.9%	6.0%
Forcible sodomy	1,303	4.3%	35.9%	27.9%	22.2%	9.6%
Statutory rape	878	0%	27.9%	0%	72.1%	0%
Lewd acts with children	7,136	6.9%	31.9%	17.9%	40.8%	2.6%
Other sexual assault	16,507	11.3%	32.9%	11.2%	40.9%	3.6%
Robbery	811	55.3%	8.4%	6.5%	22.6%	7.3%
Assault	3,895	20.3%	39.1%	4.6%	35.9%	0%
Aggravated assault	2,253	29.8%	25.7%	5.4%	39.1%	0%
Child abuse	1,390	4.3%	63.9%	4.3%	27.5%	0%
Simple assault	252	c	c	c	c	c
Other violent	288	c	c	c	c	c

[a] Includes stepchildren.

[b] Boyfriend or girlfriend.

[c] Too few sample cases for an accurate estimate.

Source: Adapted from U.S. Department of Justice, Bureau of Justice Statistics, *Child Victimizers: Violent Offenders and Their Victims* (Washington, D.C.: Government Printing Office, 1996), p. 10; BJS Survey of Inmates in State Correctional Facilities, 1991.

their own child or stepchild, while over one-third of the sexual assaults were committed against their own children. Forcible sodomy and forcible rape were the sexual assaults most often committed by imprisoned fathers. Among child victimizer assaults, more than 39 percent were committed against inmates' own children. Nearly 64 percent of such assaults were classified as child abuse. Just over 7 percent of child victimizers' kidnappings and more than 8 percent of the robberies were perpetrated against their own children.

More than 11 percent of child victimizers' violent crimes came against other family members. Of those, nearly 28 percent of the forcible sodomy was perpetrated against a family member.

It is estimated that 43 percent of the child victims and 7 percent of other victims of violent state inmates were relatives.[15] Violent prisoners were around 6 times as likely to be related to a victimized child than an adult victim.[16]

Figure 18-1 distributes offenses of own child victimizers in prison. More than 6 in 10 offenses for which the inmates were serving time were sexual assaults, while nearly 1 in 5 offenses were rapes. More than 11 percent of the offenses were assaults, and 5 percent murders of the inmate's own child. All other violent offenses against children constituted around 3 percent, and robberies less than 1 percent.

More than half the inmate child victimizers of family members or an intimate were recidivists, as shown in Figure 18-2. Among these, nearly 1 in 5 had prior histories of violence, with more than 3 percent involving child victims, including child abuse.[17] Over 47 percent of prisoners committing violent offenses against children were first-time offenders.

Inmate Child Murderers and Their Victims

According to the FBI's Supplementary Homicide Reports, between 1976 and 1994 there were 36,951 murders of children under the age of 18, constituting more than 9 percent of total murders in the United States over the time span.[18] (See also Chapter 5.) Around 20 percent of all child murder victims were killed by someone in the family.[19] Infants were far more likely to be murdered by a family member than an acquaintance, stranger, or unknown assailant.[20] Figure 18-3 breaks down family murders of child victims, by age, from 1976 to 1994. More than two-thirds of the child victims were age 4 or younger, while more than 2 in 10 were age 5 to 14. Victims age 15 to 17 accounted for less than 10 percent of the family homicides.

Most familial infant murder victims were killed by being beaten to death by the offender's hands, feet, or a blunt object.[21] Older child murder victims of family members were most often victimized by gunfire. More than 3 in 4 murder victims age 15 to 17 were killed by a firearm from 1976 to 1994.[22]

A comparison of familial child murders by age of victims in 1994 can be seen in Figure 18-4. Family members were responsible for more than 71 percent of the murders of children under the age of 1. Nearly half the child victims of murder ages 1 to 4 were killed by a family member. Around 40 percent of victims age 5 to 9 and less than 14 percent age 10 to 14 were murdered by a member of the family. Under 3 percent of murdered children between the ages of 15 and 17 were victims of someone in the family.

Figure 18-1
Violent Offenses of Prison Inmates Against Own Child

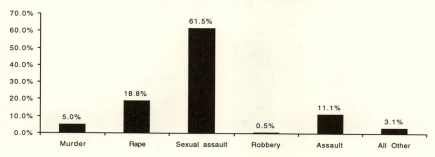

Source: Adapted from U.S. Department of Justice, Bureau of Justice Statistics, *Child Victimizers: Violent Offenders and Their Victims* (Washington, D.C.: Government Printing Office, 1996), p. 11; BJS Survey of Inmates in State Correctional Facilities, 1991.

Figure 18-2
Offense Backgrounds of Violent Inmate Family and Intimate Victimizers

[a] Includes child abuse, statutory rape, and lewd acts with children.

Source: Derived from U.S. Department of Justice, Bureau of Justice Statistics, *Child Victimizers: Violent Offenders and Their Victims* (Washington, D.C.: Government Printing Office, 1996), p. 11; BJS Survey of Inmates in State Correctional Facilities, 1991.

Around 7 percent of child victimizers incarcerated in state prisons murdered their child victims.[23] More than 4 times as many prison inmates who committed homicide against children were convicted of murder as non-negligent manslaughter.[24] Of child victimizers serving time for homicide, more than 1 in 2 killed victims age 12 or younger, while in nearly half the murders the victim was age 13 to 17.[25] Around 6 in 10 inmates imprisoned

Figure 18-3
Family Murder Victims of Violent Offenders, 1976–1994

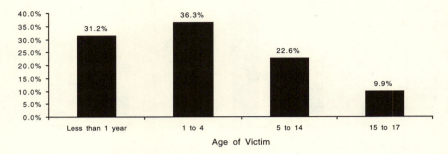

Source: Derived from U.S. Department of Justice, Bureau of Justice Statistics, *Child Victimizers: Violent Offenders and Their Victims* (Washington, D.C.: Government Printing Office, 1996), p. 17; U.S. Department of Justice, Federal Bureau of Investigation, Supplementary Homicide Reports, 1976-1994.

Figure 18-4
Percentage of Children Murdered by Family Members, by Age of Victims

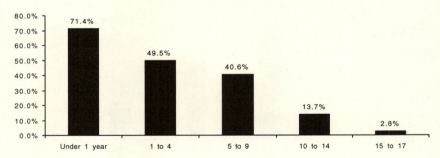

Source: Derived from U.S. Department of Justice, Bureau of Justice Statistics, *Child Victimizers: Violent Offenders and Their Victims* (Washington, D.C.: Government Printing Office, 1996), p. 27; U.S. Department of Justice, Federal Bureau of Investigation, Supplementary Homicide Reports, 1994.

for child homicides committed their crimes against single victims, whereas nearly 4 in 10 had multiple homicide victims.[26]

Sentences of Violent Child Victimizers

Median prison sentences of inmates serving time for violent crimes against children are shown in Figure 18-5. In all, child victimizers convicted

Figure 18-5
Median Sentences for Violent Prison Inmates
with Child Victims, by Offense

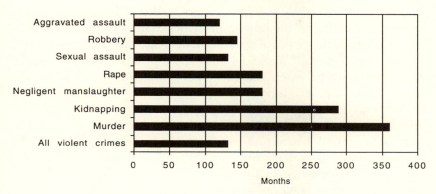

Source: Adapted from U.S. Department of Justice, Bureau of Justice Statistics, *Child Victimizers: Violent Offenders and Their Victims* (Washington, D.C.: Government Printing Office, 1996), p. 25; U.S. Department of Justice, Bureau of Justice Statistics, Survey of Inmates in State Correctional Facilities, 1991.

of violent offenses had a median sentence of 132 months or 11 years behind bars. The median sentence for child victimizers was highest for murder at 360 months, and kidnapping at 288 months. Child rape and nonnegligent manslaughter by child offender inmates resulted in a median sentence term of 180 months. For conviction on assault of a minor, the median sentence was 120 months or 10 years.

Child victimizers tended to have longer median sentences for murder, kidnapping, and nonnegligent manslaughter than inmates with adult victims for such violent crimes. The median sentences were shorter for inmates convicted of raping or sexually assaulting children than those committing the crimes against adults.[27] Around 10 percent of violent offenders with child victims were serving life sentences, while more than 60 percent of child killers, around 5 percent of child rapists, and 5 percent convicted of aggravated assault against children received life sentences.[28]

Violent offenders of children were more likely than violent offenders of adults to be required to participate in a sex offender treatment program or counseling as part of their sentence. Around 13 percent of child victimizers were ordered to undergo sex offender treatment, or psychiatric or psychological counseling; while nearly 30 percent of inmates convicted of forcible child sodomy were required to participate in a sex treatment program as a sentencing condition.[29]

Criminal History of
Inmate Child Victimizers

Most prisoners who committed crimes against children had criminal histories. According to the Bureau of Justice Statistics, among inmates where a child was the victim of the current offense, nearly 6 in 10 offenders had a criminal history.[30] Around 4 in 10 had a prior history of violence, while nearly 1 in 5 prisoners had a criminal history where a child was the victim of violence, including child abuse, lewd acts with a minor, and statutory rape. In terms of number of prior arrests as an adult or juvenile, more than 19 percent of child victimizers in prison had at least 1 previous arrest, with around 4 percent 5 priors, and more than 9 percent of the inmates committing violent crimes against children had 10 or more previous arrests.[31] These figures illustrate the recidivist nature of child victimizers, often until caught, as well as when released.

Drug and Alcohol Abuse History of
Child Victimizers in Prison

Drug or alcohol use has been shown to be a factor in the violent crimes of prisoners committed against children, though apparently not as much of a factor as when the victims of inmates were adults. According to prison survey data, around 6 in 10 inmate child victimizers reported not using drugs or alcohol when committing the violent offense, whereas around 6 in 10 adult victimizers in prison had used drugs or alcohol during the commission of the crime. Nevertheless, substance abuse by violent offenders of child victims is significant, as seen in Table 18-4. Nearly 24 percent of child victimizers used alcohol only when committing the crime. More than 5 percent used drugs, and almost 14 percent used a combination of drugs and alcohol at the time they perpetrated the crime against a child. When a drug was used by the inmate, nearly 1 in 5 used any drug. Marijuana and cocaine were the drugs used most often, followed by heroin, crack, and amphetamines.

Almost 4 in 10 victimizers of children reported drinking at the time the crime was perpetrated.[32] Among the drinkers, nearly half had been drinking for 6 or more hours prior to the offense, while almost one-quarter had been drinking between 2 and 3 hours preceding the child victimization. Approximately one-fifth of the prisoners committing violent

Table 18-4
Drug and Alcohol Use by Violent
Inmate Child Victimizers

Alcohol and drug use at time of the offense	Percent of State prison inmates serving time for a violent offense Child victims
Total[a]	100.0%
None	56.9%
Drugs only	5.3%
Alcohol only	23.9%
Both alcohol and drugs	13.9%
Type of drug used	
None	80.8%
Any drug[b]	19.2%
Marijuana	5.2%
Cocaine	4.2%
Crack	1.4%
Heroin	1.7%
LSD	0.7%
PCP	0.6%
Barbiturates	0.7%
Amphetamines	1.2%
Methamphetamines	0.9%

[a] Detail may not add to total because of rounding.

[b] Includes other drugs not separately shown. The percentages reflect the use of a hierarchy for inmates reporting more than one type of drug; only the most serious drug is considered.

Source: Adapted from U.S. Department of Justice, Bureau of Justice Statistics, *Child Victimizers: Violent Offenders and Their Victims* (Washington, D.C.: Government Printing Office, 1996), p. 7; BJS Survey of Inmates in State Correctional Facilities, 1991.

crimes against children reported using drugs at the time of the crime. Other research has supported the correlation between substance abuse and family violence (see Chapter 14).

Demographic Characteristics of Child Victimizers in Prison

Demographic characteristics of prison inmates serving time for violent crimes against children are shown in Table 18-5. Child victimizers in prison are predominantly male, white, non–Hispanic, single, under the age of 24, high school graduates, and employed. Nearly 97 percent of the inmates serving time for violent offenses against children were male, while less than 4 percent were female. Almost 70 percent of the child victimizers were white, well above the 48 percent of overall prisoners they represented. In contrast, while black inmates comprised around 48 percent of all prisoners, just over 25 percent of those victimizing children were black.

Nearly 9 in 10 child victimizers were non–Hispanic, with just over 11 percent of Hispanic origin. Around 1 in 7 Hispanic prisoners incarcerated for a crime of violence committed the offense against a victim under the age of 18.[33]

Around one-third of child victimizers were divorced and just over another one-third never married. Nearly 1 in 4 inmates serving time for violent offenses against children were married. Almost two-thirds of the child victimizers in prison had ever been married.[34]

Inmates who committed violent crimes against child victims were generally between the ages of 18 and 39 at the time of arrest, with a median age of 31 and mean age at the time of arrest of 33. Around 10 percent of child victimizers were age 50 and older when arrested. More than 45 percent of violent prisoners in their 50s were serving time for crimes against children, compared to less than 14 percent of inmates in their 20s.[35]

More than 1 in 4 child victimizers had a 12th grade education, while more than 4 in 10 had a 10th grade or less education. Nearly 2 in 10 violent inmate offenders with child victims had a college education.

Family Background Characteristics of Inmate Child Victimizers

Family background characteristics of inmate child victimizers are reflected in Table 18-6. More than half those serving state prison sentences for violent offenses against children grew up with both parents in the household. Around 3 in 10 inmates were primarily raised by a mother

Table 18-5
Demographic Characteristics of Violent Offenders,
by Victim Age

Characteristics of violent offenders	Percent of violent offenders in State prison having --		
	All	Child victims	Adult victims
Total	100.0%	100.0%	100.0%
Sex			
Male	96.2%	96.6%	96.1%
Female	3.8%	3.4%	3.9%
Race			
White	48.0%	69.7%	43.1%
Black	48.1%	25.5%	53.3%
Other	3.9%	4.8%	3.6%
Hispanic origin			
Hispanic	13.9%	11.1%	14.5%
Non-Hispanic	86.1%	88.9%	85.5%
Marital status			
Married	17.1%	23.3%	15.7%
Widowed	2.6%	2.0%	2.7%
Divorced	21.4%	32.7%	18.9%
Separated	5.6%	5.4%	5.6%
Never married	53.3%	36.5%	57.1%
Age at arrest for current offense			
17 or younger	3.0%	2.1%	3.2%
18-24	38.1%	26.1%	40.8%
25-29	22.1%	17.6%	23.1%
30-34	15.0%	16.9%	14.6%
35-39	8.8%	12.0%	8.1%
40-44	5.0%	7.9%	4.4%
45-49	3.4%	6.2%	2.7%
50-54	1.7%	4.1%	1.2%
55-59	1.5%	4.3%	0.9%
60 or older	1.4%	2.8%	1.0%
Mean age at arrest	29 yr	33 yr	28 yr
Median age at arrest	27 yr	31 yr	26 yr
Education			
8th grade or less	13.5%	17.1%	12.7%
9th grade	12.1%	11.4%	12.2%
10th grade	16.2%	12.9%	17.0%
11th grade	17.9%	14.0%	18.7%
12th grade	26.0%	26.9%	25.8%
College	14.3%	17.7%	13.6%
Employment in month before arrest			
Employed	69.6%	78.0%	67.7%
Unemployed	30.4%	22.0%	32.3%
Total number	327,958	61,037	266,920

Source: U.S. Department of Justice, Bureau of Justice Statistics, *Child Victimizers: Violent Offenders and Their Victims* (Washington, D.C.: Government Printing Office, 1996), p. 5; BJS Survey of Inmates in State Correctional Facilities, 1991.

Table 18-6
Family Background of Violent Offenders,
by Age of Victim

Characteristic of violent offenders	Percent of violent offenders in State prison having --		
	All	Child victims	Victims of other ages
Total	100.0%	100.0%	100.0%
Primarily grew up with --			
Mother only	39.0%	30.1%	41.0%
Father only	3.6%	2.8%	3.8%
Both parents	43.7%	54.2%	41.2%
Grandparents	7.3%	5.7%	7.7%
Other relatives	3.0%	2.2%	3.2%
Foster home or institution	2.7%	4.3%	2.3%
Other	0.7%	0.7%	0.8%
Ever spent time in a foster home or institution			
Yes	18.5%	16.6%	18.8%
No	81.6%	83.4%	81.2%
Parents/guardians abused drugs or alcohol			
Yes	27.7%	31.5%	26.9%
No	72.3%	68.5%	73.1%
Immediate family member ever served time			
Yes	37.0%	35.6%	37.3%
No	63.0%	64.4%	62.7%
Total number	327,958	61,037	266,920

Source: U.S. Department of Justice, Bureau of Justice Statistics, *Child Victimizers: Violent Offenders and Their Victims* (Washington, D.C.: Government Printing Office, 1996), p. 6; BJS Survey of Inmates in State Correctional Facilities, 1991.

only. More than twice the percentage of victimizers of children grew up with grandparents. Less than 3 percent of violent prison inmates who victimized children grew up with a father in the home. Under 17 percent of child victimizers had ever spent time in a foster home or institution, compared to more than 81 percent who had not.

The relationship between parental substance abuse and inmates who victimized children is significant. Almost one-third of child victimizers had parents or guardians who abused drugs or alcohol. Nearly 36 percent of state prison inmates had immediate family members who had ever served time behind bars. Prisoner data on both parent substance abuse and familial criminality support other data which indicates a familial cycle of alcohol and/or drug use that further ties in with a family cycle of violence and other forms of criminality.[36]

Physical and Sexual Abuse History of Violent Imprisoned Offenders of Child Victims

Studies show that there is a clear relationship between child physical and sexual abuse and offenders with a history of themselves being the victim of physical and/or sexual maltreatment.[37] In Table 18-7 data are presented on prior physical or sexual abuse experienced by state prison inmates serving time for violent crimes against children. Around 3 in 10 inmates were ever physically or sexually abused. This was nearly twice as many as all prisoners. Child victimizer offenders were equally likely to have been physically or sexually abused, comprising around 9 percent each. More than 13 percent had been victims of both physical and sexual abuse.

For child victimizers who were abused, more than 25 percent were under the age of 18 when the abuse occurred. Almost 4 percent experienced abuse as children and adults. The abuser was known to the inmate in more than 28 percent of the cases of abuse. The parent or guardian was the perpetrator of sexual or physical abuse in nearly 14 percent of the victimizations, while another relative was the abuser in over 6 percent of the abuse.

Inmates imprisoned for violent crimes against children were more than twice as likely to have been previously physically or sexually abused as inmates who committed violent offenses against adults.[38] The disparity is even greater with respect to sexual abuse. It is estimated that 22 percent of inmate victimizers of children were themselves victims of sexual abuse, compared to less than 6 percent of inmates with adult victims.[39] (See also Chapter 11.)

Juveniles in Custody for Child Abuse–Related Offenses

Most juvenile inmate child victimizers are incarcerated in adult or juvenile facilities for the same familial offenses against children as adults, including assaults, sexual assaults, murder, and other child abuses or family violence. Juveniles represent only a fraction of violent offenders in custody for crimes against child victims, accounting for less than 3 percent of state prison child victimizers.[40] However, persons under the age of 18 commit nearly one-third of the murders against children.[41] Around 30 percent of all murder victims in the United States were killed by family members.[42]

Many juveniles held in juvenile facilities are confined as nonoffenders,

Table 18-7
Prior Physical or Sexual Abuse Experienced by Violent Offenders, by Age of Victim

| Characteristic of violent offenders | All | Percent of violent offenders in State prison having -- | |
		Child victims	Victims of other ages
Total	100.0%	100.0%	100.0%
Ever physically or sexually abused			
No	82.9%	69.0%	86.1%
Yes	17.1%	31.0%	13.9%
Physical abuse only	8.2%	8.8%	8.1%
Sexual abuse only	3.1%	8.7%	1.9%
Both physical and sexual abuse	5.7%	13.5%	4.0%
Age at which abuse occurred			
No abuse	82.9%	69.0%	86.1%
Abused	17.1%	31.0%	13.9%
Less than 18 years old	12.4%	25.7%	9.3%
18 years or older	2.0%	1.4%	2.1%
Both as a child and an adult	2.9%	3.9%	2.6%
Who the abuser was			
No prior abuse	82.9%	69.0%	86.1%
Stranger	2.0%	2.7%	1.9%
Known	15.1%	28.3%	12.0%
Parent/guardian	7.9%	13.7%	6.5%
Other relative[a]	2.9%	6.4%	2.1%
Acquaintance	4.3%	8.1%	3.4%
Total number	327,958	61,037	266,920

[a] Other relative includes spouses and ex-spouses and acquaintances includes boyfriends and girlfriends. Detail may not add to total because of rounding.

Source: U.S. Department of Justice, Bureau of Justice Statistics, *Child Victimizers: Violent Offenders and Their Victims* (Washington, D.C.: Government Printing Office, 1996), p. 6; BJS Survey of Inmates in State Correctional Facilities, 1991.

including victims of abuse, neglect, emotional disturbance, dependency, and retardation. Approximately 1 in 4 juveniles in private juvenile detention, correctional, or shelter facilities are there as nonoffenders.[43] A recent 1-day count of juveniles in custody in public and private juvenile facilities, by gender, revealed that more than 38 percent of the females and 23 percent of the males were being held as nonoffenders, such as abuse or neglect victims.[44]

PART VII

Strategies in Response to Domestic Crimes

19. Combating Domestic Violence and Child Abuse

In response to family and intimate violence and child maltreatment, much progress has been made on the legal, social, and educational fronts as we begin life in the twenty-first century. Important federal and state legislation has been enacted in recent years aimed at protecting women, children, senior citizens, and male victims from domestic crimes and abuses in the home. Law enforcement personnel are, on the whole, better trained and equipped to handle domestic disturbance calls, as are social service workers in dealing with spouse, child, and elderly abuse cases.

Shelters for abused runaways and battered women and rape crisis centers can be found throughout the country. Other forms of assistance for victims of family or intimate violence include domestic violence hotlines; national centers on domestic violence, child abuse, and elderly abuse; and various public and private organizations offering information, referrals, support groups, and additional services. The media have also played a significant role in drawing attention to the problem of violence in the home and familial sexual abuse.

These collective efforts have not been able to eliminate domestic or family violence. But they have made it easier to detect and report suspected cases of intimate, child, or elderly abuse. These efforts have also made it easier to arrest, prosecute, and incarcerate batterers and abusers, and create a greater awareness of the issues related to violence and mistreatment between family members or intimate partners.

Responding to Domestic Violence

LEGAL RESPONSES TO THE BATTERED WOMAN SYNDROME

Recent years have seen a more appropriate response by law enforcement to domestic violence, no longer viewed as strictly a "private matter" between the abused and abuser. This shift in policy can be seen in the International Association of Chiefs of Police (IACP) training manual, which now maintains with respect to suspected domestic violence a "policy of arrest, when the elements of the offense are present, promotes the well-being of the victim.... The officer who starts legal action may give the wife the courage she needs to realistically face and correct her situation."[1] When there is not probable cause for arrest, the IACP encourages police personnel to offer assistance to battered women in seeking other support services. The idea is that "increased arrests and attention to abuse cases will be beneficial in the long run to both the public and the system of law enforcement."[2]

Legislative action on the problem of domestic violence has been made in every state and on the federal level, including:

- Laws that prohibit marital rape.[3]
- Laws that authorize the court to order a batterer to change his behavior, to evict a wife abuser from the premises shared with his victim, to require the abuser to compensate the abused partner monetarily, and to impose a jail term for batterers who violate a protective order.
- Laws authorizing law enforcement officers to make arrests in cases of domestic violence, to make arrests without a warrant when probable cause exists that there is a violation of a protective order, to transport the battered victim to a hospital, and to inform the victim of legal options available.
- Laws that require organizations which offer assistance to violent families or intimates to maintain records.[4]

Since the mid–1980s, female victims of violence have been eligible to receive financial compensation for their victimization through the 1984 Victims of Crime Act. It established a "Crime Victim Fund with monies from federal offenders (i.e., fines, penalties, forfeited bail bonds, literary royalties). The fund is used as part of state victim and compensation programs."[5] In 1990, the Office for Victims of Crime, through which the monies are obtained and dispensed, "provided a record amount of $125 million to victims programs, including more than 1,600 programs specializing in assistance for victims of sexual assault crimes and domestic violence."[6]

Most states have enacted victims' rights laws designed to protect victimized women and improve their treatment within the criminal justice system. In 1990, a Federal Victims Bill of Rights became law, strengthening the rights of battered women against victimization.[7]

Other important recent legislative advances for victims of domestic violence and battering in specific can be seen below:

- Nebraska became the first state to abolish the marital rape exemption in 1975.[8]
- Pennsylvania became the first state to enact legislation establishing orders of protection for victims of domestic violence in 1976.[9]
- Oregon became the first state to pass a law mandating an arrest be made in domestic violence disputes in 1977.[10]
- In 1978, Minnesota became the first state to authorize arrests without a warrant based on probable cause in cases of domestic violence, irrespective of whether an order of protection had been issued against a batterer.[11]
- The Family Violence Prevention and Services Act was enacted into law in 1984.[12]
- *Thurman v. Torrington* was the first federal court case in which an abused woman sued a city for the failure of the police to protect her from an abusive spouse in 1987. The suit resulted in Connecticut passing a mandatory arrest law.[13]
- *State v. Ciskie* became the first case to permit use of expert testimony in explaining the mental state and behavior of a repeat intimate rape victim in 1988.[14]
- California became the first state to enact antistalking legislation in 1990.[15] At least 37 other states have since passed antistalking laws.[16]

BATTERED WOMEN'S SHELTERS

The shelter or safe house as a place for battered women and children to seek refuge began in England in 1972, where the first official battered women's shelter was opened by Erin Pizzey.[17] The concept caught on quickly in the United States as "a way to protect women and children from the immediate threat or aftermath of domestic attack, usually at the hands of the man of the household."[18] Today, battered women's shelters can be found across the country in various shapes and sizes, with trained volunteers and paid staff whose duties include advocacy, counseling, support, medical care, and referral services.

In spite of the need for such shelters, they provide only temporary relief to a long-term problem for victims of domestic violence. Funding problems can lead to cutbacks in staff and an inability to handle the influx of battered women and children. Furthermore, strict rules and regulations as well as overcrowding can hamper the effectiveness of shelters and send victims out on the streets or back to the abusers they sought refuge from. Such problems aside, battered women's shelters continue to be an important tool in the fight against domestic violence and child abuse.

RAPE CRISIS CENTERS

The first rape crisis centers opened in the United States in the early 1970s.[19] Today, there are over 100 across the country whose purpose is to offer support, comfort, and assistance to rape victims that are often unavailable elsewhere. Many battered women are also victims of marital rape and in need of the services provided by rape crisis centers including "telephone counseling, information regarding medical and legal procedures, and support during trials."[20] Trained volunteers also educate members of the community about rape and other sexual assaults and how women can protect themselves. Many staff members live in the community, or are also rape victims. Similar to battered women's shelters, the overall effectiveness of rape crisis centers is at times weakened by lack of funding, staff, philosophical issues, or questions of professionalism. Their role as a source of assistance to victims of rape remains crucial in helping them to deal with the violation and its aftermath.

NATIONAL SERVICES FOR BATTERED WOMEN

A number of national organizations, groups, and agencies exist to offer battered women and their families aid, support, referrals, information, domestic violence hotlines, and other service to supplement local resources. These include such organizations as the Family Violence Prevention Fund, National Coalition Against Domestic Violence, National Resource Center on Domestic Violence, National Center on Elderly Abuse, and the National Center for Injury Prevention and Control. Many support services have good working relationships with state and local law enforcement as well as medical and mental health providers, allowing for cooperation in helping victims and offering them the type of assistance and referrals needed.

Responding to Child Maltreatment

LEGAL RESPONSES TO CHILD ABUSE AND NEGLECT

Legislative efforts aimed at curbing child abuse and assisting its victims and their families have resulted in a number of important laws being enacted in the '70s, '80s and '90s. This has set the groundwork for further federal and state statutes in the twenty-first century to protect children from abuse and neglect and increase penalties for child abusers.

CHILD ABUSE PREVENTION AND TREATMENT ACT

The Child Abuse Prevention and Treatment Act (P.L. 100-294) was enacted in 1974 and amended in 1978 as a direct response to increasing public concerns about abused, neglected, and exploited children.[21] The act defined child abuse and neglect and provided for several programs designed to protect all children in the United States from maltreatment, including:

> (1) the establishment of a National Center on Child Abuse and Neglect, (2) increasing public awareness on child maltreatment, detection and reporting, (3) assisting states and local communities in developing more effective mechanisms for delivery of services to families, (4) providing training and technical assistance to state and local communities in dealing with the problems of child abuse and neglect, and (5) supporting research into causal and preventative measures in child victimization.[22]

For states to qualify for federal funds, they were required to meet several criteria — including a comprehensive definition of child abuse and neglect, specifying child abuse reporting procedures, investigation of reports, and administrative procedures. Further requirements were the confidentiality of records and the appointment of guardians for child victims involved in abuse or neglect judicial proceedings.[23]

NATIONAL CENTER ON CHILD ABUSE AND NEGLECT

The National Center on Child Abuse and Neglect (NCCAN) was established by P.L. 93-247 in 1974 and reauthorized in 1988 under P.L. 100-294 (the Child Abuse Prevention, Adoption, and Family Services Act).[24] As the federal agency in charge of child abuse and neglect matters, the NCCAN "administers grants to states and territories, local agencies, and organizations nationwide for research, service programs, and assistance with respect to the identification, treatment, and prevention of child maltreatment in any form."[25]

JUVENILE JUSTICE AND DELINQUENCY PREVENTION ACT

The Juvenile Justice and Delinquency Prevention Act was enacted in 1974 and amended in 1980.[26] Its purpose was to identify victimized or troubled youth (status offenders) and divert from institutionalization. The act required: (1) a comprehensive assessment of the effectiveness of the juvenile justice system, (2) the impetus for developing and implementing innovative alternatives in delinquency prevention and diversion of status offenders from the criminal justice system, and (3) the use of resources in the juvenile justice system to deal more effectively with juvenile delinquents. In order for states to receive federal delinquency funds, the act required that they

> provide within two years after submission of the plan that juveniles who are charged with or who have committed offenses that would not be criminal if committed by an adult, shall not be placed in juvenile detention or correctional facilities, but must be placed in shelter facilities.[27]

RUNAWAY AND HOMELESS YOUTH ACT

The Runaway and Homeless Youth Act (RHYA) was enacted in 1978.[28] Its purpose was to provide assistance to local organizations for operating temporary runaway shelters. The act recognizes the seriousness of the problem of runaway children, including its relationship to child abuse, delinquency, prostitution, and substance abuse. The RHYA made grants available for the "establishment and maintenance of runaway houses by states, localities, and nonprofit groups."[29] The 1980 amendment of the act included the following provisions:

- Recognition that many "runaways" are in reality "throwaways," and thus were forced out of the home.
- Clarification of the requirement that shelter services be made available to the families of runaway and homeless children as well as to the missing youths themselves.
- Program authorities for the development of model programs designed to assist chronic runaways.[30]

PROTECTION OF CHILDREN AGAINST SEXUAL EXPLOITATION ACT

The Sexual Exploitation Act of 1978 was the result of extensive legislative hearings in both the House and Senate.[31] Its purpose was to bridge the gaps existing in federal statutes designed to protect children from sexual exploitation. The law hoped to "halt the production and dissemination of child pornography by prohibiting the transportation of children across state lines for the purpose of sexual exploitation."[32] The legislation also extended the federal government's authority to prosecute both producers and distributors of child pornography. In specific,

> the law provides punishment for persons who use, employ, or persuade minors (defined as any persons under 16) to become involved in the production of visual or print materials that depict sexually explicit conduct if the producers know or have reasons to know that the materials will be transported in interstate or foreign commerce or mailed. Punishment is also specifically provided for parents, legal guardians, or other persons having custody or control of minors and who knowingly permit a minor to participate in the production of such material.[33]

The act also provided for stiff monetary penalties against sexual exploiters of children. In 1983, the U.S. Supreme Court upheld the constitutionality of a New York law that prohibited the dissemination of child pornography "regardless of whether or not the material is judged to be legally obscene."[34] The ruling, in effect, upheld similar laws in 20 other states.[35]

FEDERAL PARENTAL KIDNAPPING PREVENTION ACT

The Federal Parental Kidnapping Prevention Act was enacted in 1980, empowering the Federal Parental Locator Service to assist in the search for parental kidnappers and abducted children.[36] The act's purpose was to determine child custody rights, enforcing them, and investigating parental kidnapping cases and prosecuting offenders. It was further designed to deter parental child snatching and make child custody decrees uniform nationwide by requiring other states to honor a custody decree from any state. Though the legislation does not make parental kidnapping a federal crime, it does allow the FBI to assist in the search for kidnapped children once a state arrest warrant has been issued against an abductor.

MISSING CHILDREN ACT

The Missing Children Act was enacted in 1982 as a response to the growing number of missing children through parental abduction, non-family kidnapping, running away, or other means.[37] The act allows parents, guardians, or next-of-kin of missing children "confirmation" of an entry into the FBI's National Crime Information Center computer in which local law enforcement have access. This clearinghouse "aids both the local police in identifying and finding children and their parents who know that the missing child is registered across the country, increasing chances of the child being located."[38] Further, the act allows for FBI intervention after proof a child has been kidnapped.

NATIONAL CHILD ABUSE AND NEGLECT DATA SYSTEM

The National Child Abuse and Neglect Data System (NCANDS) was established in 1988 by the NCCAN in response to the Child Abuse Prevention and Treatment Act, as amended, "which called for the creation of a coordinated national data collection and analysis program, both universal and case specific in scope."[39] The NCANDS is the "primary source of national information on abused and neglected children known to State child protective service agencies."[40]

The Summary Data Component of NCANDS collects "aggregate data on reports and investigations of child abuse and neglect and on the victims and perpetrators of substantiated or indicated investigations."[41] Data collected from state agencies on reported child maltreatment in the United States is made available to policy makers, child welfare practitioners, and the general public, and is meaningful in "national, State, and local program planning, design, and implementation."[42]

Child Protective Services

Child Protective Services (CPS) is the agency primarily responsible for "evaluation, intervention, prevention, protection, and treatment of child abuse and neglect cases in all states, ensuring that the services are first and foremost responsive to the needs and welfare of abused and neglected children."[43] The main purpose of CPS agencies is to "ensure that children are protected from harm and the integrity of the family maintained."[44]

Child Protective Services is responsible for establishing whether abuse or neglect has occurred or is likely to, and whether or not the child's health or life is in peril. "If CPS concludes that a child's safety is threatened, it will make all efforts to keep the family together and, at the same time, ensure a child's safety."[45] When both objectives cannot be achieved, CPS, through juvenile or family courts, removes an abused or neglected child from the custody of the parents and places them in foster care.

Though CPS agencies focus on treatment of abusers in order to possibly reestablish family stability and a safe home environment for the child, sometimes child abusers are prosecuted in criminal court (usually for cases involving child sexual abuse or severe physical abuse) to ensure that "the abuser accepts and follows through with treatment and to ensure that a criminal act is appropriately deterred."[46]

In every state there are child abuse reporting laws mandating reporting of suspected child maltreatment.

National Focus on Maltreated Children

In the effort to protect children from abuse, neglect, and exploitation, a number of national and local programs and services have been launched in recent years. Included amongst these is the National Center for Missing and Exploited Children, established in 1984.[47] The center serves as a central contact point for parents of missing children; and provides assistance and expertise in education, public awareness, advocacy, law enforcement, and legislation in locating children and preventing child exploitation.

Other national programs focusing on child maltreatment include the National Clearinghouse on Child Abuse and Neglect, the National Fingerprint Center for Missing Children, the National Committee to Prevent Child Abuse, and the National Crime Prevention Council. National and local crisis intervention hotlines can also assist families in dealing with family violence and child abuse, along with prominent local organizations or shelters such as Huckleberry House, Children of the Night, and Covenant House.

These services notwithstanding, there is still a great need for national and local resources to assist families in crisis and those seeking to break the cycle of abuse and violence.

Notes

CHAPTER 1. THE ABUSE OF WOMEN AND CHILDREN:
HISTORICAL PRECEDENTS

1. R. Barri Flowers, *The Victimization and Exploitation of Women and Children: A Study of Physical, Mental and Sexual Maltreatment in the United States* (Jefferson, N.C.: McFarland, 1994), p. 35.

2. R. Graves, *Greek Myths* (New York: Penguin, 1962).

3. Cited in M. A. Freeman, *Violence in the Home* (Farnborough, England: Saxon House, 1979), p. 4.

4. R. Barri Flowers, *Children and Criminality: The Child as Victim and Perpetrator* (Westport, Conn.: Greenwood Press, 1986), p. 49; *Oliver Twist* and *North and South* are two such examples.

5. Flowers, *Children and Criminality*, p. 49.

6. Freeman, *Violence in the Home*, p. 6.

7. Richard J. Gelles and Murray A. Straus, "Violence in the American Family," *Journal of Social Issues* 35, 2 (1979): 15–39.

8. R. Barri Flowers, *Women and Criminality: The Woman as Victim, Offender, and Practitioner* (Westport, Conn.: Greenwood Press, 1987), p. 14.

9. Terry Davidson, "Wifebeating: A Recurring Phenomenon Throughout History," as cited in Maria Roy, ed., *The Abusive Partner: An Analysis of Domestic Battering* (New York: Van Nostrand Reinhold, 1982), p. 12.

10. Maria Roy, "The Nature of Abusive Behavior," in Maria Roy, ed., *The Abusive Partner: An Analysis of Domestic Battering* (New York: Van Nostrand Reinhold, 1982), p. 12.

11. Frederick Engels, *The Origin of Family Private Property and the State* (Moscow: Progress Publishers, 1948), pp. 53–58.

12. Flowers, *Women and Criminality*, p. 15.

13. Brian G. Frazer, "The Child and His Parents: A Delicate Balance of Rights," in Ray E. Helfer and C. Henry Kempe, eds., *Child Abuse and Neglect: The Family and the Community* (Cambridge, Mass.: Ballinger, 1976).

14. Roy, *The Abusive Partner*, p. 13.

231

15. Flowers, *Women and Criminality*, p. 15.

16. *Ibid.*, p. 27.

17. Quoted in Carol V. Horos, *Rape* (New Canaan, Conn.: Tobey Publishing Co., 1974), p. 3.

18. Susan Brownmiller, *Against Our Will: Men, Women and Rape* (New York: Simon & Schuster, 1975).

19. Flowers, *Children and Criminality*, p. 4.

20. *Ibid.*, p. 5; Samuel N. Kramer, *From the Tables of Sumer: Twenty-Five Firsts in Man's Recorded History* (Indian Hills, Colo.: Falcon Wing, 1956), p. 11.

21. Samuel X. Radbill, "A History of Child Abuse and Infanticide," in Ray E. Helfer and C. Henry Kempe, eds., *The Battered Child*, 2nd ed. (Chicago: University of Chicago Press, 1974), p. 3.

22. Quoted in Pamela D. Mayhall and Katherine Norgard, *Child Abuse and Neglect: Sharing Responsibility* (Toronto: John Wiley and Sons, 1983), p. 4.

23. Flowers, *Children and Criminality*, p. 5; Mason P. Thomas, Jr., "Child Abuse and Neglect, Part I: Historical Overview, Legal Matrix and Social Perspectives," *North Carolina Law Review* 50 (1972): 293–349.

24. Flowers, *Children and Criminality*, p. 5.

25. *Ibid.*

26. Theo Solomon, "History and Demography of Child Abuse," *Pediatrics* 51, 4 (1973): 773–76.

27. Flowers, *Children and Criminality*, p. 4.

28. *The Holy Bible*, Book of Joshua, 6:17–21.

29. R. Barri Flowers, *Female Crime, Criminals and Cellmates: An Exploration of Female Criminality and Delinquency* (Jefferson, N.C.: McFarland, 1995), p. 85.

30. *Ibid.*; Solomon, "History and Demography of Child Abuse," p. 773.

31. C. Morris, *The Tudors* (London: Fontana, 1967).

32. J. E. Oliver, "The Epidemiology of Child Abuse," in Selwyn M. Smith, ed., *The Maltreatment of Children* (Baltimore, Md.: University Park Press, 1978), p. 95.

33. Shirley O'Brien, *Child Abuse: Commission and Omission* (Provo, Ut.: Brigham Young University Press, 1980), p. 5.

34. Flowers, *Female Crime, Criminals and Cellmates*, p. 85.

35. *Ibid.*

36. Flowers, *Children and Criminality*, p. 6.

37. Bernard-Benoit Remacle, *Des Hospices d'Enfants Trouvés en Europe, et Principalement en France, Despuis Leur Origine Jusqú à nos Jours* (Paris: Treuttel et Würtz, 1838), p. 347.

38. Radbill, "A History of Child Abuse and Infanticide," pp. 10–11.

39. *Ibid.*; Flowers, *Children and Criminality*, p. 6.

40. H. D. Jubainville, *La Familie Celtique: Ètude de Droit Comparé* (Paris: Librarie Emile Bouillon, 1905), p. 197.

41. *Ibid.*; A. P. Brome Weigall, *Life and Times of Cleopatra: Queen of Egypt* (New York: Putnam, 1914), pp. 45–46.

42. Theodore Schroeder, "Incest in Mormanism," *American Journal of Urology* 11 (1915): 409–16.

43. Henry Benjamin and R. L. Masters, *Prostitution and Morality* (New York: Julian Press, 1964), p. 161.

44. *Ibid.*, p. 162.

45. Flowers, *Children and Criminality*, p. 7.

46. Reay Tannahill, *Sex in History* (New York: Stein and Day, 1980), p. 370.

47. Flowers, *Children and Criminality*, pp. 8–9.

48. *Ibid.*, p. 9.

49. Robert M. Mulford, "Historical Perspectives," in Nancy B. Ebeling and Deborah A. Hill, eds., *Child Abuse and Neglect* (Boston: P. S. G., Inc., 1983), pp. 1–9.

50. Clifford E. Simonsen and Marshall S. Gordon, III, *Juvenile Justice in America* (Encino, Calif.: Glencoe Publishing Co., 1979), p. 10.

51. Robert L. Geiser, *The Illusion of Caring* (Boston: Beacon Press, 1973), pp. 137–53.

52. Louise de Koven Bowen, *Growing up with a City* (New York: Macmillan, 1926), p. 132.

53. Flowers, *Children and Criminality*, p. 9.

54. Samuel X. Radbill, "The First Treatise on Pediatrics," *American Journal of Diseases of Children* 122 (1971): 376.

55. Radbill, "A History of Child Abuse," pp. 13–14.

56. Flowers, *Children and Criminality*, p. 9.

57. *Ibid.*; J. Caffey, "Multiple Fractures in the Long Bones of Children Suffering from Chronic Subdural Hematoma," *American Journal of Roentgenology, Radium Therapy, Nuclear Medicine* 56 (1946): 163–73.

58. C. Henry Kempe, Frederic N. Silverman, Brandt F. Steele, William Droegemueller, and Henry K. Silver, "The Battered Child Syndrome," *Journal of the American Medical Association* 181 (1962): 17.

59. *Ibid.*

Chapter 2. The Magnitude of Domestic Crimes

1. Flowers, *The Victimization and Exploitation of Women and Children*, pp. 10, 23–24; U.S. Department of Justice, Bureau of Justice Statistics Factbook, *Violence by Intimates* (Washington, D.C.: Government Printing Office, 1998); U.S. Department of Health and Human Services, Children's Bureau, *Child Maltreatment 1996: Reports from the States to the National Child Abuse and Neglect Data System* (Washington, D.C.: Government Printing Office, 1998).

2. Flowers, *The Victimization and Exploitation of Women and Children*, p. 25; U.S. Department of Justice, Bureau of Justice Statistics Special Report, *Family Violence* 3 (Washington, D.C.: Government Printing Office, 1984), pp. 1–4.

3. Family Violence Prevention Fund, San Francisco.

4. Anne L. Ganley, "Understanding Domestic Violence," Family Violence Prevention Fund, San Francisco.

5. Murray A. Straus, Richard J. Gelles, and Suzanne K. Steinmetz, *Behind Closed Doors: Violence in the American Family* (Garden City, N.Y.: Doubleday/Anchor, 1980).

6. Cited in Flowers, *The Victimization and Exploitation of Women and Children*, p. 30.

7. The Commonwealth Fund, "First Comprehensive National Health Survey of American Women Finds Them at Significant Risk," news release, New York, July 14, 1993.

8. Cited in Rosemary Chalk and Patricia A. King, "Facing Up to Family Violence," *Issues in Science and Technology* 15, 2 (1998): 39.

9. George Gallup, Jr., "Many Women Cite Spousal Abuse; Job Performance Affected," *The Gallup Poll Monthly*, October 1997, p. 22.

10. *Ibid.*

11. U.S. Department of Justice, Bureau of Justice Statistics, *Sourcebook of Criminal Justice Statistics 1997* (Washington, D.C.: Government Printing Office, 1998), p. 198.

12. *Ibid.*

13. Robert Langley and Richard C. Levy, *Wife Beating: The Silent Crisis* (New York: E. P. Dutton, 1977).

14. Suzanne K. Steinmetz, "The Battered Husband Syndrome," *Victimology* 2 (1978): 507.

15. Richard J. Gelles, "The Myth of Battered Husbands," *Ms.* (October 1979): 65–66, 71–72.

16. S. Kuehl, "Legal Remedies for Teen Dating Violence," in Barbara Levy, ed., *Dating Violence: Young Women in Danger* (Seattle: Seal Press, 1998), p. 73.

17. L. Rouse, R. Breen, and M. Howell, "Abuse in Intimate Relationships: A Comparison of Married and Dating College Students," *Journal of Interpersonal Violence* 3 (1988): 415.

18. "Final Report of the Supreme Court Task Force on Courts' and Communities' Response to Domestic Abuse," submitted to the Supreme Court of Iowa, August 1994, p. 12.

19. Family Violence Prevention Fund, *Men Beating Women: Ending Domestic Violence, A Qualitative and Quantitative Study of Public Attitudes on Violence Against Women* (New York: EDK Associates, 1993).

20. *Ibid.*

21. U.S. Department of Justice, Bureau of Justice Statistics, *Female Victims of Violent Crime* (Washington, D.C.: Government Printing Office, 1991), p. 5.

22. S. McLeer and R. Anwar, "A Study of Battered Women Presenting in an Emergency Department," *American Journal of Public Health* 79, 1 (1989).

23. A. S. Helton, M. S. McFarlane, and E. T. Anderson, "Battered and Pregnant: A Prevalence Study," *American Journal of Public Health* 77, 10 (1987); A. Helton, J. McFarlane, and E. Anderson, "Prevention of Battering During Pregnancy: Focus on Behavioral Changes," *Public Health Nursing* 4, 3 (1987).

24. U.S. Department of Justice, Federal Bureau of Investigation, *Crime in the United States: Uniform Crime Reports 1988–1991* (Washington, D.C.: Government Printing Office, 1989, 1990, 1991).

25. "First Comprehensive National Health Survey of American Women."

26. *Violence by Intimates*, p. v.

27. *Ibid.*

28. *Ibid.*

29. *Ibid.*, p. 3.

30. *Ibid.*, pp. 3–4.

31. *Ibid.*, p. ix.

32. *Ibid.*

33. *Ibid.*, pp. 13–15; Flowers, *Women and Criminality*, pp. 1-20.

34. *Violence by Intimates*, pp. 19-20.

35. *Ibid.*, p. 20; Flowers, *The Victimization and Exploitation of Women and Children*, pp. 24–25.

36. *Female Victims of Violent Crime*, p. 1.

37. *Ibid.*

38. U.S. Department of Justice, Bureau of Justice Statistics Special Report, *Family Violence* (Washington, D.C.: Government Printing Office, 1984), p. 3.

39. U.S. Department of Justice, Bureau of Justice Statistics, *Criminal Victimization in the United States, 1994: A National Crime Victimization Survey Report* (Washington, D.C.: Government Printing Office, 1997), p. 42.

40. *Ibid.*

41. *Ibid.*, p. 46.

42. The Child Abuse Prevention and Treatment Act, P. L. 100-294 (1974).

43. Cited in Chalk and King, "Facing Up to Family Violence," p. 39.

44. *Child Maltreatment 1996*, p. xi.

45. John M. Leventhal, "The Challenges of Recognizing Child Abuse: Seeing Is Believing," *Journal of the American Medical Association* 281, 7 (1999): 657.

46. Alex Morales, "Seeking a Cure for Child Abuse," *USA Today* 127, 2640 (1998): 34.

47. *Child Maltreatment 1996*, p. xi.

48. *Ibid.*

49. *Ibid.*, p. 2-9.

50. *Violence by Intimates*, p. v.

51. *Child Maltreatment 1996*, p. xi.

52. Cited in Sandra Arbetter, "Family Violence: When We Hurt the Ones We Love," *Current Health* 22, 3 (1995): 6.

53. *Violence by Intimates*, p. 5.

54. *Ibid.*, p. 6.

55. Arthur Kellerman, "Men, Women and Murder," *Journal of Trauma* (July 17, 1992): 1–5.

56. Jacquelyn Campbell, "Prediction of Homicide of and by Battered Women," in J. Campbell and J. Milner, eds., *Assessing Dangerousness: Potential for Further Violence of Sexual Offenders, Batterers, and Child Abusers* (Newbury Park, Calif.: Sage, 1995).

57. *Ibid.*

58. *Violence by Intimates*, p. 7.

59. U.S. Department of Justice, Federal Bureau of Investigation, *Crime in the United States: Uniform Crime Reports 1997* (Washington, D.C.: Government Printing Office, 1998), p. 407.

60. *Violence by Intimates*, p. v.

61. *Uniform Crime Reports 1997*, p. 239.

62. *Ibid.*, p. 232.

63. *Ibid.*, p. 242.

64. *Ibid.*

CHAPTER 3. DEMOGRAPHIC FEATURES OF FAMILY VIOLENCE

1. The Commonwealth Fund, "First Comprehensive National Health Survey of American Women Finds Them at Significant Risk," news release, New York, July 14, 1993.

2. Robert Langley and Richard C. Levy, *Wife Beating: The Silent Crisis* (New York: E. P. Dutton, 1977).

3. Richard J. Gelles, *The Violent Home* (Beverly Hills: Sage, 1972).

4. Cited in R. Barri Flowers, *The Victimization and Exploitation of Women and Children*, p. 30.

5. Richard J. Gelles, "The Myth of Battered Husbands," *Ms.* (October 1979): 65–66, 71–72.

6. U.S. Department of Justice, Bureau of Justice Statistics Factbook, *Violence by Intimates* (Washington, D.C.: Government Printing Office, 1998), p. 3.

7. Gelles, *The Violent Home*, pp. 50–52.

8. M. Bulcroft and M. Straus, "Validity of Husband, Wife, and Child Reports on Conjugal Violence and Power," cited in Lewis Okun, *Woman Abuse: Facts Replacing Myths* (New York: State University of New York Press, 1985), pp. 38, 261.

9. R. Barri Flowers, *Demographics and Criminality: The Characteristics of Crime in America* (Westport, Conn.: Greenwood Press, 1989), p. 154.

10. D. A. Gaquin, "Spouse Abuse: Data from the National Crime Survey," *Victimology* 2 (1977-78): 632–43.

11. Rebecca Emerson Dobash and Russell Dobash, *Violence Against Wives* (New York: Free Press, 1979).

12. Murray A. Straus, Richard J. Gelles, and Suzanne K. Steinmetz, *Behind Closed Doors: Violence in the American Family* (Garden City, N.Y.: Doubleday/Anchor, 1980).

13. Flowers, *Demographics and Criminality*, pp. 154–55; Emily S. Adler, "Perceived Marital Power, Influence Techniques and Marital Violence," in Lee H. Bowker, ed., *Women and Crime in America* (New York: Macmillan, 1981).

14. Suzanne K. Steinmetz, "The Battered Husband Syndrome," *Victimology* 2 (1978): 499–509.

15. Flowers, *Demographics and Criminality*, p. 155.

16. *Violence by Intimates*, p. 16.

17. *Ibid.*, p. 13.

18. Kersti Yllo and Murray A. Straus, "Interpersonal Violence Among Married and Cohabiting Couples," paper presented at the annual meeting of the National Council on Family Relations, Philadelphia, 1978.

19. J. Gayford, "Wife-Battering: A Preliminary Survey of 100 Cases," *British Medical Journal* 1 (1975): 194–97; Bonnie E. Carlson, "Battered Women and Their Assailants," *Social Work* 22, #6 (1977): 456.

20. U.S. Department of Justice, Bureau of Justice Statistics, *Female Victims of Violent Crime* (Washington, D.C.: Government Printing Office, 1991), p. 5.

21. *Ibid.*

22. Jacquelyn Campbell, "Prediction of Homicide of and by Battered Women," in J. Campbell and J. Milner, eds., *Assessing Dangerousness: Potential for Further*

Violence of Sexual Offenders, Batterers, and Child Abusers (Newbury Park, Calif.: Sage, 1995).

23. Straus, Gelles, and Steinmetz, *Behind Closed Doors.*

24. *Ibid.*

25. *Violence by Intimates*, p. 13.

26. G. Levinger, "Sources of Marital Dissatisfaction Among Applicants for Divorce," *American Journal of Orthopsychiatry* 36, 5 (1966): 803–07.

27. Bulcroft and Straus, "Validity of Husband, Wife, and Child Reports."

28. Lenore E. Walker, *The Battered Woman* (New York: Harper & Row, 1979); Terry Davidson, *Conjugal Crime: Understanding and Changing the Wife-Beating Pattern* (New York: Hawthorne, 1979).

29. *Violence by Intimates*, p. 14.

30. Straus, Gelles, and Steinmetz, *Behind Closed Doors.*

31. Gelles, *The Violent Home.*

32. J. E. O'Brien, "Violence in Divorce-Prone Families," *Journal of Marriage and the Family* 33 (1971): 692–98.

33. Straus, Gelles, and Steinmetz, *Behind Closed Doors.*

34. Gelles, *The Violent Home.*

35. Straus, Gelles, and Steinmetz, *Behind Closed Doors.*

36. S. Prescott and C. Letko, "Battered: A Social Psychological Perspective," in Maria Roy, ed., *Battered Women: A Psychosociological Study of Domestic Violence* (New York: Van Nostrand Reinhold, 1977), pp. 72–96.

37. Gelles, *The Violent Home.*

38. Straus, Gelles, and Steinmetz, *Behind Closed Doors.*

39. Carlson, "Battered Women and Their Assailants;" Gelles, *The Violent Home.*

40. *Violence by Intimates*, p. 16.

41. *Ibid.*

42. *Ibid.*

43. D. J. Besharov, "U.S. National Center on Child Abuse and Neglect: Three Years of Experience," *Child Abuse and Neglect: The International Journal* 1 (1977): 173–77.

44. David G. Gil, *Violence Against Children: Physical Child Abuse in the United States* (Cambridge, Mass.: Harvard University Press, 1970).

45. Alex Morales, "Seeking a Cure for Child Abuse," *USA Today* 127, 2640 (1998): 34.

46. U.S. Department of Health and Human Services, Children's Bureau, *Child Maltreatment 1996: Reports from the States to the National Child Abuse and Neglect Data System* (Washington, D.C.: Government Printing Office, 1998), p. xi.

47. John M. Leventhal, "The Challenges of Recognizing Child Abuse: Seeing Is Believing," *Journal of the American Medical Association* 281, #17 (1999): 657.

48. R. Stark and J. McEvoy, "Middle Class Violence," *Psychology Today* 4 (1970): 52–65; H. R. Erlanger, "Social Class and Corporal Punishment: A Reassessment," *American Sociological Review* 39 (1974): 68–85.

49. Flowers, *Demographics and Criminality*, p. 152.

50. Cited in Sandra Arbetter, "Family Violence: When We Hurt the Ones We Love," *Current Health* 22, 3 (1995): 6.

51. *Child Maltreatment 1996*, p. xii.

52. *Ibid.*, p. 2-14.

53. Gelles, *The Violent Home.*

54. Brandt F. Steele and C. Pollock, "A Psychiatric Study of Parents Who Abuse Infants and Small Children," in Ray E. Helfer and C. Henry Kempe, eds., *The Battered Child* (Chicago: University of Chicago Press, 1968), pp. 89–133.

55. Gil, *Violence Against Children*, p. 109.

56. Blair Justice and Rita Justice, *The Abusing Family* (New York: Human Sciences Press, 1976), p. 90.

57. Straus, Gelles, and Steinmetz, *Behind Closed Doors.*

58. Flowers, *Demographics and Criminality*, p. 152; E. M. Thompson, N. W. Paget, D. Mesch, and T. I. Putnam, *Child Abuse: A Community Challenge* (East Aurora, N.Y.: Henry Stewart, 1971).

59. U.S. Department of Health and Human Services, *Study Findings: National Study of the Incidence and Severity of Child Abuse and Neglect* (Washington, D.C.: Government Printing Office, 1981).

60. Morales, "Seeking a Cure for Child Abuse."

61. E. Bennie and A. Sclare, "The Battered Child Syndrome," *American Journal of Psychiatry* 125, 7 (1969): 75–79.

62. Gil, *Violence Against Children.*

63. C. Henry Kempe, "Pediatric Implications of the Battered Baby Syndrome," *Archives of Diseases in Childhood* 46, 245 (1971): 28–37.

64. R. Galdston, "Observations on Children Who Have Been Physically Abused and Their Parents," *American Journal of Psychiatry* 122, 4 (1965): 440–43.

65. P. Resnick, "Child Murder by Parents: A Psychiatric Review of Filicide," *American Journal of Psychiatry* 126, 3 (1969): 325–34.

66. R. J. Gelles, "Violence Toward Children in the United States," *American Journal of Orthopsychiatry* 48, 4 (1978): 580–92.

67. Justice and Justice, *The Abusing Family*, p. 96.

68. Gil, *Violence Against Children*, p. 109.

69. Cited in Flowers, *The Victimization and Exploitation of Women and Children*, p. 16.

70. Straus, Gelles, and Steinmetz, *Behind Closed Doors.*

71. U.S. Department of Health and Human Services, *Child Abuse and Neglect: A Shared Community Concern* (Washington, D.C.: Government Printing Office, 1992), p. 6.

72. *Child Maltreatment 1996*, p. 2-11.

73. Cited in an Associated Press news report, June 26, 1998.

74. *Child Abuse and Neglect*, p. 6. See also Bennie and Sclare, "The Battered Child Syndrome."

75. Gil, *Violence Against Children*, p. 111.

CHAPTER 4. MEDICAL TREATMENT FOR VICTIMS OF FAMILY VIOLENCE

1. U.S. Department of Justice, Bureau of Justice Statistics Special Report, *Violence-Related Injuries Treated in Hospital Emergency Departments* (Washington,

D.C.: Government Printing Office, 1997); U.S. Department of Justice, Bureau of Justice Statistics, Study of Injured Victims of Violence (SIVV), 1994.

2. *Violence-Related Injuries Treated*; U.S. Department of Justice, Bureau of Justice Statistics, *Criminal Victimization in the United States, 1994: A National Crime Victimization Survey Report* (Washington, D.C.: Government Printing Office, 1997), p. 70.

3. H. Meyer, "The Billion Dollar Epidemic," *American Medical News* (January 6, 1992).

4. D. Kurz, "Emergency Department Responses to Battered Women: Resistance to Medication," *Social Problems* 34, 1 (1987); L. K. Hamberger, D. G. Saunders, and M. Hovey, "Prevalence of Domestic Violence in Community Practice and Rate of Physical Injury," *Family Medicine* 24, 4 (1992).

5. U.S. Department of Health and Human Services, *Healthy People 2000: National Health Promotion and Disease Prevention Objectives — Full Report with Commentary* (Washington, D.C.: Public Health Service, 1991).

6. *Violence by Intimates*, p. v.

7. S. McLeer and R. Anwar, "A Study of Battered Women Presenting in an Emergency Department," *American Journal of Public Health* 79, 1 (1989).

8. *Violence by Intimates*, p. v.

9. D. C. Berrios and D. Grady, "Domestic Violence: Risk Factors and Outcome," *Western Journal of Medicine* 15, 2 (1991).

10. *Ibid.*

11. *Violence by Intimates*, p. 22.

12. *Violence-Related Injuries Treated in Hospital Emergency Departments.*

13. *Ibid.*, p. 5; Joyce A. Adams, "Significance of Medical Findings in Suspected Sexual Abuse: Moving Towards Consensus," *Journal of Child Sexual Abuse* 1, 3 (1992): 91–99.

14. *Violence-Related Injuries Treated in Hospital Emergency Departments*, p. 1.

15. *Ibid.*, p. 7.

16. *Violence by Intimates*, p. 22.

17. *Violence-Related Injuries Treated in Hospital Emergency Departments*, p. 4.

18. *Ibid.*, p. 6.

19. *Ibid.*, p. 9.

20. *Ibid.*, p. 5; American Academy of Pediatrics, "Committee on Child Abuse and Neglect: Guidelines for the Evaluation of Sexual Abuse of Children," *Pediatrics* 87, 2 (1991): 254–60.

21. The Commonwealth Fund, "First Comprehensive National Health Survey of American Women Finds Them at Significant Risk," news release, New York, July 14, 1993.

22. Kurz, "Emergency Department Responses to Battered Women."

23. Hamberger, Saunders, and Hovey, "Prevalence of Domestic Violence in Community Practice and Rate of Physical Injury."

24. L. Warshaw, "Limitations of the Medical Model in the Care of Battered Women," *Gender & Society* 3, 4 (1989).

25. See, for example, Suzanne Wolfe, "As America Ages: Look for Signs of Abuse," *RN* 61, 8 (1998): 48.

26. Flowers, *The Victimization and Exploitation of Women and Children*, pp. 32–33.

27. H. A. Holtz and C. Hanes, "Education About Domestic Violence in 25 U.S. and Canadian Medical Schools, 1987–1988," *MMWR* 38, 2 (1989).

28. "Education About Adult Domestic Violence in U.S. and Canadian Medical Schools, 1987–88," *Journal of the American Medical Association* 261, 7 (1989): 972.

29. Katherine C. McKenzie, "Prevalence of Domestic Violence in an Inpatient Female Population," *Journal of the American Medical Association* 280, 5 (1998): 401.

30. "Education About Adult Domestic Violence in U.S. and Canadian Medical Schools."

31. Cited in John M. Leventhal, "The Challenges of Recognizing Child Abuse: Seeing Is Believing," *Journal of the American Medical Association* 281, 7 (1999): 657.

32. *Ibid.*

33. Martha Irvine, Associated Press news report, February 16, 1999.

34. Cited in Leventhal, "The Challenges of Recognizing Child Abuse."

35. Irvine, Associated Press news report.

36. Wolfe, "As America Ages: Look For Signs of Abuse."

CHAPTER 5. DOMESTIC FATALITIES

1. Arthur L. Kellerman, et al., "Gun Ownership as a Risk Factor for Homicide in the Home," *New England Journal of Medicine* 329, 15 (1993), 1084.

2. U.S. Department of Justice, Bureau of Justice Statistics Factbook, *Violence by Intimates* (Washington, D.C.: Government Printing Office, 1998), p. v.

3. U.S. Department of Justice, Federal Bureau of Investigation, *Crime in the United States: Uniform Crime Reports 1997* (Washington, D.C.: Government Printing Office, 1998), p. 21.

4. *Ibid.*, p. 19.

5. Flowers, *Children and Criminality*, p. 58.

6. *Ibid.*; L. Schultz, "The Victim-Offender Relationship," *Crime and Delinquency* 14, 2 (1968): 135–41; M. Houts, *They Asked for Death* (New York: Cowles, 1970), p. 241.

7. Marvin Wolfgang, "Who Kills Whom," *Psychology Today* 3, 5 (1969): 54–56.

8. *Uniform Crime Reports 1997*, p. 19.

9. Arthur Kellerman, "Men, Women and Murder," *Journal of Trauma* (July 17, 1992): 1–5.

10. Jacquelyn Campbell, "Prediction of Homicide of and by Battered Women," in J. Campbell and J. Milner, eds., *Assessing Dangerousness: Potential for Further Violence of Sexual Offenders, Batterers, and Child Abusers* (Newbury Park, Calif.: Sage, 1995).

11. *Ibid.*; *Violence by Intimates*, pp. 5–6.

12. U.S. Department of Justice, Bureau of Justice Statistics, *Female Victims of Violent Crime* (Washington, D.C.: Government Printing Office, 1991), p. 5.

13. *Ibid.*; Linda Saltzman and James Mercy, "Assaults Between Intimates: The Range of Relationships Involved," in Anna Wilson, ed., *Homicide: The Victim/Offender Connection* (Cincinnati, Ohio: Anderson, 1993).

14. *Violence by Intimates*, p. 6.

15. *Ibid.*, p. 7.

16. Vincent J. Fontana, *Somewhere a Child Is Crying* (New York: Macmillan, 1973).

17. "One Child Dies Daily from Abuse: Parent Probably Was Abuser," *Pediatric News* 9 (1975): 3.

18. Pamela D. Mayhall and Katherine Norgard, *Child Abuse and Neglect: Sharing Responsibility* (Toronto: John Wiley and Sons, 1983), p. 98.

19. Sandra Arbetter, "Family Violence: When We Hurt the Ones We Love," *Current Health* 22, 3 (1995): 6.

20. Alex Morales, "Seeking a Cure for Child Abuse," *USA Today* 127, 2640 (1998): 34.

21. Cited in Flowers, *Children and Criminality*, p. 58.

22. U.S. Department of Health and Human Services, Children's Bureau, *Child Maltreatment 1996: Reports from the States to the National Child Abuse and Neglect Data System* (Washington, D.C.: Government Printing Office, 1998), p. xi.

23. D. T. Lunde, "Hot Blood's Record Month: Our Murder Boom," *Psychology Today* 9 (1975): 35–42.

24. Carol Smart, *Women, Crime, and Criminology: A Feminist Critique* (Boston: Routledge & Kegan Paul, 1976), p. 6.

25. Flowers, *Women and Criminality*, p. 110.

26. Lawrence S. Wissow, "Infanticide," *New England Journal of Medicine* 339, 17 (1998): 1239.

27. Cited in *ibid.*

28. *Ibid.*

29. Maria Piers, *Infanticide* (New York: Norton, 1978), p. 14.

30. *Uniform Crime Reports 1997*, p. 21.

31. Flowers, *Children and Criminality*, pp. 58–59; D. Sargeant, "Children Who Kill — A Family Conspiracy?" in J. Howells, ed., *Theory and Practice of Family Psychiatry* (New York: Brunner-Mazel, 1971).

32. L. Bender and F. J. Curran, "Children and Adolescents Who Kill," *Journal of Criminal Psychopathology* 1, 4 (1940): 297.

33. Cited in Glenn Collins, "The Violent Child: Some Patterns Emerge," *New York Times* (September 27, 1982).

34. B. M. Cormier, et al., "Adolescents Who Kill a Member of the Family," in John M. Eekelaar and Sanford N. Katz, eds., *Family Violence: An International and Interdisciplinary Study* (Toronto: Butterworths, 1978), p. 468.

35. C. H. King, "The Ego and the Integration of Violence in Homicidal Youth," *American Journal of Orthopsychiatry* 45 (1975): 134–45.

36. W. M. Easson and R. M. Steinhilber, "Murderous Aggression by Children and Adolescents," *Archives of General Psychiatry* 4 (1961): 1–9.

CHAPTER 6. BATTERED WOMEN

1. Flowers, *Women and Criminality*, p. 13.

2. Mildred Pagelow, *Woman-Battering: Victims and Their Experiences* (Beverly Hills: Sage, 1981), p. 33.

3. Flowers, *Women and Criminality*, p. 14; Murray A. Straus, "Sexual Inequality, Cultural Norms, and Wife-Beating," in Jane R. Chapman and Margaret Gates, eds., *Women into Wives: The Legal and Economic Impact of Marriage* (Beverly Hills: Sage, 1976).

4. Gelles, *The Violent Home*.

5. Quoted in Cheryl Ostrom, "The Battle Scars of Emotional Abuse," *Sacramento Bee* (October 29, 1986), p. B1.

6. *Ibid.*; Lenore E. Walker, *The Battered Woman Syndrome* (New York: Springer, 1984).

7. Walker, *The Battered Woman Syndrome*.

8. Cited in Flowers, *The Victimization and Exploitation of Women and Children*, p. 163.

9. For an example of economic abuse, see "power and control" theory in Chapter 16; as well as "Final Report of the Supreme Court Task Force on Courts' and Communities' Response to Domestic Abuse," submitted to the Supreme Court of Iowa, August 1994, pp. 8–9.

10. Flowers, *Female Crime, Criminals and Cellmates*, p. 93; U.S. Department of Justice, Bureau of Justice Statistics Factbook, *Violence by Intimates* (Washington, D.C.: Government Printing Office, 1998), pp. 1–4.

11. The Commonwealth Fund, "First Comprehensive National Health Survey of American Women Finds Them at Significant Risk," news release, July 14, 1993.

12. Flowers, *The Victimization and Exploitation of Women and Children*, p. 158.

13. H. Douglas, "Assessing Violent Couples," *Families in Society* (November 1991).

14. U.S. Department of Justice, Bureau of Justice Statistics, *Highlights from 20 Years of Surveying Crime Victims: The National Crime Victimization Survey, 1973–92* (Washington, D.C.: Government Printing Office, 1993).

15. S. McLeer and R. Anwar, "A Study of Battered Women Presenting in an Emergency Department," *American Journal of Public Health* 79, 1 (1989).

16. U.S. Department of Justice, Bureau of Justice Statistics, *Sourcebook of Criminal Justice Statistics 1997* (Washington, D.C.: Government Printing Office, 1998), p. 198.

17. Based on data from the U.S. Department of Justice, Federal Bureau of Investigation, *Crime in the United States: Uniform Crime Reports 1988–1991* (Washington, D.C.: Government Printing Office, 1992). However *UCR* data from 1976 to 1996 indicated that intimate murders accounted for approximately 3 in 10 female murders each year in the U.S.

18. *Violence by Intimates*, p. 17.

19. Suzanne K. Steinmetz, *The Cycle of Violence: Assertive, Aggressive, and Abusive Family Interaction* (New York: Praeger, 1977).

20. Lenore E. Walker, "Treatment Alternatives for Battered Women," in Jane R. Chapman and Margaret Gates, eds., *Women into Wives: The Legal and Economic Impact of Marriage* (Beverly Hills: Sage, 1976), p. 144.

21. Lee H. Bowker, *Women, Crime, and the Criminal Justice System* (Lexington, Mass.: Lexington Books, 1978), p. 125.

22. P. D. Scott, "Battered Wives," *British Journal of Psychiatry* 125 (1975): 441.

23. Rebecca Emerson Dobash and Russell Dobash, *Violence Against Wives* (New York: Free Press, 1979), pp. 19–20.

24. Diana E. Russell, *Rape in Marriage* (New York: Macmillan, 1982).

25. *Violence by Intimates*, p. 3.

26. Flowers, *Women and Criminality*, p. 16.

27. *Ibid.*, pp. 16–17.

28. Flowers, *The Victimization and Exploitation of Women and Children*, p. 159.

29. *Ibid.*; Terry Davidson, *Conjugal Crime: Understanding and Changing the Wife-Beating Pattern* (New York: Hawthorne, 1979).

30. Flowers, *Women and Criminality*, p. 17.

31. Maria Roy, "Four Thousand Partners in Violence: A Trend Analysis," in Maria Roy, ed., *The Abusive Partner: An Analysis of Domestic Battering* (New York: Van Nostrand Reinhold, 1982), pp. 34–35.

32. Lenore E. Walker, *The Battered Woman* (New York: Harper & Row, 1979).

33. Flowers, *The Victimization and Exploitation of Women and Children*, p. 165.

34. Walker, *The Battered Woman*, p. 59.

35. Quoted in Nancy Baker, "Why Women Stay with Men Who Beat Them," *Glamour* (August 1983), p. 366.

36. P. M. Lewinsohn, "The Behavioral Study and Treatment of Depression," in M. Hersen, M. Eisler, and P. M. Miller, eds., *Progress in Behavior Modification* (New York: Academic Press, 1975).

37. E. M. Lewis, "An Experiment Analogue of the Spouse Abuse Cycle." Paper presented at the National Conference for Family Violence Researchers, University of New Hampshire, Durham, July 1981.

38. Kathleen H. Hofeller, *Social, Psychological and Situational Factors in Wife Abuse* (Palo Alto, Calif.: R & E Research Associates, 1982), p. 48.

39. Flowers, *The Victimization and Exploitation of Women and Children*, p. 165; Lewis Okun, *Woman Abuse: Facts Replacing Myths* (New York: State University of New York Press, 1985).

40. Rebecca Bettin, Young Women's Resource Center, testimony at Iowa House of Representatives Public Hearing on Dating Violence, March 31, 1992.

41. *Violence by Intimates*, pp. 1–4.

42. S. Kuehl, "Legal Remedies for Teen Dating Violence," in Barbara Levy, ed., *Dating Violence: Young Women in Danger* (Seattle: Seal Press, 1998), p. 73.

43. L. Rouse, R. Breen, and M. Howell, "Abuse in Intimate Relationships: A Comparison of Married and Dating College Students," *Journal of Interpersonal Violence* 3 (1988): 415.

44. "Final Report of the Supreme Court Task Force," p. 12.

45. D. Sugarman and G. Hotaling, "Dating Violence: A Review of Contextual and Risk Factors," in Barbara Levy, ed., *Dating Violence: Young Women in Danger* (Seattle: Seal Press, 1998).

46. "Final Report of the Supreme Court Task Force," p. 13; Sugarman and Hotaling, "Dating Violence," pp. 116–17.

47. *Ibid.*; M. D. Fields, "Wife Beating: The Hidden Offense," *New York Law Journal* 175, 83 (1976): 1–7.

48. T. Tatara, *Summaries of the Statistical Data on Elder Abuse in Domestic Settings for FY 95 and FY 96* (Washington, D.C.: National Center on Elder Abuse, 1997).

49. K. Pillemer and D. Finkelhor, "The Prevalence of Elder Abuse: A Random Sample Survey," *Gerontologist* 28, 10 (1988): 51.

50. *Ibid.*

51. "Final Report of the Supreme Court Task Force," p. 13.

52. *Ibid.*, p. 11.

53. *Ibid.*

54. *Ibid.*

55. *Ibid.*, p. 15.

56. *Ibid.*, pp. 15, 19.

57. *Ibid.*, p. 15.

58. John Leo, "Things That Go Bump in the Home," *U.S. News & World Report* 120, 19 (May 13, 1996), p. 25.

59. "Final Report of the Supreme Court Task Force," p. 16.

60. *Ibid.*

61. *Ibid.*

62. *Ibid.*; Tani Takagi, "Violence Against Women," *Women of Color and Violence Against Women* (Spring 1991).

63. R. Barri Flowers, *The Prostitution of Women and Girls* (Jefferson, N.C.: McFarland, 1998), p. 103.

64. *Ibid.*; Anastasia Volkonsky, "Legalizing the 'Profession' Would Sanction the Abuse," *Insight on the News* 11 (1995): 20.

65. Flowers, *The Prostitution of Women and Girls*, p. 103.

66. *Ibid.*, pp. 51–52; "Final Report of the Supreme Court Task Force," p. 17.

67. Cited in Beth J. Harpaz, Associated Press news report, January 18, 1999.

68. Quoted in *ibid.*

69. *Ibid.*

70. *Ibid.*

CHAPTER 7. MARITAL RAPE AND SEXUAL FACTORS IN BATTERING

1. Flowers, *Women and Criminality*, p. 28.

2. *Ibid.*; Battelle Law and Justice Study Center Report, *Forcible Rape: An Analysis of Legal Issues* (Washington, D.C.: Government Printing Office, 1977), p. 11.

3. *Forcible Rape: An Analysis of Legal Issues*, p. 34.

4. Flowers, *Women and Criminality*, p. 29.

5. Quoted in Andrea Gross, "A Question of Rape," *Ladies Home Journal* 110, 11 (November 1993), p. 170.

6. *Ibid.*

7. Flowers, *Women and Criminality*, p. 29.

8. Gross, "A Question of Rape."

9. Cited in *ibid.*

10. *Ibid.*

11. U.S. Department of Justice, Bureau of Justice Statistics, *Criminal Victimization in the United States, 1994: A National Crime Victimization Survey Report* (Washington, D.C.: Government Printing Office, 1997), p. 42.

12. "Marital Rape: Drive for Tougher Laws Is Pressed," *New York Times* (May 15, 1987), p. A16.

13. *Ibid.*; Kersti Yllo and David Finkelhor, *License to Rape: Sexual Abuse of Wives* (New York: Free Press, 1985), p. 22.

14. Diana E. Russell, *Rape in Marriage* (New York: Macmillan, 1982).

15. Cited in "Final Report of the Supreme Court Task Force on Courts' and Communities' Response to Domestic Abuse," submitted to the State Supreme Court of Iowa, August 1994, p. 10.

16. *Ibid.*; Evan Stark and Anne Flitcraft, *Surgeon General's Workshop on Violence and Public Health Source Book*, presented at the Surgeon General's Workshop on Violence and Public Health, Leesburg, Va., October 1985, p. 16.

17. Russell, *Rape in Marriage.*

18. Lenore E. Walker, *The Battered Woman Syndrome* (New York: Springer, 1984), pp. 48–49.

19. Quoted in Gross, "A Question of Rape."

20. Kersti Yllo, *Types of Marital Rape: Three Case Studies*, presented at the National Conference for Family Violence Researchers, University of New Hampshire, Durham, July 1981.

21. Quoted in "Marital Rape," p. A16.

22. Gross, "A Question of Rape."

23. A Nicholas Groth, Ann W. Burgess, and Lynda L. Holmstrom, "Rape: Power, Anger, and Sexuality," *American Journal of Psychiatry* 34 (1977): 1239–43.

24. Paul H. Gebhard, John H. Gagnon, Wardell B. Pomeroy, and Cornelia V. Christenson, *Sex Offenders: An Analysis of Types* (New York: Harper & Row, 1965), pp. 198–204; Richard T. Rada, *Clinical Aspects of the Rapist* (New York: Grune and Stratton, 1978), pp. 122–30.

25. Flowers, *The Victimization and Exploitation of Women and Children*, p. 153.

26. Julia R. Schwendinger and Herman Schwendinger, *Rape and Inequality* (Beverly Hills: Sage, 1983), p. 65.

27. Flowers, *The Victimization and Exploitation of Women and Children*, p. 153.

28. Menachem Amir, *Patterns in Forcible Rape* (Chicago: University of Chicago Press, 1971), p. 261.

29. Flowers, *The Victimization and Exploitation of Women and Children*, p. 153; Schwendinger and Schwendinger, *Rape and Inequality*, p. 71.

30. Flowers, *The Victimization and Exploitation of Women and Children*, p. 153.

31. Lorenne M. Clark and Debra J. Lewis, *Rape: The Price of Coercive Sexuality* (Toronto: Canadian Women's Educational Press, 1977), pp. 128–31.

32. Cited in "The Date Who Rapes," *Newsweek* (April 9, 1984), p. 91.

33. Cited in Ellen Sweet, "Date Rape," *Ms./Campus Times* (October 1985), p. 58.

34. Barbara Levy, ed., *Dating Violence: Young Women in Danger* (Seattle: Seal Press, 1998).

35. S. Kuehl, "Legal Remedies for Teen Dating Violence," in Barbara Levy, ed., *Dating Violence: Young Women in Danger* (Seattle: Seal Press, 1998), p. 73.

36. Rebecca Bettin, Young Woman's Resource Center, testimony at Iowa House of Representatives Public Hearing on Dating Violence, March 31, 1992.

37. R. Barri Flowers, *Drugs, Alcohol and Criminality in American Society* (Jefferson, N.C.: McFarland, 1999), p. 150.

38. Flowers, *The Victimization and Exploitation of Women and Children*, pp. 150–51.

39. Quoted in "Final Report of the Supreme Court Task Force," p. 10.

40. A. S. Helton, M. S. McFarlane, and E. T. Anderson, "Battered and Pregnant: A Prevalence Study," *American Journal of Public Health* 77, 10 (1987).

41. J. McFarlane, B. Parker, K. Soeken, and L. Bullock, "Assessing for Abuse During Pregnancy: Severity and Frequency of Injuries and Associated Entry into Prenatal Care," *Journal of American Medical Association* 267, 23 (1992); A. Helton, J. McFarlane, and E. Anderson, "Prevention of Battering During Pregnancy: Focus on Behavioral Change," *Public Health Nursing* 4, 3 (1987).

42. Cited in "Final Report of the Supreme Court Task Force," pp. 17–18.

43. *Ibid.*, p. 17.

44. *Ibid.*

45. Cited in Cynthia Gillespie, *Justifiable Homicide: Battered Women, Self-Defense, and the Law* (Columbus, Ohio: Ohio State University Press, 1989), p. 52.

46. Walker, *The Battered Woman Syndrome*, p. 51.

47. Richard J. Gelles, "Violence and Pregnancy: A Note on the Extent of the Problem and Needed Services," *Family Coordinator* 24 (1975): 81–86.

48. "Final Report of the Supreme Court Task Force," p. 18.

49. *Ibid.*, pp. 17–18; Flowers, *The Victimization and Exploitation of Women and Children*, p. 161.

50. "Final Report of the Supreme Court Task Force," pp. 18–19.

51. Susan S. Glander, "The Prevalence of Domestic Violence Among Women Seeking Abortion," *Journal of the American Medical Association* 280, 5 (1998): 401.

52. Flowers, *Women and Criminality*, p. 19; E. Hilberman and L. Munson, "Sixty Battered Women," *Victimology* 2, 3-4 (1978): 460–71.

53. Maria Roy, "Four Thousand Partners in Violence: A Trend Analysis," in Maria Roy, ed., *The Abusive Partner: An Analysis of Domestic Battering* (New York: Van Nostrand Reinhold, 1982), p. 32.

54. Flowers, *Women and Criminality*, pp. 19–20.

55. Walker, *The Battered Woman Syndrome*, p. 55.

CHAPTER 8. BATTERED MEN

1. Robert Langley and Richard C. Levy, *Wife Beating: The Silent Crisis* (New York: E. P. Dutton, 1977).

2. Suzanne K. Steinmetz, "The Battered Husband Syndrome," *Victimology* 2 (1978): 507.

3. M. Fields and R. Kirchner, "Battered Women Are Still in Need: A Reply to Steinmetz," *Victimology* 3, 1-2 (1978): 216–26; Steinmetz reply, pp. 222–24.

4. Richard J. Gelles, "The Myth of Battered Husbands," *Ms.* (October 1979), pp. 65–66, 71–72.

5. Cited in Flowers, *Female Crime, Criminals and Cellmates*, p. 93.

6. Richard J. Gelles, *The Violent Home* (Beverly Hills: Sage, 1985), pp. 50–52.

7. M. Bulcroft and M. Straus, "Validity of Husband, Wife, and Child Reports of Conjugal Violence and Power," cited in Lewis Okun, *Woman Abuse: Facts Replacing Myths* (New York: State University of New York Press, 1985), pp. 38, 261.

8. G. Levinger, "Sources of Marital Dissatisfaction Among Applicants for Divorce," *American Journal of Orthopsychiatry* 36, 5 (1966): 803–07.

9. U.S. Department of Justice, Bureau of Justice Statistics Factbook, *Violence by Intimates* (Washington, D.C.: Government Printing Office, 1998), pp. 3–4.

10. *Ibid.*

11. John Leo, "Things That Go Bump in the Home," *U.S. News & World Report* 120, 19 (May 13, 1996), p. 25.

12. *Ibid.*; Flowers, *Female Crime, Criminals and Cellmates*, p. 93.

13. Leo, "Things That Go Bump in the Home"; Gelles, "The Myth of Battered Husbands," pp. 65–66, 71–72.

14. Cited in Leo, "Things That Go Bump in the Home."

15. *Violence by Intimates*, pp. 5–10; Arthur Kellerman, "Men, Women and Murder," *Journal of Trauma* (July 17, 1992): 1–5.

16. *Violence by Intimates*, pp. 5–6; Flowers, *Female Crime, Criminals and Cellmates*, p. 87.

17. *Violence by Intimates*, pp. 5–10; U.S. Department of Justice, Federal Bureau of Investigation, *Crime in the United States: Uniform Crime Reports 1997* (Washington, D.C.: Government Printing Office, 1998), p. 21.

18. *Violence by Intimates*, p. 6; *Uniform Crime Reports 1997*, pp. 19, 21.

19. G. Rasko, "The Victim of the Female Killer," *Victimology* 1 (1976): 396–402.

20. J. Totman, *The Murderess: A Psychosocial Study of the Process* (Ann Arbor: University Microfilms, 1971).

21. Cited in Sandy Nelson, "Women Who Kill," *Sacramento Bee* (December 30, 1986), p. B1.

22. D. Ward, M. Jackson, and R. Ward, "Crimes of Violence by Women," in D. Mulvill, M. M. Tumin, and L. A. Curtis, ed., *Crimes of Violence* (Washington, D.C.: Government Printing Office, 1969).

23. Quoted in Nick Jordan, "Till Murder Us Do Part," *Psychology Today* 19 (July 1985): 7.

24. Flowers, *Female Crime, Criminals and Cellmates*, pp. 84–88.

25. Cited in Jordan, "Till Murder Us Do Part."

26. *Ibid.*

27. Elissa P. Benedek, "Women and Homicide," in Bruce L. Danto, John Bruhns, and Austin H. Kutscher, eds., *The Human Side of Homicide* (New York: Columbia University Press, 1982), p. 155.

28. Flowers, *Women and Criminality*, p. 109.

29. Lenore E. Walker, *The Battered Woman Syndrome* (New York: Springer, 1984), p. 40.

30. Flowers, *Female Crime, Criminals and Cellmates*, pp. 93–94.

Chapter 9. Elderly Abuse

1. U.S. Department of Justice, Bureau of Justice Statistics, National Crime Victimization Survey, *Elderly Crime Victims* (Washington, D.C.: Government Printing Office, 1994), p. 1.

2. *Ibid.*

3. *Ibid.*, p. 2.

4. *Ibid.*

5. *Ibid.*

6. *Ibid.*

7. *Ibid.*

8. *Ibid.*

9. *Ibid.*, p. 3.

10. Herbert C. Covey and Scott Menard, "Trends in Elderly Criminal Victimization from 1973 to 1984," *Research on Aging* 10 (1988): 329–41.

11. Peter Yin, *Victimization and the Aged* (Springfield, Ill.: Charles C Thomas, 1985).

12. Barry D. Lebowitz, "Age and Fearfulness: Personal and Situational Factors," *Journal of Gerontology* 30 (1975): 696–700.

13. C. J. Wiltz, "Fear of Crime, Criminal Victimization and Elderly Blacks," *Phylon* 43 (1982): 283–94.

14. Mary L. Hummert, "Age and Typical Judgments of Stereotypes of the Elderly: Perceptions of Elderly vs. Young Adults," *International Journal of Aging and Human Development* 37 (1993): 217–26.

15. Jane C. Ollenberger, "Criminal Victimization and Fear of Crime," *Research on Aging* 29 (1981): 317–27.

16. John H. Linquist and Janice M. Duke, "The Elderly Victim at Risk," *Criminology* 20 (1982): 115–26.

17. James A. Fox and Jack Levin, "Homicides Against the Elderly: A Research Note," *Criminology* 29 (1991): 317–27; Ronald L. Akers, Anthony J. LaGrecca, Christine Sellers, and John Cochran, "Fear of Crime and Victimization Among the Elderly in Different Types of Communities," *Criminology* 25 (1987): 487–505.

18. Kimberly A. McCabe and Sharon S. Gregory, "Elderly Victimization: An Examination Beyond the FBI's Index Crimes," *Research on Aging* 20, 3 (1998): 363.

19. Jaber Gubrium, "Victimization in Old Age: Available Evidence and Three Hypotheses," *Crime & Delinquency* 20 (1974): 245–50.

20. McCabe and Gregory, "Elderly Victimization."

21. Wiltz, "Fear of Crime, Criminal Victimization and Elderly Blacks," pp. 283–94.

22. McCabe and Gregory, "Elderly Victimization," p. 363.

23. Susan Wolfe, "As America Ages: Look for Signs of Abuse," *RN* 61, 8 (1998): 48.

24. Cited in Sandra Arbetter, "Family Violence: When We Hurt the Ones We Love," *Current Health* 22, 3 (1995): 6.

25. *Ibid.*; Wolfe, "As America Ages," p. 48.

26. K. Pillemer and D. Finkelhor, "The Prevalence of Elder Abuse: A Random Sample Survey," *Gerontologist* 28, 10 (1988): 51.

27. T. Tatara, *Summaries of the Statistical Data on Elder Abuse in Domestic Settings for FY 95 and FY 96* (Washington, D.C.: National Center on Elder Abuse, 1997).

28. Pillemer and Finkelhor, "The Prevalence of Elder Abuse," p. 51.

29. Cited in Paul Chance, "Attacking Elderly Abuse," *Psychology Today* 21 (September 1987), p. 24.

30. Tatara, *Summaries of the Statistical Data on Elderly Abuse*; Flowers, *The Victimization and Exploitation of Women and Children*, p. 33.

31. McCabe and Gregory, "Elderly Victimization."

32. Marjorie Valbrun, "Problem of Abuse of Elderly by the Elderly Grows as Longevity Increases," *Knight-Ridder/Tribune News Service* (February 9, 1994).

33. *Ibid.*

34. *Ibid.*

35. *Ibid.*

36. T. Lay, "The Flourishing Problem of Elder Abuse in Our Society," *AACN Clinical Issues* 5, 4 (1994): 507.

37. *Ibid.*; M. S. Lachs and K. Pillemer, "Abuse and Neglect of Elderly Persons," *New England Journal of Medicine* 332 (1995): 437.

38. Arbetter, "Family Violence," p. 6.

39. *Ibid.*

40. *Ibid.*; J. I. Kosberg and D. Nahmiash, "Characteristics of Victims and Perpetrators and Milieus of Abuse and Neglect," in L. A. Baumhover and S. C. Beall, eds., *Abuse, Neglect, and Exploitation of Older Persons* (Baltimore, Md.: Health Professions Press, 1996), p. 5164.

41. Flowers, *The Victimization and Exploitation of Women and Children*, p. 33; Arbetter, "Family Violence."

42. Lachs and Pillemer, "Abuse and Neglect of Elderly Persons," p. 437.

43. Flowers, *Children and Criminality*, p. 51.

44. Chance, "Attacking Elderly Abuse," p. 24.

CHAPTER 10. CHILD ABUSE AND NEGLECT

1. David G. Gil, *Violence Against Children: Physical Child Abuse in the United States* (Cambridge, Mass.: Harvard University Press, 1970).

2. Flowers, *Children and Criminality*, p. 58.

3. U.S. Department of Health and Human Services, Children's Bureau, *Child Maltreatment 1996: Reports from the States to the National Child Abuse and Neglect Data System* (Washington, D.C.: Government Printing Office, 1998), p. xi.

4. C. Henry Kempe, Frederic N. Silverman, Brandt F. Steele, William Droegemueller, and Henry K. Silver, "The Battered Child Syndrome," *Journal of the American Medical Association* 181 (1962): 17–24.

5. Vincent J. Fontana, *The Maltreated Child: The Maltreatment Syndrome in Children*, 2nd ed. (Springfield, Ill.: Charles C Thomas, 1971).

6. Cited in Alfred Kadushin and Judith A. Martin, *Child Abuse: An Interactional Event* (New York: Columbia University Press, 1981), p. 6.

7. Quoted in L. Whiting, "Defining Emotional Neglect," *Children Today* 5 (1976): 2–5.

8. David A. Mrazek and Patricia Mrazek, "Psychosexual Development Within the Family," in Patricia Mrazek and C. Henry Kempe, eds., *Sexually Abused Children and Their Families* (New York: Pergamon Press, 1981), pp. 17–30.

9. K. T. Alvy, "On Child Abuse: Values and Analytic Approaches," *Journal of Clinical Child Psychology* 4 (1975): 36–37.

10. Flowers, *The Victimization and Exploitation of Women and Children*, p. 6; Public Law 98-457.

11. National Association of Public Child Welfare Administrators, *Guidelines for the Development of a Model System of Protective Services for Abused and Neglected Children and Their Families* (Washington, D.C.: American Public Welfare Association, 1987), p. 5.

12. Gertrude J. Williams, "Child Abuse and Neglect: Problems of Definition and Incidence," in Gertrude J. Williams and John Money, eds., *Traumatic Abuse and Neglect of Children at Home* (Baltimore, Md.: Johns Hopkins University Press, 1980), p. 2.

13. Cited in John M. Leventhal, "The Challenges of Recognizing Child Abuse: Seeing Is Believing," *Journal of the American Medical Association* 281, 7 (1999): 657.

14. *Child Maltreatment 1996*, p. xi.

15. *Ibid.*

16. *Ibid.*

17. Flowers, *The Victimization and Exploitation of Women and Children*, p. 10.

18. F. J. Bishop, "Children at Risk," *Medical Journal of Australia* 1 (1971): 623.

19. Richard J. Gelles, "Violence Towards Children in the United States," *American Journal of Orthopsychiatry* 48, 4 (1978): 580–92.

20. Brandt F. Steele and C. Pollock, "A Psychiatric Study of Parents Who Abuse Infants and Small Children," in Ray E. Helfer and C. Henry Kempe, eds., *The Battered Child* (Chicago: University of Chicago Press, 1968), p. 128.

21. Gil, *Violence Against Children*, p. 110.

22. R. J. Light, "Abused and Neglected Children in America: A Study of Alternative Politics," *Harvard Educational Review* 143 (1973): 574.

23. Ray E. Helfer, *The Diagnostic Process and Treatment Programs* (Washington, D.C.: Office of Child Development, 1975).

24. Blair Justice and Rita Justice, *The Abusing Family* (New York: Human Sciences Press, 1976), p. 27.

25. *Ibid.*

26. J. Milowe and R. Lourie, "The Child's Role in the Battered Child Syndrome," *Journal of Pediatrics* 65 (1964): 1079–81.

27. William N. Friedrick and Jerry A. Boriskin, "The Role of the Child in Abuse: A Review of the Literature," in Gertrude J. Williams and John Money, eds., *Traumatic Abuse and Neglect of Children at Home* (Baltimore, Md.: Johns Hopkins University Press, 1980), p. 194.

28. Flowers, *Children and Criminality*, p. 65.

29. James Garbarino and Deborah Sherman, "High-Risk Neighborhoods and High-Risk Families: The Human Ecology of Child Maltreatment," *Child Development* 51 (1980): 188–98.

30. Flowers, *Children and Criminality*, p. 65.

31. *Ibid.*; Michael J. Martin and James Walters, "Familial Correlates of Selected Types of Child Abuse and Neglect," *Journal of Marriage and the Family* 5 (1982): 267–76.

32. Theo Solomon, "History and Demography of Child Abuse," *Pediatrics* 51, 4 (1973): 773–76.

33. Cited in Flowers, *Children and Criminality*, pp. 72, 74.

34. *Ibid.*, pp. 97–98.

35. *Ibid.*

36. Pamela D. Mayhall and Katherine Norgard, *Child Abuse and Neglect: Sharing Responsibility* (Toronto: John Wiley and Sons, 1983), pp. 103–07.

37. A. J. Ebbin, et al., "Battered Child Syndrome at the Los Angeles County General Hospital," *American Journal of Diseases in Children* 118 (1969): 660–67.

38. Flowers, *Children and Criminality*, pp. 97–98.

39. *Ibid.*, p. 98; H. P. Martin and P. Beezley, "Behavioral Observations of Abused Children," *Developmental Medicine and Child Neurology* 19 (1977): 373–87.

40. Flowers, *Children and Criminality*, p. 98; A. H. Green, "Psychopathology of Abused Children," *Journal of the American Academy of Child Psychiatry* (1978): 92–103.

41. J. Roberts, M. M. Lynch, and P. Duff, "Abused Children and Their Siblings: A Teacher's View," *Therapeutic Education* 6 (1978): 25–31.

42. Ann Buchanan and J. E. Oliver, "Abuse and Neglect as a Cause of Mental Retardation: A Study of 140 Children Admitted to Subnormality Hospitals in Wiltshire," in Gertrude J. Williams and John Money, eds., *Traumatic Abuse and Neglect of Children at Home* (Baltimore, Md.: Johns Hopkins University Press, 1980), pp. 311–12.

43. H. P. Martin, et al., "The Development of Abused Children: I. A Review of the Literature, II. Physical, Neurological and Intellectual Outcomes," *Advances in Pediatrics* 21 (1974): 25–73.

44. C. W. Morse, O. Z. Sahler, and S. F. Friedman, "A Three-Year Study of Abused and Neglected Children," *American Journal of Diseases in Childhood* 120 (1970): 439–46.

45. C. H. Kempe, et al., "The Battered Child Syndrome," pp. 17–24.

46. E. Elmer, *Children in Jeopardy* (Pittsburgh: University of Pittsburgh Press, 1967); R. G. Birrell and J. W. Birrell, "The Maltreatment Syndrome in Chicago: A Hospital Survey," *Medical Journal of Australia* 2 (1968): 1023–29.

47. Flowers, *Children and Criminality*, p. 99.

48. H. P. Martin, "The Child and His Development," in C. Henry Kempe and Ray E. Helfer, eds., *Helping the Battered Child and His Family* (Philadelphia: J. B. Lippincott, 1972).

49. Elmer, *Children in Jeopardy*.

50. Flowers, *Children and Criminality*, p. 99.

51. *Ibid.*

52. Sandra Arbetter, "Family Violence: When We Hurt the Ones We Love," *Current Health* 22, 3 (1995): 6.

53. Deborah Blum, "Attention Deficit: Physical and Sexual Child Abuse Grab All the Headlines. But What You May Not Realize Is That Neglect Can Be the Worst," *Mother Jones* 24 (1999): 58.

54. Arbetter, "Family Violence: When We Hurt the Ones We Love."

55. Flowers, *Children and Criminality*, p. 97.

56. Blum, "Attention Deficit: Physical and Sexual Child Abuse."

57. *Ibid.*

58. *Ibid.*

59. Quoted in *ibid.*

60. Flowers, *Children and Criminality*, pp. 86–87.

61. Sally Abrahams, "Parental Kidnapping Is the Agony of the '80s," *USA Today* (July 16, 1983), p. 4D.

62. Cited in *ibid.*

63. Flowers, *The Victimization and Exploitation of Women and Children*, p. 46.

64. *Ibid.*, p. 47.

65. *Ibid.*

66. *Child Maltreatment 1996.*

67. John K. Miller, "Perspectives on Child Maltreatment in the Military," in Ray E. Helfer and C. Henry Kempe, eds., *Child Abuse and Neglect: The Family and the Community* (Cambridge, Mass.: Ballinger, 1976), pp. 267–91.

68. Flowers, *Children and Criminality*, p. 92.

69. John K. Miller, "The Maltreatment Syndrome in the Military Community," presented to the Current Trends in Army Social Work Conference, William Beaumont Army Medical Center in El Paso, Texas, August 1972.

70. Miller, "Perspectives on Child Maltreatment," p. 279; J. D. Delsordo, "Protective Casework for Abused Children," *Children* 10 (1963): 11–12.

CHAPTER 11. CHILD SEXUAL ABUSES

1. Flowers, *Children and Criminality*, p. 75; Gerald M. Caplan, "Sexual Exploitation of Children: The Conspiracy of Silence," *Police Magazine* 5, 1 (1982): 46–51; David Finkelhor, *Sexually Victimized Children* (New York: Free Press, 1979).

2. Flowers, *The Victimization and Exploitation of Women and Children*, p. 53. See also Leroy C. Schultz, "The Child as a Sex Victim: Socio-Legal Perspectives," in Israel Drapkin and Emilo Viano, eds., *Victimology: A New Focus*, Vol. 5 (Toronto: D. C. Heath, 1975), p. 178.

3. Flowers, *The Victimization and Exploitation of Women and Children*, p. 53.

4. Flowers, *Children and Criminality*, p. 75.

5. Child Abuse Prevention and Treatment Act, Public Law 100–294.

6. *Child Abuse and Neglect Reporting and Investigation: Policy Guidelines for Decision-Making* (Denver: American Humane Association, 1987), p. 7.

7. *Ibid.*; Flowers, *The Victimization and Exploitation of Women and Children*, p. 55.

8. Flowers, *The Victimization and Exploitation of Women and Children*, p. 55.

9. *Protecting the Child Victim of Sex Crimes* (Denver: American Humane Association, 1966), p. 2.

10. *Child Victims of Incest* (Denver: American Humane Association, 1968), p. 5.

11. *Sexual Abuse of Children: Implications for Casework* (Denver: American Humane Association, 1967), p. 10.

12. Schultz, "The Child As a Sex Victim," p. 172.

13. Karen McCurdy and Deborah Daro, *Current Trends in Child Abuse Reporting and Fatalities: The Results of the 1992 Annual Fifty State Survey* (Chicago: National Committee for Prevention of Child Abuse, 1993), p. 10.

14. U.S. Department of Health and Human Services, *National Child Abuse and Neglect Data System: Working Paper 2 — 1991 Summary Data Component* (Washington, D.C.: National Center on Child Abuse and Neglect, 1984).

15. Cited in John M. Leventhal, "The Challenges of Recognizing Child Abuse: Seeing Is Believing," *Journal of the American Medical Association* 281, 7 (1999): 657.

16. David Finkelhor, "How Widespread Is Child Abuse?" in *Perspectives on Child Maltreatment in the Mid '80s* (Washington, D.C.: National Center on Child Abuse and Neglect Information, 1984).

17. Flowers, *The Victimization and Exploitation of Women and Children*, p. 56.

18. *Ibid.*

19. *Ibid.*; *American Association for Protecting Children, Highlights of Official Child Abuse and Neglect Reporting 1984* (Denver: American Humane Association, 1985).

20. Cited in Flowers, *The Victimization and Exploitation of Women and Children*, p. 57.

21. Peggy Smith and Marvin Bohnstedt, *Child Victimization Study Highlights* (Sacramento: Social Research Center of the American Justice Institute, 1981), p. 2.

22. Flowers, *The Victimization and Exploitation of Women and Children*, p. 57; Flowers, *Children and Criminality*, pp. 69, 75.

23. See, for example, Phil M. Coons, "Psychiatric Problems Associated with Child Abuse: A Review," in J. J. Jacobsen, *Psychiatric Sequelae of Child Abuse* (Springfield, Ill.: Charles C Thomas, 1986); Diana E. Russell, *Intrafamilial Child Sexual Abuse: A San Francisco Survey* (Berkeley, Calif.: Wright Institute, 1983).

24. U.S. Department of Health and Human Services, *Research Symposium on Child Sexual Abuse* (Washington, D.C.: National Center on Child Abuse and Neglect, 1988), pp. 3–4.

25. *Ibid.*, p. 4. *See also* B. G. Braun, "The Transgenerational Incidence of Disassociation and Multiple Personality Disorder: A Preliminary Report," in R. P. Kluft, ed., *Childhood Antecedents of Multiple Personalities* (Washington, D.C.: American Psychiatric Press, 1985).

26. U.S. Department of Health and Human Services, Children's Bureau, *Child Maltreatment 1996: Reports from the States to the National Child Abuse and Neglect Data System* (Washington, D.C.: Government Printing Office, 1998).

27. Flowers, *The Victimization and Exploitation of Women and Children*, p. 58; P. H. Gebhard, J. H. Gagnon, W. B. Pomery, and C. V. Christenson, *Sex Offenders* (New York: Harper & Row, 1965).

28. Flowers, *The Victimization and Exploitation of Women and Children*, p. 58; D. Abrahamsen, *The Psychology of Crime* (New York: Columbia University Press, 1960); B. Karpman, *The Sex Offender and His Offenses* (New York: Julian Press, 1962).

29. Flowers, *The Victimization and Exploitation of Women and Children*, p. 58.

30. B. G. Braun, "The Role of the Family in the Development of Multiple Personality," *International Journal of Family Psychiatry* 5, 4 (1984): 303–13.

31. Flowers, *Children and Criminality*, pp. 76–83.

32. David Finkelhor, Sharon Araji, Larry Baron, Angela Browne, Stephanie Peters, and Gail Wyatt, *A Sourcebook on Child Sexual Abuse* (Beverly Hills: Sage, 1986), p. 201.

33. John E. Henderson, Diana J. English, and Ward R. MacKenzie, "Family Centered Casework Practice with Sexually Aggressive Children," *Journal of Social Work and Human Sexuality* 7, 2 (1988).

34. The National Adolescent Predator Network, "Preliminary Report from the National Task Force on Juvenile Sexual Offending 1988," *Juvenile & Family Court Journal* 39, 2 (1988): 5.

35. Flowers, *Children and Criminality*, p. 96.

36. *Ibid.*; p. 97; Judianne Densen-Gerber and S. F. Hutchinson, "Medical-Legal and Societal Problems Involving Children — Child Prostitution, Child Pornography and Drug-Related Abuse: Recommended Legislation," in Selwyn M. Smith, ed., *The Maltreatment of Children* (Baltimore, Md.: University Park Press, 1978), p. 322.

37. Flowers, *The Victimization and Exploitation of Women and Children*, p. 59.

38. *Ibid.*

39. *Ibid.*; Jeanne Cyriaque, "The Chronic Serious Offender: How Illinois Juveniles 'Match Up,'" Illinois Department of Corrections, *Illinois* (February 1982): pp. 4–5; Flowers, *The Prostitution of Women and Girls*, pp. 83, 119.

CHAPTER 12. INCEST AND OTHER CHILD SEXUAL VICTIMIZATION

1. Flowers, *The Victimization and Exploitation of Women and Children*, p. 60.

2. Patricia Mrazek, "Definition and Recognition of Child Sexual Abuse: Historical and Cultural Perspectives," in Patricia Mrazek and C. Henry Kempe, eds., *Sexually Abused Children and Their Families* (New York: Pergamon Press, 1981), p. 7.

3. Flowers, *The Victimization and Exploitation of Women and Children*, p. 61.

4. *Ibid.*

5. Flowers, *Female Crime, Criminals and Cellmates*, p. 97.

6. Flowers, *The Victimization and Exploitation of Women and Children*, p. 62; S. Kirson Weinberg, *Incest Behavior* (New York: Citadel Press, 1955); Flowers, *Children and Criminality*, p. 79.

7. Cited in Carol L. Mithers, "Incest: The Crime That's All in the Family," *Mademoiselle* 96 (June 1984), p. 18.

8. Heidi Vanderbilt, "Incest: A Chilling Report," *Lear's* (February 1992), p. 52.

9. Cited in Kathy McCoy, "Incest: The Most Painful Family Problem," *Seventeen* 43 (June 1984), p. 18.

10. Cited in Anita Manning, "Victims Must Face the Hurt," *USA Today* (January 10, 1984), p. 5D.

11. Judy Howard, "Incest Victims Speak Out," *Teen* (July 1985), p. 30.

12. Cited in Jean Renvoize, *Incest: A Family Pattern* (London: Routledge & Kegan Paul, 1982), p. 51.

13. Marshall D. Schechter and Leo Roberge, "Sexual Exploitation," in Ray E. Helfer and C. Henry Kempe, eds., *Child Abuse and Neglect: The Family and the Community* (Cambridge, Mass.: Ballinger, 1976), p. 129.

14. Cited in Howard, "Incest Victims Speak Out," p. 31.

15. Flowers, *The Victimization and Exploitation of Women and Children*, p. 62.

16. *Ibid.*; Howard, "Incest Victims Speak Out," p. 31.

17. Flowers, *Women and Criminality*, p. 61.

18. H. Stoenner, *Child Sexual Abuse Seen Growing in the United States* (Denver: American Humane Association, 1972).

19. Weinberg, *Incest Behavior*, pp. 34–40.

20. Quoted in Howard, "Incest: Victims Speak Out," p. 31. See also Susan Forward and C. Buck, *Betrayal of Innocence: Incest and Its Devastation* (Los Angeles: J. P. Tarcher, 1978).

21. Flowers, *Children and Criminality*, p. 79.

22. *Ibid.*; Flowers, *The Victimization and Exploitation of Women and Children*, p. 63.

23. Adele Mayer, *Incest: A Treatment Manual for Therapy with Victims, Spouses, and Offenders* (Holmes Beach, Fla.: Learning Publications, 1983), p. 22.

24. Flowers, *Children and Criminality*, p. 79; Flowers, *The Victimization and Exploitation of Women and Children*, pp. 62–63.

25. Flowers, *The Victimization and Exploitation of Women and Children*, p. 63.

26. Cited in Vanderbilt, "Incest: A Chilling Report," pp. 60–62.

27. *Ibid.*

28. *Ibid.*

29. Herbert L. Packer, *The Limits of the Criminal Sanction* (Stanford, Calif.: Stanford University Press, 1968), pp. 296–316.

30. Flowers, *The Victimization and Exploitation of Women and Children*, p. 64.

31. *Ibid.*, p. 66.

32. See, for instance, P. Machotka, F. S. Pittman, and K. Flomenhaft, "Incest as a Family Matter," *Family Process* 6 (1967): 98.

33. Flowers, *The Victimization and Exploitation of Women and Children*, p. 66.

34. Flowers, *Female Crime, Criminals and Cellmates*, p. 97.

35. Cited in Vanderbilt, "Incest: A Chilling Report," p. 62.

36. Flowers, *The Victimization and Exploitation of Women and Children*, p. 65.

37. *Ibid.*

38. *Ibid.*, pp. 64–65.

39. Flowers, *Female Crime, Criminals and Cellmates*, p. 98.

40. *Ibid.*

41. *Ibid.*, p. 99.

42. *Ibid.*; Vanderbilt, "Incest: A Chilling Report," p. 63.

43. Quoted in Vanderbilt, "Incest: A Chilling Report," p. 62.

44. *Ibid.*

45. *Ibid.*, p. 63.

46. Flowers, *The Victimization and Exploitation of Women and Children*, p. 65.

47. R. Medlicott, "Parent-Child Incest," *Australian Journal of Psychiatry* 1 (1967): 180.

48. R. Lidz and T. Lidz, "Homosexual Tendencies in Mothers of Schizophrenic Women," *Journal of Nervous and Mental Disorders* 149 (1969): 229.

49. Vanderbilt, "Incest: A Chilling Report," p. 63.

50. Quoted in *ibid.*

51. See, for example, A. C. Kinsey, W. B. Pomeroy, and C. E. Martin, *Sexual Behavior in the Human Male* (Philadelphia: W. B. Saunders, 1948).

52. Flowers, *The Victimization and Exploitation of Women and Children*, p. 66.

53. *Ibid.*, p. 67.

54. *Ibid.*

55. Jean Goodwinn, Lawrence Cormier, and John Owen, "Grandfather-Granddaughter Incest: A Trigenerational View," *Child Abuse and Neglect* 7 (1983): 163–70.

56. K. C. Meiselman, *Incest: A Psychological Study of Causes and Effects with Treatment Recommendations* (San Francisco: Jossey-Bass, 1978).

57. Flowers, *The Victimization and Exploitation of Women and Children*, p. 67.

58. L. Bender and A. Blau, "The Reactions of Children to Sexual Problems with Adults," *American Journal of Orthopsychiatry* 8, 4 (1937): 500–18.

59. Mayer, *Incest: A Treatment Manual*, p. 13.

60. Schecter and Roberge, "Sexual Exploitation," p. 131.

61. Flowers, *The Victimization and Exploitation of Women and Children*, p. 68.

62. Susan Forward as quoted in Howard, "Incest Victims Speak Out," p. 80.

63. Flowers, *The Victimization and Exploitation of Women and Children*, p. 68.

64. *Ibid.*; Joel Greenberg, "Incest Out of Hiding," *Science News* 117, 4 (1980): 218–20.

65. Flowers, *Women and Criminality*, pp. 61–63; Flowers, *Children and Criminality*, pp. 3–12.

66. Flowers, *The Victimization and Exploitation of Women and Children*, p. 68.

67. *Ibid.*, p. 73.

68. *Ibid.*

69. E. P. Sarafino, "An Estimate of the Nationwide Incidence of Sexual Offenses Against Children," *Child Welfare* 58, 2 (1979): 127–34.

70. Susan Brownmiller, *Against Our Will: Men, Women, and Rape* (New York: Simon & Schuster, 1975), pp. 278–79.

71. Flowers, *The Victimization and Exploitation of Women and Children*, p. 74.

72. J. M. Reinhardt, *Sexual Perversions and Sex Crimes* (Springfield, Ill.: Charles C Thomas, 1957).

73. Flowers, *The Victimization and Exploitation of Women and Children*, p. 74.

74. *Ibid.*, p. 79.

75. *Ibid.*

76. David Finkelhor, Linda Williams, Nanci Burns, and Michael Kalinowski, *Sexual Abuse in Day Care: A National Study Executive Summary* (Durham: University of New Hampshire, 1988).

77. Flowers, *The Victimization and Exploitation of Women and Children*, pp. 77–80.

78. National Center on Child Abuse and Neglect, *Research Symposium on*

Child Sexual Abuse: May 17–19, 1988 (Washington, D.C.: U. S. Department of Health and Human Services, 1988), p. 3.

79. Flowers, *The Victimization and Exploitation of Women and Children*, p. 80.

80. Flowers, *Children and Criminality*, pp. 134–36; Flowers, *The Prostitution of Women and Girls*, pp. 71–72.

81. Flowers, *The Victimization and Exploitation of Women and Children*, pp. 81–88.

82. Flowers, *The Prostitution of Women and Girls*, p. 80.

83. *Ibid.*; Joan J. Johnson, *Teen Prostitution* (Danbury, Conn.: Franklin Watts, 1992), p. 87.

84. Flowers, *The Prostitution of Women and Girls*, p. 80.

85. Margot Hornblower, "The Skin Trade," *Time* 141 (June 21, 1993), p. 44.

86. Flowers, *The Prostitution of Women and Girls*, p. 122; Johnson, *Teen Prostitution*, p. 90.

87. Flowers, *The Prostitution of Women and Girls*, p. 122.

88. *Ibid.*, pp. 122–24; Flowers, *The Victimization and Exploitation of Women and Children*, pp. 90–93.

89. Flowers, *The Prostitution of Women and Girls*, pp. 123–24.

90. Flowers, *Children and Criminality*, p. 82.

CHAPTER 13. SIBLING ABUSE AND PARENT ABUSE

1. Quoted in Heidi Vanderbilt, "Incest: A Chilling Report," *Lear's* (February 1992), p. 63; Vernon R. Wiehe, *Sibling Abuse: Hidden Physical, Emotional, and Sexual Trauma* (Newbury Park, Calif.: Sage, 1997).

2. Sandra Arbetter, "Family Violence: When We Hurt the Ones We Love," *Current Health* 22, 3 (1995): 6.

3. *Ibid.*

4. *Ibid.*; Flowers, *The Victimization and Exploitation of Women and Children*, pp. 31–32.

5. Flowers, *The Victimization and Exploitation of Women and Children*, pp. 31–32; Gail Ryan, "Sibling Abuse: Hidden Physical, Emotional, and Sexual Trauma," *Child Abuse and Neglect* 16, 2 (1992): 312.

6. U.S. Department of Justice, Bureau of Justice Statistics, *Criminal Victimization in the United States, 1994: A National Crime Victimization Survey Report* (Washington, D.C.: Government Printing Office, 1997), p. 42.

7. *Ibid.*, p. 46.

8. U.S. Department of Justice, Federal Bureau of Investigation, *Crime in the United States: Uniform Crime Reports 1997* (Washington, D.C.: Government Printing Office, 1998), p. 227.

9. *Ibid.*, p. 226.

10. Suzanne K. Steinmetz, "The Use of Force for Resolving Family Conflicts: The Training Ground for Abuse," *Family Coordinator* 26 (1977): 19.

11. Murray A. Straus, Richard J. Gelles, and Suzanne K. Steinmetz, *Behind Closed Doors: Violence in the American Family* (Garden City, N.Y.: Doubleday/Anchor, 1980).

12. *Ibid.*

13. *Ibid.*

14. Ellen E. Whippie and Sara E. Finton, "Psychological Maltreatment by Siblings: An Unrecognized Form of Abuse," *Child & Adolescent Social Work Journal* 12, 2 (1995): 35.

15. Quoted in Arbetter, "Family Violence: When We Hurt the Ones We Love," p. 6.

16. *Ibid.*

17. Quoted in "Parental Abuse," *USA Today* (March 18, 1983), p. 1D.

18. *Ibid.*

19. Cited in Karen S. Peterson, "The Nightmare of a Battered Parent," *USA Today* (March 18, 1983), p. A6.

20. Straus, Gelles, and Steinmetz, *Behind Closed Doors.*

21. Flowers, *The Victimization and Exploitation of Women and Children*, p. 32.

22. Carol A. Warren, "Parent Batterers: Adolescent Violence and the Family," Pacific Sociological Association, Anaheim, Calif., April 1978, pp. 3–5.

23. Flowers, *Children and Criminality*, p. 53.

24. Quoted in Cliff Yudell, "I'm Afraid of My Own Children," *Reader's Digest* (August 1983), p. 79.

25. Flowers, *Children and Criminality*, p. 53.

26. Quoted in *ibid.*

27. Rudolf Dreikers and Vicki Saltz, *Children: The Challenge* (New York: Hawthorne Books, 1964), p. 201.

28. Suzanne Wolfe, "As America Ages: Look for Signs of Abuse," *RN* 61, 8 (1998): 48.

29. Flowers, *The Victimization and Exploitation of Women and Children*, p. 33.

30. Flowers, *Children and Criminality*, p. 51. *See also* M. A. Freeman, *Violence in the Home* (Farnborough, England: Saxon House, 1979), p. 239.

CHAPTER 14. SUBSTANCE ABUSE, INTIMATE ABUSE, AND FAMILY ABUSES

1. Flowers, *Drugs, Alcohol and Criminality*; U.S. Department of Justice, Bureau of Justice Statistics Factbook, *Violence by Intimates* (Washington, D.C.: Government Printing Office, 1998), pp. 26–27; U.S. Department of Justice, Bureau of Justice Statistics, *Child Victimizers: Violent Offenders and Their Victims* (Washington, D.C.: Government Printing Office, 1996), pp. 6–7.

2. Office of National Drug Control Policy, *Fact Sheet: Drug Data Summary* (Rockville, Md.: ONDCP Drugs and Crime Clearinghouse, 1996), p. 1.

3. *Ibid.*

4. *Ibid.*

5. See, for example, Flowers, *Drugs, Alcohol and Criminality*; *Violence by Intimates*, pp. 26–27; *Child Victimizers*, p. 7; Flowers, *Female Crime, Criminals and Cellmates*, pp. 227–28.

6. *Violence by Intimates; Child Victimizers.*

7. U.S. Department of Justice, Federal Bureau of Investigation, *Crime in the*

United States: Uniform Crime Reports 1997 (Washington, D.C.: Government Printing Office, 1998), p. 232.

8. *Violence by Intimates*, pp. 26–27; Flowers, *Female Crime, Criminals and Cellmates*, pp. 227–30.

9. Flowers, *Demographics and Criminality*, pp. 125–38; Erich Goode, "Drugs and Crime," in Abraham S. Blumberg, ed., *Current Perspectives on Criminal Behavior: Essays on Criminology*, 2nd ed. (New York: Knopf, 1981), pp. 227–72; L. W. Gerson, "Alcohol Consumption and the Incidence of Violent Crime," *Journal for the Study of Alcoholism* 40 (1978): 307–12.

10. Jeffrey Fagan, "Interactions Among Drugs, Alcohol and Violence," *Health Affairs* 12, 4 (1993): 65–79; Sara Markowitz and Michael Grossman, "Alcohol Regulation and Domestic Violence Towards Children," *Contemporary Economic Policy* 16, 3 (1998): 309.

11. *Violence by Intimates*, pp. 26–27.

12. *Ibid.*, p. 27.

13. U.S. Department of Health and Human Services, National Institute on Drug Abuse, *Substance Abuse Among Women and Parents* (Washington, D.C.: Government Printing Office, 1994).

14. *Ibid.*

15. Michael J. Martin and James Walters, "Familial Correlates of Selected Types of Child Abuse and Neglect," *Journal of Marriage and the Family* 5 (1982): 267–76.

16. David G. Gil, *Violence Against Children: Physical Child Abuse in the United States* (Cambridge, Mass.: Harvard University Press, 1970).

17. R. Famularo, K. Stone, R. Barnum, and R. Wharton, "Alcoholism and Severe Child Maltreatment," *American Journal of Orthopsychiatry* 56 (1986): 481–85.

18. Children of Alcoholics Foundation, *Helping Children Affected by Parental Addiction and Family Violence: Collaboration, Coordination, and Cooperation* (New York: Children of Alcoholics Foundation, 1996).

19. B. Miketic, "The Influence of Parental Alcoholism in the Development Disturbance in Children," *Alcoholism* 8 (1972): 135–39.

20. Z. Popisil, K. Turcin, and R. Turcin, "Alcoholism and Article 196 of Criminal Law Abuse and Neglect of Minors," *New Ossihijatrya Zagreb* 16 (1968): 49–53.

21. D. W. Behling, "History of Alcohol Abuse in Clinical Child Abuse Cases Reported at Naval Regional Medical Center," paper presented at the National Child Abuse Forum, Long Beach, Calif., June 1971.

22. *Child Victimizers*, p. 7.

23. *Ibid.*

24. *Ibid.*, pp. 6–7; Flowers, *Children and Criminality*, pp. 87–88.

25. Patricia Mrazek and David A. Mrazek, "The Effects of Child Sexual Abuse: Methodological Considerations," in Patricia Mrazek and C. Henry Kempe, eds., *Sexually Abused Children and Their Families* (New York: Pergamon Press, 1981), p. 236.

26. Patricia Mrazek, "The Nature of Incest: A Review of Contributing Factors," in Patricia Mrazek and C. Henry Kempe, eds., *Sexually Abused Children and Their Families* (New York: Pergamon Press, 1981), p. 99.

27. Flowers, *Children and Criminality*, p. 58; D. T. Lunde, "Hot Blood's Record Month: Our Murder Boom," *Psychology Today* 9 (1975): 35–42.

28. *Child Victimizers*, p. 7.

29. Alfred Kadushin and Judith A. Martin, *Child Abuse: An Interactional Event* (New York: Columbia University Press, 1981), p. 141.

30. Brandt F. Steele, "Violence Within the Family," in Ray E. Helfer and C. Henry Kempe, eds., *Child Abuse and Neglect: The Family and the Community* (Cambridge, Mass.: Ballinger, 1976), p. 12.

31. Cited in Flowers, *The Victimization and Exploitation of Women and Children*, p. 64.

32. Flowers, *Children and Criminality*, p. 88; E. H. Newberger, et al., "Pediatric Social Illness: Toward an Etiologic Classification," *Pediatrics* 60 (1977): 178–85.

33. Kadushin and Martin, *Child Abuse*, pp. 125–28; Jerry P. Flanzer, *The Many Faces of Family Violence* (Springfield, Ill.: Charles C. Thomas, 1982), p. 38.

34. Flowers, *Children and Criminality*, p. 88. *See also* M. S. Dine, "Tranquilizer Poisoning: An Example of Child Abuse," *Pediatrics* 36 (1965): 782–85.

35. *Substance Abuse Among Women and Parents.*

36. *Ibid.*

37. Alex Morales, "Seeking a Cure for Child Abuse," *USA Today* 127, 2640 (1998): 34.

38. Flowers, *Female Crime, Criminals and Cellmates*, pp. 116–19; U.S. Department of Justice, Bureau of Justice Statistics Special Report, *Women in Prison* (Washington, D.C.: Government Printing Office, 1994).

39. Flowers, *Female Crime, Criminals and Cellmates*, p. 119; Flowers, *Children and Criminality*, pp. 65, 87–88.

40. Martin and Walters, "Familial Correlates of Selected Types of Child Abuse and Neglect," pp. 267–76.

41. G. C. Murdock, "The Abused Child and the School System," *American Journal of Public Health* 60 (1970): 105.

42. U.S. Department of Health and Human Services, National Institute on Drug Abuse, "Summary Tables: Annualized Estimates from the National Pregnancy and Health Survey," *NIDA Press Briefing*, September 12, 1994.

43. Flowers, *Female Crime, Criminals and Cellmates*, pp. 115–24; Flowers, *Drugs, Alcohol and Criminality in American Society*; Anne Geller and Helene MacLean, "Substance Abuse," in Helene MacLean, ed., *Every Woman's Health: The Complete Guide to Body and Mind*, 5th ed. (Garden City, N.Y.: Guild American Books, 1993), p. 392.

44. Flowers, *Female Crime, Criminals and Cellmates*, p. 121; U.S. Department of Justice, National Institute of Justice, *Characteristics of Different Types of Drug-Involved Offenders* (Washington, D.C.: Government Printing Office, 1988), pp. 20–21.

45. Flowers, *Female Crime, Criminals and Cellmates*, pp. 120–21, 227–29.

46. Carol A. Warren, "Parent Batterers: Adolescent Violence and the Family," Pacific Sociological Association, Anaheim, Calif., April 1978, pp. 3–5.

47. George Gallup, Jr., *The Gallup Poll Monthly*, No. 384 (Princeton, N.J.: The Gallup Poll, 1997), p. 24.

48. Quoted in Robert Straus, "The Social Costs of Alcohol," in Edith Gomberg, Helen White, and John A. Carpenter, eds., *Alcohol, Science and Society Revisited* (Ann Arbor: University of Michigan Press, 1982), p. 143.

49. Flowers, *Demographics and Criminality*, pp. 129–35; Flowers, *Children and Criminality*, pp. 65, 87–88; *Violence by Intimates*, pp. 26–27; *Child Victimizers*, p. 7.

50. Flowers, *The Victimization and Exploitation of Women and Children*, pp. 79–80.

51. Flowers, *Children and Criminality*, pp. 87–88, 95–97; Flowers, *Demographics and Criminality*, pp. 157, 169–70.

52. *Child Victimizers*, pp. 6–7.

Chapter 15. Cycle of Family Violence and Other Crimes

1. Murray A. Straus, "A General Systems Theory Approach to a Theory of Violence Between Family Members," *Social Science Information* 12 (1972): 105–25.

2. G. V. Laury, "The Battered Child Syndrome: Parental Motivation, Clinical Aspects," *Bulletin of the New York Academy of Medicine* 46, 9 (1970): 676–85.

3. Vincent J. Fontana, *The Maltreated Child: The Maltreatment Syndrome in Children* (Springfield, Ill.: Charles C Thomas, 1964).

4. T. C. Gibbons and A. Walker, *Cruel Parents* (London: Institute for the Study and Treatment of Delinquency, 1965).

5. Christopher Ounsted, Rhoda Oppenheimer, and Janet Lindsay, "The Psychopathology and Psychotherapy of the Families, Aspects Bounding Failure," in A. Franklin, ed., *Concerning Child Abuse* (London: Churchill Livingston, 1975).

6. Mia K. Pringle, "Towards the Prediction of Child Abuse," in Neil Fruce, ed., *Psychological Approaches to Child Abuse* (Totowa, N.J.: Rowman and Littlefield, 1981), p. 208.

7. Flowers, *Children and Criminality*, pp. 95–97; "Preventing Sexual Abuse of Children," *Parade Magazine* (May 26, 1985), p. 16; U.S. Department of Justice, Bureau of Justice Statistics, *Child Victimizers: Violent Offenders and Their Victims* (Washington, D.C.: Government Printing Office, 1996), p. 6.

8. "Preventing Sexual Abuse of Children," p. 16.

9. Jean Goodwinn, Lawrence Cormier, and John Owen, "Grandfather-Granddaughter Incest: A Trigenerational View," *Child Abuse and Neglect* 7 (1983): 163–70.

10. See, for examples, Flowers, *The Prostitution of Women and Girls*, p. 83; Sandra Arbetter, "Family Violence: When We Hurt the Ones We Love," *Current Health* 22, 3 (1995): 6.

11. C. Henry Kempe and Ray E. Helfer, eds., *Helping the Battered Child and His Family* (Philadelphia: J. B. Lippincott, 1972).

12. E. Rathbone and R. Pierce, "Intergenerational Treatment Approach," in Robert J. Hunner and Yvonne E. Walker, eds., *Exploring the Relationship Between Child Abuse and Delinquency* (Montclair, N.J.: Allanheld, Osmun and Co., 1981), p. 66; Norman Polansky, Christine De Saix, and Schlomo A. Sharlin, *Child Neglect: Understanding and Reaching the Parents* (New York: Child Welfare League of America, 1972).

13. *Child Victimizers*, p. 6.

14. *Ibid.*

15. Cited in Flowers, *Children and Criminality*, p. 53.

16. *Ibid.*, p. 51; M. A. Freeman, *Violence in the Home* (Farnsborough, England: Saxon House, 1979), p. 239.

17. Flowers, *Children and Criminality*, p. 96.

18. Monica Holmes, *Child Abuse and Neglect Programs: Practice and Theory* (Rockville, Md.: National Institute of Mental Health, 1977).

19. Flowers, *Children and Criminality*, p. 96; L. DeMause, "Our Forebearers Made Childhood a Nightmare," *Psychology Today* 8 (1975): 85–88.

20. Flowers, *Children and Criminality*, p. 96

21. *Ibid.*, p. 52; Linda S. King, "Responding to Spouse Abuse: The Mental Health Profession," in *Response to Family Violence* 4, 5 (1981): 7–9; Bonnie E. Carlson, "Battered Women and Their Assailants," *Social Work* 22, 6 (1977): 456.

22. Kathleen H. Hofeller, *Social, Psychological and Situational Factors in Wife Abuse* (Palo Alto, Calif.: R & E Research Associates, 1982), p. 39.

23. Carlson, "Battered Women and Their Assailants," p. 456.

24. J. Gayford, "Wife Battering: A Preliminary Survey of 100 Cases," *British Medical Journal* 1 (1975): 194–97.

25. U.S. Department of Justice, Bureau of Justice Statistics Special Report, *Women in Prison* (Washington, D.C.: Government Printing Office, 1994).

26. "Final Report of the Supreme Court Task Force on Courts' and Communities' Response to Domestic Abuse," submitted to the Supreme Court of Iowa, August 1994, pp. 14–15.

27. *Women in Prison*.

28. *Ibid.*; *Child Victimizers*, p. 6; Jeanne Cyriaque, "The Chronic Serious Offender: How Illinois Juveniles 'Match Up,'" Illinois Department of Corrections, *Illinois* (February 1982): 4–5.

29. Cathy Widom, "Childhood Sexual Abuse and Its Criminal Consequences," *Society* 33, 4 (1996): 47.

30. Joan Petersilia, Peter Greenwood, and Marvin Lavin, *Criminal Careers of Habitual Felons* (Washington, D.C.: National Institute of Justice, 1978).

31. *Women in Prison*.

32. R. Barri Flowers, *The Sex Slave Murders* (New York: St. Martin's Press, 1996).

33. Martin R. Haskell and Lewis Yablonsky, *Crime and Delinquency*, 2nd ed. (Chicago: Rand McNally, 1974).

34. Brandt F. Steele, "Violence Without the Family," in Ray E. Helfer and C. Henry Kempe, eds., *Child Abuse and Neglect: The Family and the Community* (Cambridge, Mass.: Ballinger, 1976).

35. Cited in Glenn Collins, "The Violent Child: Some Patterns Emerge," *New York Times* (September 27, 1982), p. B10.

36. D. E. Adams, H. A. Ishizuka, and K. S. Ishizuka, *The Child Abuse Delinquent: An Exploration/Descriptive Study*, unpublished MSW thesis, University of South Carolina, South Carolina, 1977.

37. W. McCord, "The Biological Basis of Juvenile Delinquency," in J. S. Roucek, ed., *Juvenile Delinquency* (Freeport, N.Y.: Philosophical Library, 1958).

38. H. E. Simmons, *Protective Services for Children*, 2nd ed. (Sacramento: Citadel Press, 1970).

39. Cyriaque, "The Chronic Serious Offender," pp. 4–5.

40. Sheldon Glueck and Eleanor Glueck, *Delinquents and Non-Delinquents in Perspective* (Cambridge, Mass.: Harvard University Press, 1968).

41. E. Y. Deykin, "Life Functioning in Families of Delinquent Boys: An Assessment Model," *Social Services Review* 46, 1 (1971): 90–91.

42. M. F. Shore, "Psychological Theories on the Causes of Antisocial Behavior," *Crime and Delinquency* 17, 4 (1971): 456–58.

43. James Garbarino, "Child Abuse and Juvenile Delinquency: The Developmental Impact of Social Isolation," in Robert J. Hunner and Yvonne E. Walker, eds., *Exploring the Relationship Between Child Abuse and Delinquency* (Montclair, N.J.: Allanheld, Osmun and Co., 1981), p. 117.

44. B. D. Schmitt and C. H. Kempe, "Neglect and Abuse in Children," in V. C. Vaugh and R. J. McKay, eds., *Nelson Textbook of Pediatrics*, 10th ed. (Philadelphia: W. B. Saunders Co., 1975), pp. 107–11.

45. Robert Weinback, et al., "Theoretical Linkages Between Child Abuse and Juvenile Delinquency," in Robert J. Hunner and Yvonne E. Walker, eds., *Exploring the Relationship Between Child Abuse and Delinquency* (Montclair, N.J.: Allanheld, Osmun and Co., 1981), p. 162.

46. R. Barri Flowers, *The Adolescent Criminal: An Examination of Today's Juvenile Offender* (Jefferson, N.C.: McFarland, 1990), p. 49; Flowers, *The Victimization and Exploitation of Women and Children*, pp. 36–42.

47. Flowers, *The Victimization and Exploitation of Women and Children*, pp. 39–44; John Zaccaro, Jr., "Children of the Night," *Woman's Day* (March 29, 1988), p. 138; Patricia Hersch, "Coming of Age on City Streets," *Psychology Today* (January 1988), pp. 31–32.

48. Cited in Hersch, "Coming of Age on City Streets," p. 31.

49. Cited in Stephanie Arbarbanel, "Women Who Make a Difference," *Family Circle* 107 (January 11, 1994), p. 11.

50. Cited in Hersch, "Coming of Age on City Streets," p. 32.

51. Widom, "Childhood Sexual Abuse and Its Criminal Consequences."

52. Flowers, *The Victimization and Exploitation of Women and Children*, p. 44.

53. *Ibid.*, pp. 43–45; Flowers, *The Adolescent Criminal*, pp. 51–52.

54. Flowers, *Children and Criminality*, pp. 87–88, 95–96, 101–02; Widom, "Childhood Sexual Abuse and Its Criminal Consequences."

55. Flowers, *The Victimization and Exploitation of Women and Children*, pp. 84–86; Flowers, *The Prostitution of Women and Girls*, pp. 52, 83–84, 178.

56. Sparky Harlan, Luanne L. Rodgers, and Brian Slattery, *Male and Female Adolescent Prostitution: Huckleberry House Sexual Minority Youth Services Project* (Washington, D.C.: U.S. Department of Health and Human Services, 1981), p. 21.

57. Mimi H. Silbert, "Delancey Street Study: Prostitution and Sexual Assault," summary of results (Delancey Street Foundation: San Francisco, 1982), p. 3.

58. Flowers, *The Prostitution of Women and Girls*, pp. 49–50; Barbara Goldsmith, "Women on the Edge: A Reporter at Large," *The New Yorker* 69 (April 26, 1993), pp. 65–66.

59. Flowers, *Children and Criminality*, pp. 81–82, 97; Flowers, *The Prostitution of Women and Girls*, p. 83.

60. Maura G. Crowley, "Female Runaway Behavior and Its Relationship to Prostitution," master's thesis, Sam Houston State University, Institute of Contemporary Corrections and Behavioral Sciences, 1977, p. 63.

61. Harlan, Rodgers, and Slattery, *Male and Female Adolescent Prostitution*, p. 15.

62. Flowers, *The Prostitution of Women and Girls*, p. 64; Flowers, *Women and Criminality*, p. 128.

63. Flowers, *The Adolescent Criminal*, p. 62; Hilary Abramson, "Sociologists Try to Reach Young Hustlers," *Sacramento Bee* (September 3, 1984), p. A8.

64. Cited in Anastasia Volkonsky, "Legalizing the 'Profession' Would Sanction the Abuse," *Insight on the News* 11 (1995): 21.

65. Flowers, *The Prostitution of Women and Girls*, p. 83.

66. Cited in Sam Meddis, "Teen Prostitution Rising, Study Says," *USA Today* (April 23, 1984), p. 3A.

67. Volkonsky, "Legalizing the 'Profession' Would Sanction the Abuse," p. 103.

68. Crowley, "Female Runaway Behavior and Its Relationship to Prostitution."

69. Harlan, Rodgers, and Slattery, *Male and Female Adolescent Prostitution*, p. 15.

70. Jennifer James, *Entrance into Juvenile Prostitution* (Washington, D.C.: National Institute of Mental Health, 1980), p. 88.

71. Diana Gray, "Turning Out: A Study of Teenage Prostitution," master's thesis, University of Washington, 1971, p. 25.

72. Harlan, Rodgers, and Slattery, *Male and Female Adolescent Prostitution*, p. 15.

73. Flowers, *The Prostitution of Women and Girls*, pp. 52, 85; Flowers, *Children and Criminality*, p. 81.

74. Flowers, *The Victimization and Exploitation of Women and Children*, p. 88; Harlan, Rodgers, and Slattery, *Male and Female Adolescent Prostitution*, p. 22; Donald M. Allen, "Young Male Prostitutes: A Psychosocial Study," *Archives of Sexual Behavior* 9, 5 (1980).

75. Flowers, *The Prostitution of Women and Girls*, p. 85.

CHAPTER 16. CAUSES OF DOMESTIC VIOLENCE AND CHILD ABUSE

1. W. Goode, "Violence Among Intimates," *Crimes and Violence* 13 (1969): 941–77.

2. R. Chester and J. Streather, "Cruelty in English Divorce: Some Empirical Findings," *Journal of Marriage and the Family* 34, 4 (1972): 706–10. See also B. M. Cormier, "Psychodynamics of Homicide Committed in a Marital Relationship," *Corrective Journal of Orthopsychiatry* 36, 5 (1966): 803–07.

3. L. Eron, "Symposium: The Application of Role and Learning Theories to the Study of the Development of Aggression in Children," *Proceedings of the Rip Van Winkle Clinic* 10, 1-2 (1959): 3–61.

4. L. Kopernik, "The Family as a Breeding Ground for Violence," *Corrective Psychiatric Journal of Sociology Therapy* 10, 6 (1964).

5. Flowers, *Demographics and Criminality*, p. 159.

6. See, for example, S. Zalba, "The Abused Child: A Survey of the Problem," *Social Work* 11, 4 (1966): 3–16.

7. S. Kirson Weinberg, *Incest Behavior* (New York: Citadel Press, 1966); Flowers, *The Victimization and Exploitation of Women and Children*, pp. 34–35, 65.

8. Weinberg, *Incest Behavior*; R. Lidz and T. Lidz, "Homosexual Tendencies in Mothers of Schizophrenic Women," *Journal of Nervous and Mental Disorders* 149 (1969): 229.

9. Brandt F. Steele, "Violence Within the Family," in Ray E. Helfer and C. Henry Kempe, eds., *Child Abuse and Neglect: The Family and the Community* (Cambridge, Mass.: Ballinger, 1976), p. 12.

10. Flowers, *Demographics and Criminality*, p. 159; Richard J. Gelles and Murray A. Straus, "Determinants of Violence in the Family: Toward a Theoretical Integration," in W. R. Burr, R. Hill, F. I. Nye, and I. L. Reiss, eds., *Contemporary Theories About the Family* (New York: Free Press, 1979).

11. Flowers, *Demographics and Criminality*, p. 159; Flowers, *Children and Criminality*, pp. 42–44, 50.

12. *Ibid.*, p. 50; F. Ilfeld, Jr., "Environmental Theories of Violence," in D. Danield, M. Gilula, and F. Ochberg, eds., *Violence and the Struggle for Existence* (Boston: Little, Brown, 1970).

13. Murray A. Straus, "A General Systems Theory Approach to a Theory of Violence Between Family Members," *Social Science Information* 12, 3 (1973): 105–25.

14. Flowers, *Demographics and Criminality*, p. 159.

15. *Ibid.*

16. *Ibid.*

17. David G. Gil, *Violence Against Children: Physical Child Abuse in the United States* (Cambridge, Mass.: Harvard University Press, 1970).

18. D. Abrahamsen, *Our Violent Society* (New York: Funk and Wagnalls, 1970).

19. D. Owens and M. Straus, "The Social Structure of Violence in Childhood and Approved as an Adult," presented to the 1973 annual meeting of the American Orthopsychiatric Association, New York.

20. Flowers, *The Victimization and Exploitation of Women and Children*, p. 35.

21. *Ibid.*

22. Flowers, *Women and Criminality*, p. 20. See also Kathleen H. Hofeller, *Social, Psychological and Situational Factors in Wife Abuse* (Palo Alto, Calif.: R & E Research Associates, 1982), p. 39.

23. Flowers, *Women and Criminality*, p. 20.

24. Terry Davidson, *Conjugal Crime: Understanding and Changing the Wife-Beating Pattern* (New York: Hawthorne, 1979), p. 29.

25. Flowers, *Women and Criminality*, pp. 20–21.

26. *Ibid.*, p. 21.

27. Davidson, *Conjugal Crime*, p. 51.

28. Flowers, *Women and Criminality*, p. 21.

29. Richard J. Gelles, *The Violent Home: A Study of the Physical Aggression Between Husbands and Wives* (Beverly Hills: Sage, 1972).

30. Flowers, *Children and Criminality*, p. 22.

31. Murray A. Straus, "Sexual Inequality, Cultural Norms, and Wife-Beating," *Victimology* 1 (1976): 62–66.

32. Flowers, *Women and Criminality*, pp. 22–23.

33. Lee H. Bowker, *Women, Crime, and the Criminal Justice System* (Lexington, Mass.: Lexington Books, 1978), p. 128.

34. Flowers, *Women and Criminality*, p. 23; Robert N. Whitehurst, "Violence in Husband-Wife Interaction," in Suzanne K. Steinmetz and Murray A. Straus, eds., *Violence in the Family* (New York: Dodd, Mead, 1974), pp. 75–82.

35. Ellen Pence, Domestic Abuse Intervention Project, Duluth, Minnesota.

36. "Final Report of the Supreme Court Task Force on Courts' and Communities' Response to Domestic Violence," submitted to the Supreme Court of Iowa, August 1994, p. 8.

37. *Ibid.*

38. *Ibid.*, p. 9.

39. C. Henry Kempe, "Pediatric Implications of the Battered Baby Syndrome," *Archives of Diseases in Childhood* 46, 245 (1971): 28–37.

40. Flowers, *Children and Criminality*, p. 42.

41. *Ibid.*, p. 43.

42. E. J. Merrill, "Physical Abuse of Children: An Agency Study," in V. De Francis, ed., *Protecting the Battered Child* (Denver: American Humane Association, 1962).

43. Flowers, *Children and Criminality*, p. 43.

44. *Ibid.*

45. M. H. Lystad, "Violence at Home: A Review of the Literature," *American Journal of Orthopsychiatry* 45 (1975): 328–45.

46. Flowers, *Children and Criminality*, p. 43.

47. *Ibid.*, p. 44.

48. *Ibid.*

49. D. Bakan, *Slaughter of the Innocents* (San Francisco: Jossey-Bass, 1971); M. L. Blumberg, "Psychopathology of the Abusing Parent," *American Journal of Psychotherapy* 28 (1974): 21–29.

50. Gil, *Violence Against Children*.

51. Flowers, *Children and Criminality*, p. 44; J. J. Spinetta and D. Rigler, "The Child-Abusing Parent: A Psychological Review," *Psychological Bulletin* 77 (1972): 296–304.

52. Richard J. Gelles, "Child Reformation," *American Journal of Orthopsychiatry* 43 (1973): 611–21.

53. Flowers, *Children and Criminality*, p. 45.

54. *Ibid.*; A. Lascari, "The Abused Child," *Journal of the Iowa Medical Society* 62 (1972): 229–32.

55. P. V. Wooley and W. A. Evans, "Significance of Skeletal Lesions in Infants Resembling Those of Traumatic Origin," *Journal of the American Medical Association* 158 (1955): 539–43.

56. E. Lard and D. Weisfeld, "The Abused Child," in A. Roberts, ed., *Childhood Deprivation* (Springfield, Ill.: Charles C Thomas, 1974).

57. Flowers, *The Victimization and Exploitation of Women and Children*, pp. 65–66; Weinberg, *Incest Behavior*.

58. Zalba, "The Abused Child," pp. 3–16.

59. Flowers, *Children and Criminality*, p. 45.

60. Blair Justice and Rita Justice, *The Abusing Family* (New York: Human Sciences Press, 1976), pp. 55–80.

61. Flowers, *Children and Criminality*, p. 46.

62. F. J. Bishop, "Children at Risk," *Medical Journal of Australia* 1 (1971): 623–28.

Chapter 17. Inmates and Intimate Violence

1. U.S. Department of Justice, Bureau of Justice Statistics Factbook, *Violence by Intimates* (Washington, D.C.: Government Printing Office, 1998), pp. 1–4; U.S. Department of Justice, Bureau of Justice Statistics, *Child Victimizers: Violent Offenders and Their Victims* (Washington, D.C.: Government Printing Office, 1996), pp. 1–13.

2. *Ibid.*

3. Ann Jones, *Women Who Kill* (New York: Fawcett Crest, 1980), p. 9; Charles P. Ewing, *Battered Women Who Kill: Psychological Self-Defense as Legal Justification* (Lexington, Mass.: Lexington Books, 1987).

4. Flowers, *Demographics and Criminality*, p. 169; Flowers, *Female Crime, Criminals and Cellmates*, pp. 234–35.

5. *Violence by Intimates*, p. 23.

6. *Ibid.*, p. 26.

7. *Ibid.*

8. *Ibid.*, p. 23.

9. *Ibid.*, p. 28.

10. *Ibid.*

11. *Ibid.*, p. 29.

12. *Ibid.*

13. *Ibid.*

14. Cited in Nick Jordan, "Till Murder Us Do Part," *Psychology Today* 19 (July 1985), p. 7.

15. *Ibid.*

16. "Final Report of the Supreme Court Task Force on Courts' and Communities' Response to Domestic Abuse," submitted to the Supreme Court of Iowa, August 1994, p. 14.

17. *Ibid.*, pp. 14, 19.

18. Jones, *Women Who Kill*, p. 9.

19. *Battered Women and Criminal Justice: The Unjust Treatment of Battered Women in a System Controlled by Men*, a report of the Committee on Domestic Violence and Incarcerated Women, June 1987, p. 3A.

20. "National Estimates & Facts About Domestic Violence," *NCADV Voice* (Winter 1989): 12.

21. Ewing, *Battered Women Who Kill*.

22. Lenore E. Walker, "Legal Self-Defense Issues for Women of Color," unpublished paper, 1988, p. 4.

23. Flowers, *Drugs, Alcohol and Criminality*, pp. 168–73.

24. *Violence by Intimates*, pp. 25, 29.

25. *Ibid.*; *Child Victimizers*, p. 6; Flowers, *Demographics and Criminality*, pp. 169–70.

26. U.S. Department of Justice, Bureau of Justice Statistics, *Report to the Nation on Crime and Justice: The Data* (Washington, D.C.: Government Printing Office, 1983), pp. 30–40.

27. *Child Victimizers*, p. 6; Flowers, *Female Crime, Criminals and Cellmates*, pp. 233–34; U.S. Department of Justice, Bureau of Justice Statistics Special Report, *Women in Prison* (Washington, D.C.: Government Printing Office, 1994), p. 5.

28. Flowers, *Demographics and Criminality*, p. 169; *Report to the Nation on Crime and Justice*.

29. Flowers, *Drug, Alcohol and Criminality*, pp. 163–64.

30. Flowers, *Demographics and Criminality*, p. 169; Flowers, *Female Crime, Criminals and Cellmates*, pp. 234–35.

31. U.S. Department of Justice, Bureau of Justice Statistics, *Survey of State Prison Inmates, 1991* (Washington, D.C.: Government Printing Office, 1994), p. 6.

32. Law Enforcement Assistance Administration, *Profile of State Prison Inmates: Sociodemographic Findings from the 1974 Survey of Inmates of State Correctional Facilities* (Washington, D.C.: Government Printing Office, 1979).

33. *Report to the Nation*.

34. Flowers, *Drugs, Alcohol and Criminality*, p. 165.

35. *Profile of State Prison Inmates*.

36. Flowers, *Demographics and Criminality*, p. 169.

Chapter 18. Prisoners and Child Abuse

1. U.S. Department of Justice, Bureau of Justice Statistics, *Child Victimizers: Violent Offenders and Their Victims* (Washington, D.C.: Government Printing Office, 1996), pp. 4–14.

2. *Ibid.*, p. 17.

3. *Ibid.*

4. *Ibid.*, p. 6.

5. *Ibid.*, p. 7.

6. *Ibid.*, pp. 1–3.

7. *Ibid.*, pp, 1–14; Flowers, *The Victimization and Exploitation of Women and Children*, pp. 97–110.

8. *Child Victimizers*, p. 12.

9. *Ibid.*

10. *Ibid.*, pp. 1–2.

11. *Ibid.*, pp. 1–13; Flowers, *The Victimization and Exploitation of Women and Children*, pp. 103–09.

12. *Child Victimizers*, pp. 1–13; Flowers, *Children and Criminality*, pp. 95–97, 101–02.

13. *Child Victimizers*; Flowers, *Demographics and Criminality*, pp. 165–79.

14. *Child Victimizers*, p. 10.

15. *Ibid.*

16. *Ibid.*, p. 11.

17. *Ibid.*

18. *Child Victimizers*, p. 15; U.S. Department of Justice, Federal Bureau of Investigation, Supplementary Homicide Reports, 1976–1994.

19. *Child Victimizers*, pp. 15–17.

20. *Ibid.*, p. 17.

21. *Ibid.*, p. 19.

22. *Ibid.*

23. *Ibid.*, pp. 1–3.

24. *Ibid.*

25. *Ibid.*

26. *Ibid.*, p. 9.

27. *Ibid.*, p. 8.

28. *Ibid.*

29. *Ibid.*, p. 4.

30. *Ibid.*

31. *Ibid.*

32. *Ibid.*, p. 7.

33. *Ibid.*, p. 5.

34. *Ibid.*

35. *Ibid.*, pp. 5–6.

36. *Ibid.*, pp. 6–7; Flowers, *Children and Criminality*, pp. 87–88, 95–96, 101–02.

37. *Child Victimizers*, p. 6; Flowers, *Children and Criminality*, pp. 101–02; Martin R. Haskell and Lewis Yablonsky, *Crime and Delinquency*, 2nd ed. (Chicago: Rand McNally, 1974); M. F. Shore, "Psychological Theories on the Causes of Antisocial Behavior," *Crime and Delinquency* 17, 4 (1971): 456–58.

38. *Child Victimizers*, p. 6.

39. *Ibid.*, p. 7.

40. *Ibid.*, p. 5.

41. *Ibid.*, p. 18.

42. *Ibid.*, pp. 11, 15–17.

43. U.S. Department of Justice, Office of Juvenile Justice and Delinquency Prevention, *Juveniles Taken Into Custody: FY 93* (Washington, D.C.: Government Printing Office, 1995). See also U.S. Department of Justice, Office of Justice Programs, *Children in Custody 1989* (Washington, D.C.: Government Printing Office, 1991).

44. *Juveniles Taken Into Custody.*

CHAPTER 19. COMBATING DOMESTIC VIOLENCE AND CHILD ABUSE

1. Anna Kurl and Linda E. Saltzman, "Battered Women and the Criminal Justice System," in Imogene L. Moyer, ed., *The Changing Roles of Women in the Criminal Justice System: Offenders, Victims, and Professionals* (Prospect Heights, Ill.: Waveland Press, 1985), p. 188; International Association of Chiefs of Police, Wife Beating: Training Key, No. 245, 1976.

2. Flowers, *Women and Criminality*, p. 187.

3. *Ibid.*

4. *Ibid.*

5. Flowers, *The Victimization and Exploitation of Women and Children*, pp. 200–01.

6. *Ibid.*, p. 201.

7. *Ibid.*

8. Andrea Gross, "A Question of Rape," *Ladies Home Journal* 110, 11 (November 1993), p. 170.

9. National Resource Center on Domestic Violence, Harrisburg, Penn.

10. *Ibid.*

11. *Ibid.*

12. *Ibid.*

13. *Ibid.*

14. *Ibid.*

15. Flowers, *The Victimization and Exploitation of Women and Children*, p. 202.

16. *Ibid.*

17. Erin Pizzey, *Scream Quietly or the Neighbors Will Hear* (London: Penguin, 1974).

18. Flowers, *Women and Criminality*, p. 190.

19. *Ibid.*, p. 191.

20. *Ibid.*

21. 42 U.S.C. §5101–5106 (1974); as amended by Child Abuse Prevention and Treatment and Adoption Reform Act of 1978, P.L. No. 95-266, 92 Stat. 205 (1978).

22. *Ibid.*

23. Flowers, *The Victimization and Exploitation of Women and Children*, p. 196.

24. *Ibid.*, pp. 196–97; Child Abuse Prevention, Adoption, and Family Services Act of 1988, P.L. 100-294 (1988).

25. Flowers, *The Victimization and Exploitation of Women and Children*, p. 196.

26. Juvenile Justice and Delinquency Prevention Act of 1974, P.L. 93-415 (1974).

27. P.L. 93-415, Title II, Part B., Sec. 223 (a), (12) (1974).

28. The Runaway and Homeless Youth Act, 42 U.S.C. §5701–5702 (Supp. II, 1978).

29. Flowers, *Children and Criminality*, p. 190.

30. *Ibid.*

31. The Sexual Exploitation Act of 1978, 18 U.S.C. §2251, 2253–2254 (1978).

32. Flowers, *Children and Criminality*, p. 190.

33. 18 U.S.C. §2251, 2253–2254 (1978).

34. Flowers, *The Victimization and Exploitation of Women and Children*, p. 199.

35. Flowers, *Children and Criminality*, p. 191.

36. Federal Parental Kidnapping Prevention Act of 1980, 18 U.S.C. §1073 (1980).

37. 128 Cong. Rec. 8, 566 (1982).

38. *Ibid.*; Flowers, *Children and Criminality*, p. 191.

39. U.S. Department of Health and Human Services, Children's Bureau, *Child Maltreatment 1996: Reports from the States to the National Child Abuse and Neglect Data System* (Washington, D.C.: Government Printing Office, 1998), p. 1-1.

40. *Ibid.*

41. *Ibid.*

42. *Ibid.*

43. Flowers, *The Victimization and Exploitation of Women and Children*, p. 200.

44. *Child Abuse and Neglect: A Shared Community Concern* (Washington, D.C.: National Center on Child Abuse and Neglect, 1992), p. 10.

45. *Ibid.*

46. *Ibid.*

47. Flowers, *Children and Criminality*, p. 192.

Bibliography

Adams, Joyce A. "Significance of Medical Findings in Suspected Sexual Abuse: Moving Towards Consensus." *Journal of Child Sexual Abuse* 1, 3 (1992): 91–99.

Akers, Ronald L., Anthony J. LaGrecca, Christine Sellers, and John Cochran. "Fear of Crime and Victimization Among the Elderly in Different Types of Communities." *Criminology* 25 (1987): 487–505.

Alvy, K. T. "On Child Abuse: Values and Analytic Approaches." *Journal of Clinical Child Psychology* 4 (1975): 36–37.

Amir, Menachem. *Patterns in Forcible Rape.* Chicago: University of Chicago Press, 1971.

Anglin, M. Douglas, and Yih Ing Hser. "Addicted Women and Crime." *Criminology* 25 (1987): 359–97.

Appel, Anne E., and George W. Holden. "The Co-Occurrence of Spouse and Physical Child Abuse: A Review and Appraisal." *Journal of Family Psychology* 12 (1998): 578.

Arbetter, Sandra. "Family Violence: When We Hurt the Ones We Love." *Current Health* 22, 3 (1995): 6.

Bachman, Jerald G., J. M. Wallace, Jr., Patrick O'Malley, Lloyd D. Johnston, C. L. Kurth, and H. W. Neighbors. "Racial/Ethnic Differences in Smoking, Drinking, and Illicit Drug Use Among American High School Seniors, 1975–1989." *American Journal of Public Health* 81 (1991): 372–77.

Bakan, D. *Slaughter of the Innocents.* San Francisco: Jossey-Bass, 1971.

Barbour, Krista A., et al. "The Experience and Expression of Anger in Maritally Discordant-Nonviolent Men." *Behavior Therapy* 29, 2 (1998): 173.

Battelle Law and Justice Study Center Report. *Forcible Rape: An Analysis of Legal Issues.* Washington, D.C.: Government Printing Office, 1977.

Baumhover, L. A., and S. C. Beall, eds. *Abuse, Neglect, and Exploitation of Older Persons.* Baltimore, Md.: Health Professions Press, 1996.

Behling, D. W. "Alcohol Abuse Encountered in 51 Instances of Reported Child Abuse." *Clinical Pediatrics* 18 (1979): 87–91.

_____. "History of Alcohol Abuse in Clinical Child Abuse Cases Reported at

Naval Regional Medical Center." Paper presented at the National Child Abuse Forum. Long Beach, Calif., June 1971.

Bender, L., and A. Blau. "The Reactions of Children to Sexual Problems with Adults." *American Journal of Orthopsychiatry* 8, 4 (1937): 500–18.

_____, and F. J. Curran. "Children and Adolescents Who Kill." *Journal of Criminal Psychopathology* 1, 4 (1940): 297.

Benedek, Elissa P. "Women and Homicide." In Bruce L. Danto, John Bruhns, and Austin H. Kutscher, eds. *The Human Side of Homicide.* New York: Columbia University Press, 1982.

Bennie, E., and A. Sclare. "The Battered Child Syndrome." *American Journal of Psychiatry* 125, 7 (1969): 75–79.

Berrios, D. C., and D. Grady. "Domestic Violence: Risk Factors and Outcomes." *Western Journal of Medicine* 15, 2 (1991).

"Beyond the Boundaries of Child Welfare: Connecting with Welfare, Juvenile Justice, Family Violence and Mental Health." *Spectrum: The Journal of State Government* 72 (1999): 14.

Bishop, F. J. "Children at Risk." *Medical Journal of Australia* 1 (1971): 623–28.

Blum, Deborah. "Attention Deficit: Physical and Sexual Child Abuse Grab All the Headlines. But What You May Not Realize Is That Neglect Can Be Worse." *Mother Jones* 24 (1999): 58.

Blumberg, M. L. "Psychopathology of the Abusing Parent." *American Journal of Psychotherapy* 28 (1974): 21–29.

Brookoff, Daniel, et al. "Characteristics of Participants in Domestic Violence: Assessment at the Scene of Domestic Assault." *Journal of the American Medical Association* 277, 17 (1997): 1369.

Brownmiller, Susan. *Against Our Will: Men, Women, and Rape.* New York: Simon & Schuster, 1975.

Burt, Marvin R., Thomas J. Glynn, and Barbara J. Sowder. *Psychosocial Characteristics of Drug-Abusing Women.* Rockville, Md.: U.S. Department of Health, Education, and Welfare, 1979.

Caffey, J. "Multiple Fractures in the Long Bones of Children Suffering from Chronic Subdural Hematoma." *American Journal of Roentgenology, Radium Therapy, Nuclear Medicine* 56 (1946): 163–73.

Campbell, C. A. "Prostitution, AIDS and Preventive Health Behavior." *Social Science and Medicine* 32 (1991): 1367–78.

Campbell, Jacquelyn. "Prediction of Homicide of and by Battered Women." In Jacquelyn Campbell and J. Milner, eds. *Assessing Dangerousness: Potential for Further Violence of Sexual Offenders, Batterers, and Child Abusers.* Newbury Park, Calif.: Sage, 1995.

_____, and J. Milner, eds. *Assessing Dangerousness: Potential for Further Violence of Sexual Offenders, Batterers, and Child Abusers.* Newbury Park, Calif.: Sage, 1995.

Caplan, Gerald M. "Sexual Exploitation of Children: The Conspiracy of Silence." *Police Magazine* 5, 1 (1982): 46–51.

Carlson, Bonnie E. "Battered Women and Their Assailants." *Social Work* 22, 6 (1977): 456.

Carpenter, Cheryl, Barry Blassner, Bruce D. Johnson, and Julia Loughlin. *Kids, Drugs, and Crime.* Lexington, Mass.: Lexington Books, 1988.

Chalk, Rosemary, and Patricia A. King. "Facing Up to Family Violence." *Issues in Science and Technology* 15, 2 (1998): 39.

_____, eds. *Violence in Families: Assessing Prevention and Treatment Programs.* Washington, D.C.: National Academy Press, 1998.

Chance, Paul. "Attacking Elderly Abuse." *Psychology Today* 21 (September 1987): 24.

Chapman, Jane R., and Margaret Gates, eds. *The Victimization of Women.* Beverly Hills: Sage, 1978.

Chester, R., and J. Streather. "Cruelty in English Divorce: Some Empirical Findings." *Journal of Marriage and the Family* 34, 4 (1972): 706–10.

Child Victims of Incest. Denver: American Humane Association, 1968.

Children of Alcoholics Foundation. *Helping Children Affected by Parental Addiction and Family Violence: Collaboration, Coordination, and Cooperation.* New York: Children of Alcoholics Foundation, 1996.

Clark, Alan H., and Margaret J. Lewis. "Fear of Crime Among the Elderly." *British Journal of Criminology* 22 (1982): 49–62.

Clark, Lorenne M., and Debra J. Lewis. *Rape: The Price of Coercive Sexuality.* Toronto: Canadian Women's Educational Press, 1977.

Collins, James J., ed. *Drinking and Crime: Perspectives in the Relationships Between Alcohol Consumption and Criminal Behavior.* New York: Guilford Press, 1981.

Cormier, B. M. "Psychodynamics of Homicide Committed in a Marital Relationship." *Corrective Journal of Orthopsychiatry* 36, 5 (1966): 803–07.

_____, et al. "Adolescents Who Kill a Member of the Family." In John M. Eekelaar and Sanford N. Katz., eds. *Family Violence: An International and Interdisciplinary Study.* Toronto: Butterworths, 1978.

Covey, Herbert C., and Scott Menard. "Trends in Elderly Criminal Victimization from 1973 to 1984." *Research on Aging* 10 (1988): 329–41.

Darrow, William. "Prostitution, Intravenous Drug Use, and HIV-1 in the United States." In Martin A. Plant, ed. *AIDS, Drugs, and Prostitution.* London: Routledge, 1990.

Davidson, Terry. *Conjugal Crime: Understanding and Changing the Wife-Beating Pattern.* New York: Hawthorne, 1979.

_____. "Wifebeating: A Recurring Phenomenon Throughout History." In Maria Roy, ed. *The Abusive Partner: An Analysis of Domestic Battering.* New York: Van Nostrand Reinhold, 1982.

DeMause, L. "Our Forebearers Made Childhood a Nightmare." *Psychology Today* 8 (1975): 85–88.

Densen-Gerber, Judianne, and S. F. Hutchinson. "Medical-Legal and Societal Problems Involving Children — Child Prostitution, Child Pornography, and Drug-Related Abuse: Recommended Legislation." In Selwyn M. Smith, ed., *The Maltreatment of Children.* Baltimore, Md.: University Park Press, 1978.

Dine, M. S. "Tranquilizer Poisoning: An Example of Child Abuse." *Pediatrics* 36 (1965): 782–85.

Dobash, Rebecca Emerson, and Russell Dobash. *Violence Against Wives.* New York: Free Press, 1979.

Dreikers, Rudolf, and Vicki Saltz. *Children: The Challenge.* New York: Hawthorne Books, 1964.

Dutton, D. G. "The Criminal Justice Response to Wife Assault." *Law and Human Behavior* II, 3 (1987): 189–206.

Easson, W. M., and R. M. Steinhilber. "Murderous Aggression by Children and Adolescents." *Archives of General Psychiatry* 4 (1961): 1–9.

"Education About Adult Domestic Violence in U.S. and Canadian Medical Schools, 1987–88." *Journal of the American Medical Association* 261, 7 (1989): 972.

Elmer, E. *Children in Jeopardy*. Pittsburgh: University of Pittsburgh Press, 1967.

The Enablers. *Juvenile Prostitution in Minnesota: The Report of a Research Project*. St. Paul: The Enablers, 1978.

Engels, Frederick. *The Origin of Family Private Property and the State*. Moscow: Progress Publishers, 1948.

Ewing, Charles P. *Battered Women Who Kill: Psychological Self-Defense as Legal Justification*. Lexington, Mass.: Lexington Books, 1987.

Family Violence Prevention Fund. *Men Beating Women: Ending Domestic Violence, A Qualitative and Quantitative Study of Public Attitudes on Violence Against Women*. New York: EDK Associates, 1993.

Famularo, R., K. Stone, R. Barnum, and R. Wharton. "Alcoholism and Severe Child Maltreatment." *American Journal of Orthopsychiatry* 56 (1986): 481–85.

Fields, M. D. "Wife Beating: The Hidden Offense." *New York Law Journal* 175, 83 (1976): 1–7.

"Final Report of the Supreme Court Task Force on Courts' and Communities' Response to Domestic Abuse." Submitted to the Supreme Court of Iowa, August 1994.

Finkelhor, David. "How Widespread Is Child Abuse?" In *Perspectives on Child Maltreatment in the Mid '80s*. Washington, D.C.: National Center on Child Abuse and Neglect Information, 1984.

_____. *Sexually Victimized Children*. New York: Free Press, 1979.

_____, Sharon Araji, Larry Baron, Angela Browne, Stephanie Peters, and Gail Wyatt. *A Sourcebook on Child Sexual Abuse*. Beverly Hills: Sage, 1986.

_____, Linda Williams, Nanci Burns, and Michael Kalinowski. *Sexual Abuse in Day Care: A National Study Executive Summary*. Durham: University of New Hampshire, 1988.

_____, and Kersti Yllo. *License to Rape: Sexual Abuse of Wives*. New York: Free Press, 1985.

Flanzer, Jerry P. *The Many Faces of Family Violence*. Springfield, Ill.: Charles C Thomas, 1982.

Flowers, R. Barri. *The Adolescent Criminal: An Examination of Today's Juvenile Offender*. Jefferson, N.C.: McFarland, 1990.

_____. *Children and Criminality: The Child as Victim and Perpetrator*. Westport, Conn.: Greenwood Press, 1986.

_____. *Demographics and Criminality: The Characteristics of Crime in America*. Westport, Conn.: Greenwood Press, 1989.

_____. *Drugs, Alcohol and Criminality in American Society*. Jefferson, N.C.: McFarland, 1999.

_____. *Female Crime, Criminals and Cellmates: An Exploration of Female Criminality and Delinquency*. Jefferson, N.C.: McFarland, 1995.

_____. *Minorities and Criminality*. Westport, Conn.: Greenwood Press, 1990.

_____. *The Prostitution of Women and Girls.* Jefferson, N.C.: McFarland, 1998.

_____. *The Sex Slave Murders.* New York: St. Martin's Press, 1996.

_____. *The Victimization and Exploitation of Women and Children: A Study of Physical, Mental and Sexual Maltreatment in the United States.* Jefferson, N.C.: McFarland, 1994.

_____. *Women and Criminality: The Woman as Victim, Offender, and Practitioner.* Westport, Conn.: Greenwood Press, 1987.

Fontana, Vincent J. *The Maltreated Child: The Maltreatment Syndrome in Children.* Springfield, Ill.: Charles C Thomas, 1964; 2nd ed., 1971.

Forward, Susan, and C. Buck. *Betrayal of Innocence: Incest and Its Devastation.* Los Angeles: J. P. Tarcher, 1978.

Fox, James A., and Jack Levin. "Homicides Against the Elderly: A Research Note." *Criminology* 29 (1991): 317–27.

Freeman, M. A. *Violence in the Home.* Farnborough, England: Saxon House, 1979.

Galdston, R. "Observations on Children Who Have Been Physically Abused and Their Parents." *American Journal of Psychiatry* 122, 4 (1965): 440–43.

Garbarino, James, and Deborah Sherman. "High-Risk Neighborhoods and High-Risk Families: The Human Ecology of Child Maltreatment." *Child Development* 51 (1980): 188–98.

Gayford, J. "Wife Battering: A Preliminary Survey of 100 Cases." *British Medical Journal* 1 (1975): 194–97.

Gebhard, Paul H., John H. Gagnon, Wardell B. Pomeroy, and Cornelia V. Christenson. *Sex Offenders: An Analysis of Types.* New York: Harper & Row, 1965.

Geller, Anne, and Helene MacLean. "Substance Abuse." In Helene MacLean, ed. *Every Woman's Health: The Complete Guide to Body and Mind.* 5th ed. Garden City, N.Y.: Guild American Books, 1993.

Gelles, Richard J. "Child Reformation." *American Journal of Orthopsychiatry* 43 (1973): 611–21.

_____, and Murray A. Straus. "Determinants of Violence in the Family: Toward a Theoretical Integration." In W. R. Burr, R. Hill, F. I. Nye, and I. L. Reiss, eds. *Contemporary Theories About the Family.* New York: Free Press, 1979.

_____, and Claire P. Cornell. *Intimate Violence in Families.* Beverly Hills, Calif.: Sage, 1990.

_____. "The Myth of Battered Husbands." *Ms.* (October 1979): 65–72.

_____. "Violence and Pregnancy: A Note on the Extent of the Problem and Needed Services." *Family Coordinator* 24 (1975): 81–86.

_____, and Murray A. Straus. "Violence in the American Family." *Journal of Social Issues* 35, 2 (1979): 15–39.

_____. "Violence Toward Children in the United States." *American Journal of Orthopsychiatry* 48, 4 (1978): 580–92.

_____. *The Violent Home: A Study of the Physical Aggression Between Husbands and Wives.* Beverly Hills: Sage, 1972; reprint, 1985.

Gerson, L. W. "Alcohol Consumption and the Incidence of Violent Crime." *Journal for the Study of Alcoholism* 40 (1978): 307–12.

Gibbons, T. C., and A. Walker. *Cruel Parents.* London: Institute for the Study and Treatment of Delinquency, 1965.

Gil, David G. *Violence Against Children: Physical Child Abuse in the United States.* Cambridge, Mass.: Harvard University Press, 1970.

Gillespie, Cynthia. *Justifiable Homicide: Battered Women, Self-Defense, and the Law.* Columbus, Ohio: Ohio State University Press, 1989.

Glander, Susan S. "The Prevalence of Domestic Violence Among Women Seeking Abortion." *Journal of the American Medical Association* 280, 5 (1998): 401.

Goldsmith, Barbara. "Women on the Edge: A Reporter at Large." *New Yorker* 69 (April 26, 1993): 65–66.

Goode, W. "Violence Among Intimates." *Crimes and Violence* 13 (1969): 941–77.

Glueck, Sheldon, and Eleanor Glueck. *Delinquents and Non-Delinquents in Perspective.* Cambridge, Mass.: Harvard University Press, 1968.

Goldsmith, Barbara. "Women on the Edge: A Reporter at Large." *The New Yorker* 69 (April 26, 1993): 64–67, 74–78.

Goldstein, Paul J. "Drugs and Violent Crime." In Neil A. Weiner and Marvin E. Wolfgang, eds. *Pathways to Criminal Violence.* Beverly Hills, CA: Sage, 1989.

_____. *Prostitution and Drugs.* Lexington, Mass.: Lexington Books, 1979.

Gomby, Deanna S., and Patricia H. Shiono. "Estimating the Number of Substance-Exposed Infants." *The Future of Children* 1 (1991): 17–25.

Goodwinn, Jean, Lawrence Cormier, and John Owen. "Grandfather-Granddaughter Incest: A Trigenerational View." *Child Abuse and Neglect* 7 (1983): 163–70.

Graves, R. *Greek Myths.* New York: Penguin, 1962.

Green, A. H. "Psychopathology of Abused Children." *Journal of the American Academy of Child Psychiatry* (1978): 92–103.

Gross, Andrea. "A Question of Rape." *Ladies Home Journal* 110, 11 (November 1993): 170.

Groth, A. Nicholas, Ann W. Burgess, and Lynda L. Holmstrom. "Rape: Power, Anger, and Sexuality." *American Journal of Psychiatry* 34 (1977): 1239–43.

Gubrium, Jaber. "Victimization in Old Age: Available Evidence and Three Hypotheses." *Crime & Delinquency* 20 (1974): 245–50.

Hancock, D. N. "Alcohol and Crime." In G. Edwards and M. Grant, ed. *Alcoholism: New Knowledge and New Responses.* London: Croom Helm, 1977.

Harlan, Sparky, Luanne L. Rodgers, and Brian Slattery. *Male and Female Adolescent Prostitution: Huckleberry House Sexual Minority Youth Services Project.* Washington, D.C.: U.S. Department of Health and Human Services, 1981.

Haskell, Martin R., and Lewis Yablonsky. *Crime and Delinquency.* 2nd ed. Chicago: Rand McNally, 1974.

Helfer, M. E., R. S. Kempe, and R. D. Krugman, eds. *The Battered Child.* 5th ed. Chicago: University of Chicago Press, 1997.

Helfer, Ray E., and C. Henry Kempe, eds. *Child Abuse and Neglect: The Family and the Community.* Cambridge, Mass.: Ballinger, 1976.

Helton, A. S., M. S. McFarlane, and E. T. Anderson. "Battered and Pregnant: A Prevalence Study." *American Journal of Public Health* 77, 10 (1987).

_____, J. McFarlane, and E. Anderson. "Prevention of Battering During Pregnancy: Focus on Behavioral Change." *Public Health Nursing* 4, 3 (1987).

Hersch, Patricia. "Coming of Age on City Streets." *Psychology Today* (January 1988): 28–37.

Hofeller, Kathleen H. *Social, Psychological and Situational Factors in Wife Abuse.* Palo Alto, Calif.: R & E Research Associates, 1982.

Holmes, Monica. *Child Abuse and Neglect Programs: Practice and Theory.* Rockville, Md.: National Institute of Mental Health, 1977.

Holtz, H. A., and C. Hanes. "Education About Domestic Violence in 25 U.S. and Canadian Medical Schools, 1987–1988." *MMWR* 38, 2 (1989).

Horn, Patricia. "Beating Back the Revolution: Domestic Violence's Economic Toll on Women." *Dollars & Sense* 182 (1992): 12.

Hornblower, Margot. "The Skin Trade." *Time* 141 (June 21, 1993): 44–51.

Houts, M. *They Asked for Death.* New York: Cowles, 1970.

Howard, Judy. "Incest Victims Speak Out." *Teen* (July 1985): 30.

Hummert, Mary L. "Age and Typical Judgments of Stereotypes of the Elderly: Perceptions of Elderly vs. Young Adults." *International Journal of Aging and Human Development* 37 (1993): 217–26.

Jacobsen, J. J., ed. *Psychiatric Sequelae of Child Abuse.* Springfield, Ill.: Charles C Thomas, 1986.

James, J., C. Fosho, and R. W. Wohl. "The Relationship Between Female Criminality and Drug Use." *International Journal of the Addictions* 14 (1979): 115–229.

James, Jennifer. *Entrance into Juvenile Prostitution.* Washington, D.C.: National Institute of Mental Health, 1980.

_____. "Motivations for Entrance into Prostitution." In Laura Crites, ed. *The Female Offender.* Lexington, Mass.: Lexington Books, 1976.

Jenny, C., K. P. Hymel, A. Ritzen, S. E. Reinert, and T. C. Hay. "Analysis of Missed Cases of Head Trauma." *Journal of the American Medical Association* 281 (1999): 621–26.

Johnson, Bruce D., and Eric Walsh, eds. *Crime Rates Among Drug Abusing Offenders.* New York: Interdisciplinary Research Center, 1986.

Johnson, Joan J. *Teen Prostitution.* Danbury, Conn.: Franklin Watts, 1992.

Jones, Ann. *Women Who Kill.* New York: Fawcett Crest, 1980.

Jordan, Nick. "Till Murder Us Do Part." *Psychology Today* 19 (July 1985): 7.

Justice, Blair, and Rita Justice. *The Abusing Family.* New York: Human Sciences Press, 1976.

Kadushin, Alfred, and Judith A. Martin. *Child Abuse: An Interactional Event.* New York: Columbia University Press, 1981.

Kandel, Denise B., Ora Simcha-Fagan, and Mark Davies. "Risk Factors for Delinquency and Illicit Drug Use From Adolescence to Young Adulthood." *Journal of Drug Issues* (Winter 1986): 67–90.

Kellerman, Arthur L., et al. "Gun Ownership as a Risk Factor for Homicide in the Home." *New England Journal of Medicine* 329, 15 (1993): 1084.

Kempe, C. Henry, "Pediatric Implications of the Battered Baby Syndrome." *Archives of Diseases in Childhood* 46, 245 (1971): 28–37.

_____, and Ray E. Helfer, eds. *Helping the Battered Child and His Family.* Philadelphia: J. B. Lippincott, 1972.

_____, Frederic N. Silverman, Brandt F. Steele, William Droegemueller, and Henry K. Silver. "The Battered Child Syndrome." *Journal of the American Medical Association* 181 (1962): 17–24.

King, Linda S. "Responding to Spouse Abuse: The Mental Health Profession." In *Response to Family Violence* 4, 5 (1981): 7–9.

Kluft, R. P., ed. *Childhood Antecedents of Multiple Personalities*. Washington, D.C.: American Psychiatric Press, 1985.

Kopernik, L. "The Family as a Breeding Ground for Violence." *Corrective Psychiatric Journal of Sociology Therapy* 10, 6 (1964).

Kramer, Samuel N. *From the Tables of Sumer: Twenty-Five Firsts in Man's Recorded History*. Indian Hills, Colo.: Falcon Wing, 1956.

Kuehl, S. "Legal Remedies for Teen Dating Violence." In Barbara Levy, ed. *Dating Violence: Young Women in Danger*. Seattle: Seal Press, 1998.

Kurl, Anna, and Linda E. Saltzman. "Battered Women and the Criminal Justice System." In Imogene L. Moyer, ed. *The Changing Roles of Women in the Criminal Justice System: Offenders, Victims, and Professionals*. Prospect Heights, Ill.: Waveland Press, 1985.

Kurz, D. "Emergency Department Responses to Battered Women: Resistance to Medication." *Social Problems* 34, 1 (1987).

Langley, Robert, and Richard C. Levy. *Wife Beating: The Silent Crisis*. New York: E. P. Dutton, 1977.

Lard, E., and D. Weisfeld. "The Abused Child." In A. Roberts, ed. *Childhood Deprivation*. Springfield, Ill.: Charles C Thomas, 1974.

Lascari, A. "The Abused Child." *Journal of the Iowa Medical Society* 62 (1972): 229–32.

Laury, G. V. "The Battered Child Syndrome: Parental Motivation, Clinical Aspects." *Bulletin of the New York Academy of Medicine* 46, 9 (1970): 676–85.

Law Enforcement Assistance Administration. *Profile of State Prison Inmates: Sociodemographic Findings from the 1974 Survey of Inmates of State Correctional Facilities*. Washington, D.C.: Government Printing Office, 1979.

Lay, T. "The Flourishing Problem of Elder Abuse in Our Society." *AACN Clinical Issues* 5, 4 (1994): 507.

Leo, John. "Things That Go Bump in the Home." *U.S. News & World Report* 120, 19 (May 13, 1996): 25.

Leventhal, John M. "The Challenges of Recognizing Child Abuse: Seeing Is Believing." *Journal of the American Medical Association* 281, 7 (1999): 657.

Levy, Barbara, ed. *Dating Violence: Young Women in Danger*. Seattle: Seal Press, 1998.

Liang, Jersey, and Mary C. Sengstock. "Personal Crimes Against the Elderly." In J. Kosberg, ed. *Abuse and Mistreatment of the Elderly: Causes and Interventions*. Little John, Mass.: John Wright-PGS, 1983.

Lidz, R., and T. Lidz. "Homosexual Tendencies in Mothers of Schizophrenic Women." *Journal of Nervous and Mental Disorders* 149 (1969): 229.

Light, R. J. "Abused and Neglected Children in America: A Study of Alternative Politics." *Harvard Educational Review* 143 (1973): 574.

Linquist, John H., and Janice M. Duke. "The Elderly Victim at Risk." *Criminology* 20 (1982): 115–26.

Lloyd, Robin. *For Money or Love: Boy Prostitution in America*. New York: Ballantine, 1976.

Lowinson, Joyce H., Pedro Ruiz, and Robert B. Millman, eds. *Substance Abuse: A Comprehensive Textbook*. Baltimore: Williams and Wilkins, 1992.

Lunde, D. T. "Hot Blood's Record Month: Our Murder Boom." *Psychology Today* 9 (1975): 35–42.

Lystad, M. H. "Violence At Home: A Review of the Literature." *American Journal of Orthopsychiatry* 45 (1975): 328–45.

Machotka, P., F. S. Pittman, and K. Flomenhaft. "Incest as a Family Matter." *Family Process* 6 (1967): 98.

Mahan, Sue. *Crack Cocaine, Crime & Women: Legal, Social & Treatment Issues.* Beverly Hills: Sage, 1996.

Markowitz, Sara, and Michael Grossman. "Alcohol Regulation and Domestic Violence Towards Children." *Contemporary Economic Policy* 16, 3 (1998): 309.

Martin, H. P., and P. Beezley. "Behavioral Observations of Abused Children." *Developmental Medicine and Child Neurology* 19 (1977): 373–87.

_____, et al. "The Development of Abused Children: I. A Review of the Literature, II. Physical, Neurological and Intellectual Outcomes." *Advances in Pediatrics* 21 (1974): 25–73.

Martin, Michael J., and James Walters. "Familial Correlates of Selected Types of Child Abuse and Neglect." *Journal of Marriage and the Family* 5 (1982): 267–76.

Mayer, Adele. *Incest: A Treatment Manual for Therapy with Victims, Spouses, and Offenders.* Holmes Beach, Fla.: Learning Publications, 1983.

Mayhall, Pamela D., and Katherine Norgard. *Child Abuse and Neglect: Sharing Responsibility.* Toronto: John Wiley and Sons, 1983.

McCabe, Kimberly A., and Sharon S. Gregory. "Elderly Victimization: An Examination Beyond the FBI's Index Crimes." *Research on Aging* 20, 3 (1998): 363.

McCord, W. "The Biological Basis of Juvenile Delinquency." In J. S. Roucek, ed. *Juvenile Delinquency.* Freeport, N.Y.: Philosophical Library, 1958.

McCoy, Kathy. "Incest: The Most Painful Family Problem." *Seventeen* 43 (June 1984): 18.

McCurdy, Karen, and Deborah Daro. *Current Trends in Child Abuse Reporting and Fatalities: The Results of the 1992 Annual Fifty State Survey.* Chicago: National Committee for Prevention of Child Abuse, 1993.

McGlothlin, William H., M. Douglas Anglin, and Bruce D. Wilson. "Narcotic Addiction and Crime." *Criminology* 16 (November 1978): 293–315.

McKenzie, Katherine C. "Prevalence of Domestic Violence in an Inpatient Female Population." *Journal of the American Medical Association* 280, 5 (1998): 401.

McLeer, S., and R. Anwar. "A Study of Battered Women Presenting in an Emergency Department." *American Journal of Public Health* 79, 1 (1989).

Medlicott, R. "Parent-Child Incest." *Australian Journal of Psychiatry* 1 (1967): 180.

Meiselman, K. C. *Incest: A Psychological Study of Causes and Effects with Treatment Recommendations.* San Francisco: Jossey-Bass, 1978.

Melton, G., and F. Burry, eds. *Protecting Children from Abuse and Neglect.* New York: Guilford, 1994.

Miketic, B. "The Influence of Parental Alcoholism in the Development Disturbance of Children." *Alcoholism* 8 (1972): 135–39.

Miles-Doan, Rebecca. "Violence Between Spouses and Intimates: Does Neighborhood Context Matter?" *Social Forces* 77 (1998): 623.

Miller, John K. "Perspectives on Child Maltreatment in the Military." In Ray E.

Helfer and C. Henry Kempe, eds. *Child Abuse and Neglect: The Family and the Community*. Cambridge, Mass.: Ballinger, 1976.

Milowe, J., and R. Lourie. "The Child's Role in the Battered Child Syndrome." *Journal of Pediatrics* 65 (1964): 1079–81.

Mithers, Carol L. "Incest: The Crime That's All in the Family." *Mademoiselle* 96 (June 1984): 18.

Morales, Alex. "Seeking a Cure for Child Abuse." *USA Today* 127, 2640 (1998): 34.

Morris, C. *The Tudors*. London: Fontana, 1967.

Morse, C. W., O. Z. Sahler, and S. F. Friedman. "A Three-Year Study of Abused and Neglected Children." *American Journal of Diseases in Childhood* 120 (1970): 439–46.

Mrazek, Patricia. "The Nature of Incest: A Review of Contributing Factors." In Patricia Mrazek and C. Henry Kempe, eds. *Sexually Abused Children and Their Families*. New York: Pergamon Press, 1981.

_____, and C. Henry Kempe, eds. *Sexually Abused Children and Their Families*. New York: Pergamon Press, 1981.

Mulford, Robert M. "Historical Perspectives." In Nancy B. Ebeling and Deborah A. Hill, eds. *Child Abuse and Neglect*. Boston: P. S. G., Inc., 1983.

National Center on Addiction and Substance Abuse at Columbia University. *National Survey of American Attitudes on Substance Abuse II: Teens and Their Parents*. New York: National Center on Addiction and Substance Abuse at Columbia University, 1996.

Newberger, E. H., and R. Bourne, eds. *Unhappy Families: Clinical and Research Perspectives on Family Violence*. Littleton, Mass.: PSG Publishing, 1985.

O'Brien, J. E. "Violence in Divorce-Prone Families." *Journal of Marriage and the Family* 33 (1971): 692–98.

O'Brien, Shirley. *Child Abuse: Commission and Omission*. Provo, Ut.: Brigham Young University Press, 1980.

Office of National Drug Control Policy. *Fact Sheet: Drug Data Summary*. Rockville, Md.: ONDCP Drugs and Crime Clearinghouse, 1996.

_____. *Minorities and Drugs: Facts and Figures*. Rockville, Md.: White House Drug Policy Clearinghouse, 1997.

_____. *Pulse Check: National Trends in Drug Abuse*. Washington, D.C.: Office of National Drug Control Policy, 1997.

_____. *Women and Drugs: Facts and Figures*. Rockville, Md.: ONDCP Drugs and Crime Clearinghouse, 1997.

Okun, Lewis. *Woman Abuse: Facts Replacing Myths*. New York: State University of New York Press, 1985.

Oliver, J. E. "The Epidemiology of Child Abuse." In Selwyn M. Smith, ed. *The Maltreatment of Children*. Baltimore, Md.: University Park Press, 1978.

Ollenberger, Jane C. "Criminal Victimization and Fear of Crime." *Research on Aging* 29 (1981): 317–27.

Ounsted, Christopher, Rhoda Oppenheimer, and Janet Lindsay. "The Psychopathology and Psychotherapy of the Families, Aspects Bounding Failure." In A. Franklin, ed. *Concerning Child Abuse*. London: Churchill Livingston, 1975.

Pagelow, Mildred D. *Woman-Battering: Victims and Their Experiences*. Beverly Hills: Sage, 1981.

Petersilia, Joan, Peter Greenwood, and Marvin Lavin. *Criminal Careers of Habitual Felons*. Washington, D.C.: National Institute of Justice, 1978.

Piers, Maria. *Infanticide*. New York: Norton, 1978.

Pillemer, K., and D. Finkelhor. "The Prevalence of Elder Abuse: A Random Sample Survey." *Gerontologist* 28, 10 (1988): 51.

Pizzey, Erin. *Scream Quietly or the Neighbors Will Hear*. London: Penguin, 1974.

Plant, Martin A. and M. L. Plant. *Risk-Takers: Alcohol, Drugs, Sex and Youth*. London: Routledge, 1992.

Plass, Peggy S. "African American Family Homicide: Patterns in Partner, Parent, & Child Victimization, 1985–87." *Journal of Black Studies* 23 (1993): 515–38.

Polansky, Norman, Christine De Saix, and Schlomo A. Sharlin. *Child Neglect: Understanding and Reaching the Parents*. New York: Child Welfare League of America, 1972.

Popisil, Z., K. Turcin, and R. Turcin. "Alcoholism and Article 196 of Criminal Law Abuse and Neglect of Minors." *New Ossihijatrya Zagreb* 16 (1968): 49–53.

Pringle, Mia K. "Towards the Prediction of Child Abuse." In Neil Fruce, ed. *Psychological Approaches to Child Abuse*. Totowa, N.J.: Rowman and Littlefield, 1981.

Protecting the Child Victims of Sex Crimes. Denver: American Humane Association, 1966.

Rada, Richard T. *Clinical Aspects of the Rapist*. New York: Grune and Stratton, 1978.

Radbill, Samuel X. "A History of Child Abuse and Infanticide." In Ray E. Helfer and C. Henry Kempe, eds. *The Battered Child*. 2nd ed. Chicago: University of Chicago Press, 1974.

_____. "The First Treatise on Pediatrics." *American Journal of Diseases of Children* 122 (1971): 376.

Rasko, G. "The Victim of the Female Killer." *Victimology* 1 (1976): 396–402.

Rathbone, E., and R. Pierce. "Intergenerational Treatment Approach." In Robert J. Hunner. *Between Child Abuse and Delinquency*. Montclair, N.J.: Allanheld, Osmun and Co., 1981.

Reinhardt, J. M. *Sexual Perversions and Sex Crimes*. Springfield, Ill.: Charles C Thomas, 1957.

Renvoize, Jean. *Incest: A Family Pattern*. London: Routledge & Kegan Paul, 1982.

Resnick, P. "Child Murder by Parents: A Psychiatric Review of Filicide." *American Journal of Psychiatry* 126, 3 (1969): 325–34.

Roberts, Albert R. "Substance Abuse Among Men Who Batter Their Mates." *Journal of Substance Abuse Treatment* 5 (1988): 83–87.

Roberts, J., M. M. Lynch, and P. Duff. "Abused Children and Their Siblings: A Teacher's View." *Therapeutic Education* 6 (1978): 25–31.

Rouse, L., R. Breen, and M. Howell. "Abuse in Intimate Relationships: A Comparison of Married and Dating College Students." *Journal of Interpersonal Violence* 3 (1988): 415.

Roy, Maria, ed. *The Abusive Partner: An Analysis of Domestic Battering*. New York: Van Nostrand Reinhold, 1982.

Russell, Diana E. *Intrafamilial Child Sexual Abuse: A San Francisco Survey*. Berkeley, Calif.: Wright Institute, 1983.

_____. *Rape in Marriage*. New York: Macmillan, 1982.

Saltzman, Linda, and James Mercy. "Assaults Between Intimates: The Range of Relationships Involved." In Anna Wilson, ed. *Homicide: The Victim/Offender Connection*. Cincinnati, Ohio: Anderson, 1993.

Sanchez, Jose, E., and Bruce D. Johnson. "Women and the Drugs-Crime Connection: Crime Rates Among Drug-Abusing Women at Rikers Island." *Journal of Psychoactive Drugs* 19, 2 (1987): 205–16.

Sargeant, D. "Children Who Kill — A Family Conspiracy?" In J. Howells, ed. *Theory and Practice of Family Psychiatry*. New York: Brunner-Mazel, 1971.

Schmitt, B. D., and C. H. Kempe. "Neglect and Abuse in Children." In V. C. Vaugh and R. J. McKay, eds. *Nelson Textbook of Pediatrics*. 10th ed. Philadelphia: W. B. Saunders Co., 1975.

Schroeder, Theodore. "Incest in Mormanism." *American Journal of Urology* 11 (1915): 409–16.

Schultz, Leroy C. "The Child as a Sex Victim: Socio-Legal Perspectives." In Israel Drapkin and Emilo Viano, eds. *Victimology: A New Focus*. Vol. 5. Toronto: D. C. Heath, 1975.

_____. "The Victim-Offender Relationship." *Crime and Delinquency* 14, 2 (1968): 135–41.

Schwendinger, Julia R., and Herman Schwendinger. *Rape and Inequality*. Beverly Hills: Sage, 1983.

Sexual Abuse of Children: Implications for Casework. Denver: American Humane Association, 1967.

Shore, M. F. "Psychological Theories on the Causes of Antisocial Behavior." *Crime and Delinquency* 17, 4 (1971): 456–58.

Silbert, Mimi H. "Delancey Street Study: Prostitution and Sexual Assault." Summary of Results. Delancey Street Foundation: San Francisco, 1982.

Smith, Peggy, and Marvin Bohnstedt. *Child Victimization Study Highlights*. Sacramento: Social Research Center of the American Justice Institute, 1981.

Solomon, Theo. "History and Demography of Child Abuse." *Pediatrics* 51, 4 (1973): 773–76.

Spinetta, J. J., and D. Rigler. "The Child-Abusing Parent: A Psychological Review." *Psychological Bulletin* 77 (1972): 296–304.

Steele, Brandt F., and C. Pollock. "A Psychiatric Study of Parents Who Abuse Infants and Small Children." In Ray E. Helfer and C. Henry Kempe, eds. *The Battered Child*. Chicago: University of Chicago Press, 1968.

Steinman, Michael, ed. *Woman Battering: Policy Responses*. Cincinnati, Ohio: Anderson, 1991.

Steinmetz, Suzanne K. "The Battered Husband Syndrome." *Victimology* 2 (1978): 499–509.

_____. *The Cycle of Violence: Assertive, Aggressive, and Abusive Family Interaction*. New York: Praeger, 1977.

_____. "The Use of Force for Resolving Family Conflicts: The Training Ground for Abuse." *Family Coordinator* 26 (1977): 19.

Straus, Murray A. "A General Systems Theory Approach to a Theory of Violence Between Family Members." *Social Science Information* 12 (1972): 105–25.

_____. "Sexual Inequality, Cultural Norms, and Wife-Beating." *Victimology* 1 (1976): 62–66.

_____, Richard J. Gelles, and Suzanne K. Steinmetz. *Behind Closed Doors: Violence in the American Family*. Garden City, N.Y.: Doubleday/Anchor, 1980.

_____, and Richard J. Gelles. *Physical Violence in American Families: Risk Factors and Adaptations to Violence in 8,145 Families*. New Brunswick, N.J.: Transaction Publishers, 1990.

Sugarman, D., and G. Hotaling. "Dating Violence: A Review of Contextual and Risk Factors." In Barbara Levy, ed. *Dating Violence: Young Women in Danger*. Seattle: Seal Press, 1998.

Sweet, Ellen. "Date Rape." *Ms./Campus Times* (October 1985): 58.

Tannahill, Reay. *Sex in History*. New York: Stein and Day, 1980.

Tatara, T. *Summaries of the Statistical Data on Elder Abuse in Domestic Settings for FY 95 and FY 96*. Washington, D.C.: National Center on Elder Abuse, 1997.

Thomas, Mason P., Jr. "Child Abuse and Neglect, Part I: Historical Overview, Legal Matrix and Social Perspectives." *North Carolina Law Review* 50 (1972): 293–349.

Turner, C. F., H. G. Miller, and L. E. Moses, eds. *AIDS, Sexual Behavior and Intravenous Drug Use*. Washington, D.C.: National Academy Press, 1989.

U.S. Department of Health and Human Services. *Child Abuse and Neglect: A Shared Community Concern*. Washington, D.C.: Government Printing Office, 1992.

_____. Children's Bureau. *Child Maltreatment 1996: Reports from the States to the National Child Abuse and Neglect Data System*. Washington, D.C.: Government Printing Office, 1998.

_____. Substance Abuse and Mental Health Services Administration. *National Household Survey on Drug Abuse: Main Findings 1995*. Washington, D.C.: Government Printing Office, 1997.

U.S. Department of Health, Education and Welfare. *Marijuana and Health: Eighth Annual Report on the U.S. Congress*. Washington, D.C.: Government Printing Office, 1980.

U.S. Department of Justice. Bureau of Justice Statistics. *Child Victimizers: Violent Offenders and Their Victims*. Washington, D.C.: Government Printing Office, 1996.

_____. Bureau of Justice Statistics. *Criminal Victimization in the United States, 1994: A National Crime Victimization Survey Report*. Washington, D.C.: Government Printing Office, 1997.

_____. Bureau of Justice Statistics. *Fact Sheet: Drug Use Trends*. Rockville, Md.: Drugs and Crime Data Center and Clearinghouse, 1992.

_____. Bureau of Justice Statistics. *Female Victims of Violent Crime*. Washington, D.C.: Government Printing Office, 1991.

_____. Bureau of Justice Statistics. National Crime Victimization Survey. *Elderly Crime Victims*. Washington, D.C.: Government Printing Office, 1994.

_____. Bureau of Justice Statistics. *Preventing Domestic Violence Against Women*. Washington, D.C.: Government Printing Office, 1986.

_____. Bureau of Justice Statistics. *Sourcebook of Criminal Justice Statistics 1997*. Washington, D.C.: Government Printing Office, 1998.

_____. Bureau of Justice Statistics. *Study of Injured Victims of Violence*.

_____. Bureau of Justice Statistics. Survey of Inmates in Local Jails, 1995.

_____. Bureau of Justice Statistics. *Survey of State Prison Inmates, 1991*. Washington, D.C.: Government Printing Office, 1994.

_____. Bureau of Justice Statistics. *Violence Between Intimates*. Washington, D.C.: Government Printing Office, 1994.

_____. Bureau of Justice Statistics Factbook. *Violence by Intimates*. Washington, D.C.: Government Printing Office, 1998.

_____. Bureau of Justice Statistics Special Report. *Violence-Related Injuries Treated in Hospital Emergency Departments*. Washington, D.C.: Government Printing Office, 1997.

_____. Bureau of Justice Statistics Special Report. *Women in Prison*. Washington, D.C.: Government Printing Office, 1994.

_____. Federal Bureau of Investigation. *Crime in the United States: Uniform Crime Reports 1988–1991*. Washington D.C.: Government Printing Office, 1989–1992.

_____. Federal Bureau of Investigation. National Incident-Based Reporting Program.

_____. Federal Bureau of Investigation. Supplementary Homicide Reports, 1976–1994.

_____. National Institute of Justice. *Characteristics of Different Types of Drug-Involved Offenders*. Washington, D.C.: Government Printing Office, 1988.

_____. Office of Juvenile Justice and Delinquency Prevention. *Juveniles Taken Into Custody: FY93*. Washington, D.C.: Government Printing Office, 1995.

Vanderbilt, Heidi. "Incest: A Chilling Report." *Lear's* (February 1992): 52–62.

Voss, Harwin L., and John R. Hepburn. "Patterns in Criminal Homicide in Chicago. *Journal of Criminal Law, Criminology, and Political Science* 59 (1968): 499–508.

Walker, Lenore E. *The Battered Woman*. New York: Harper & Row, 1979.

_____. *The Battered Woman Syndrome*. New York: Springer, 1984.

_____. "Psychology and Domestic Violence Around the World." *American Psychologist* 54 (1999): 21.

Warshaw, L. "Limitations of the Medical Model in the Care of Battered Women." *Gender & Society* 3, 4 (1989).

Weinberg, S. Kirson. *Incest Behavior*. New York: Citadel Press, 1966.

Whippie, Ellen E., and Sara E. Finton. "Psychological Maltreatment by Siblings: An Unrecognized Form of Abuse." *Child & Adolescent Social Work Journal* 12, 2 (1995): 135.

Whitehurst, Robert N. "Violence in Husband-Wife Interaction." In Suzanne K. Steinmetz and Murray A. Straus, eds. *Violence in the Family*. New York: Dodd, Mead, 1974.

Whiting, L. "Defining Emotional Neglect." *Children Today* 5 (1976): 2–5.

Widom, Cathy Spatz. "Childhood Sexual Abuse and Its Criminal Consequences." *Society* 33, 4 (1996): 47.

Wiehe, Vernon. *Sibling Abuse: Hidden Physical, Emotional, and Sexual Trauma*. Newbury Park, Calif.: Sage, 1997.

Williams, Gertrude J., and John Money, eds. *Traumatic Abuse and Neglect of Children at Home*. Baltimore, Md.: Johns Hopkins University Press, 1980.

Wiltz, C. J. "Fear of Crime, Criminal Victimization and Elderly Blacks." *Phylon* 43 (1982): 283–94.

Wissow, Lawrence S. "Infanticide." *New England Journal of Medicine* 339, 17 (1998): 1239.

Wolfe, Suzanne. "As America Ages: Look for Signs of Abuse." *RN* 61, 8 (1998): 48.

Wolfgang, Marvin E., *Patterns in Criminal Homicide* (Philadelphia: University of Pennsylvania Press, 1958).

_____. "Who Kills Whom." *Psychology Today* 3, 5 (1969): 54–56.

_____, and R. B. Strohm. "The Relationship Between Alcohol and Criminal Homicide." *Quarterly Journal of Studies on Alcoholism* 17 (1956): 411–26.

Wooley, P. V., and W. A. Evans. "Significance of Skeletal Lesions in Infants Resembling Those of Traumatic Origin." *Journal of the American Medical Association* 158 (1955): 539–43.

Yin, Peter. *Victimization and the Aged.* Springfield, Ill.: Charles C Thomas, 1985.

Yllo, Kersti, and David Finkelhor. *License to Rape: Sexual Abuse of Wives.* New York: Free Press, 1985.

_____, and Murray A. Straus. "Interpersonal Violence Among Married and Cohabitating Couples." Paper presented at the annual meeting of the National Council on Family Relations. Philadelphia, 1978.

Zalba, S. "The Abused Child: A Survey of the Problem." *Social Work* 11, 4 (1966): 3–16.

Recommended Readings

Child Abuse

Ascione, Frank R., and Phil Arkow. *Child Abuse, Domestic Violence and Animal Abuse.* Lafayette, Ind.: Purdue University Press, 1998.

Campbell, Jacquelyn. *Empowering Survivors of Abuse.* Newbury Park, Calif.: Sage, 1998.

Edmonson-Nelson, Gloria. *Child Abuse and Domestic Violence.* Oakland, Calif.: Gloria Edmonson-Nelson, 1999.

Firstman, R., and J. Talan. *The Death of Innocents.* New York: Bantam, 1997.

Fontana, Vincent J., and Douglas J. Besharov. *The Maltreated Child.* Springfield, Ill.: Charles C Thomas, 1995.

Hurley, Jennifer A. *Child Abuse.* San Diego: Greenhaven Press, 1999.

Monteleone, James A. *Child Maltreatment: Identifying, Interpreting and Reporting Child Abuse.* St. Louis: G. W. Medical Publishing, Inc., 1999.

Multiple Victimization of Children. Uplands, Calif.: Diane Publishing Co., 1998.

Perry, Bruce D. *Maltreated Children.* New York: W. W. Norton, 1998.

Russell, Lisa. *Child Maltreatment and Psychological Distress Among Urban Homeless Youth.* New York: Garland, 1998.

Saunders, Pete, and Steve Myers. *Child Abuse.* Brookfield, Conn.: Milbrook Press, 1996.

Tooley, Michael. *Abortion and Infanticide.* New York: Oxford University Press, 1985.

Tower, Cynthia C. *Understanding Child Abuse and Neglect.* Needham Heights, Mass.: Allyn & Bacon, Inc., 1998.

Van Bueren, Geraldine. *Childhood Abused.* Holmes Beach, Fla.: Gaunt, Inc., 1998.

Waldfogel, Jane. *The Future of Child Protection.* Cambridge, Mass.: Harvard University Press, 1998.

Child Sexual Abuse

Brohl, Kathryn, and Joyce Case. *When Your Child Has Been Molested.* San Francisco: Jossey-Bass, 1998.

Colin, Crawford. *Forbidden Femininity*. Fitchburg, Mass.: Ashgate, 1997.

Female Sexual Abuse of Children. New York: John Wiley and Sons, 1998.

Hyde, Margaret O., and Elizabeth H. Forsyth. *The Sexual Abuse of Children and Adolescents*. Brookfield, Conn.: Millbrook Press, 1997.

Jackson, Helene, and Ronald Nuttall. *Childhood Abuse*. Newbury Park, Calif.: Sage, 1997.

Kinkaid, James R. *Erotic Innocence*. Durham, N.C.: Duke University Press, 1998.

Leberg, Eric. *Understanding Child Molesters*. Newbury Park, Calif.: Sage, 1997.

Levesque, Roger I. *Sexual Abuse of Children*. Bloomington: Indiana University Press, 1999.

MacGregor, Cynthia. *Stranger Danger*. New York: Rosen Publishing Group, 1997.

Mains, Karen B., and Maxine Hancock. *Child Sexual Abuse*. Wheaton, Ill.: Harold Shaw Publishers, 1997.

Saradjian, Jacqui, and Helga G. Hanks. *Women Who Sexually Abuse Children*. New York: John Wiley and Sons, 1996.

Winters, Paul A. *Child Sexual Abuse*. San Diego: Greenhaven Press, 1997.

Domestic Violence

Asher, Alexis. *Don't Let Him Hurt Me Anymore: A Self-Help Guide for Women in Abusive Relationships*. Tarzana, Calif.: Burning Gate Press, 1994.

Barnett, Ola W., and Alyce D. LaViolette. *It Could Happen to Anyone: Why Battered Women Stay*. Newbury Park: Sage, 1993.

Bergen, Raquel K. *Issues in Intimate Violence*. Newbury Park, Calif.: Sage, 1998.

Cook, Philip W. *Abused Men*. Westport, Conn.: Greenwood Press, 1997.

Crowell, N., and A. Burgess, eds. *Understanding Violence Against Women*. Washington, D.C.: National Academy Press, 1996.

Dobash, R. Emerson, and Russell Dobash. *Rethinking Violence Against Women*. Newbury Park, Calif.: Sage, 1998.

Domestic Violence, Stalking and Antistalking Legislation. Uplands, Calif.: Diane Publishing Co., 1996.

Evans, Patricia. *The Verbally Abusive Relationship: How to Recognize it and How to Respond*. Holbrook, Mass.: Bob Adams, 1992.

Fazzone, Patricia A., John Holton, and Beth Reed. *Substance Abuse Treatment and Domestic Violence*. Uplands, Calif.: Diane Publishing Co., 1998.

Fuzy, Jean. *Recognizing Domestic Violence*. Albuquerque, N.M.: Hartman Publishing, Inc., 1998.

Hague, Gill, and Ellen Malos. *Domestic Violence*. Concord, Mass.: New Clarion Press, 1999.

Hoyle, Carolyn. *Negotiating Domestic Violence*. New York: Oxford University Press, 1998.

Jones, Ann. *Next Time She'll Be Dead: Battering & How to Stop It*. Boston: Beacon Press, 1994.

Jukes, Adam. *Men Who Batter*. New York: Routledge, 1999.

Marecek, Mary. *Breaking Free from Partner Abuse*. Buena Park, Calif.: Morning Glory Press, Inc., 1999.

Mullender, Audrey. *Rethinking Domestic Violence*. New York: Routledge, 1996.

National Research Council. *Understanding Child Abuse and Neglect*. Washington, D.C.: National Academy Press, 1993.

Nelson, Noelle. *Dangerous Relationships*. New York: Plenum, 1997.

NiCarthy, Ginny. *The Ones Who Got Away: Women Who Left Abusive Partners*. Seattle: Seal Press, 1987.

Pryke, Julie, and Martin Thomas. *Domestic Violence and Social Work*. Fitchburg, Mass.: Ashgate, 1998.

Schechter, Susan. *Women and Male Violence: The Visions and Struggles of the Battered Women's Movement*. Boston: South End Press, 1982.

Schornstein, Sherri L. *Domestic Violence*. Newbury Park, Calif.: Sage, 1997.

Stark, Evan, and Anne Flitcraft. *Women at Risk*. Newbury Park, Calif.: 1996.

Women and Domestic Violence. Binghamton, N.Y.: Haworth Press, 1999.

Elderly Abuse

Biggs, Simon, et al. *Elder Abuse in Perspective*. Buckingham, England: Open University Press, 1995.

Brownell, Patricia J. *Family Crimes Against the Elderly: Elderly Abuse and the Criminal Justice System*. New York: Garland Publishers, 1998.

Decalmer, Peter, and Frank Glendenning, eds. *The Mistreatment of Elderly People*. Newbury Park, Calif.: Sage, 1997.

Kakar, Suman. *Domestic Abuse: Public Policy/Criminal Justice Approaches Towards Child, Spousal, and Elderly Abuse*. Lanham, Md.: Austin & Winfield, 1997.

Miller, Thomas W., et al. *Clinical Handbook of Adult Exploitation and Abuse*. Madison, Conn.: International University Press, 1998.

Quinn, Mary Joy, et al. *Elder Abuse and Neglect: Causes, Diagnosis, and Intervention Strategies*. New York: Springer Publishers, 1997.

Ruben, Douglas H. *Drug Abuse and the Elderly: An Annotated Bibliography*. Lanham, Md.: Scarecrow Press, 1984.

Victims of Child Abuse: Domestic Violence; Elderly Abuse; Rape, Robbery, Assault; & Violent Death: A Manual for Clergy & Congregations. Uplands, Calif.: Diane Publishing Co., 1992.

Wolfe, Rosalie S., et al. *Helping Elderly Victims: The Reality of Elder Abuse*. New York: Columbia University Press, 1989.

Family Violence

Family Violence from a Communication Perspective. Newbury Park, Calif.: Sage, 1996.

Hampton, Robert L., and Vincent Senatore. *Substance Abuse, Family Violence and Child Welfare*. Newbury Park, Calif.: Sage, 1998.

Snow, Robert L. *Family Abuse*. New York: Plenum, 1997.

Index